JOHN SKELTON

PRIEST AS POET

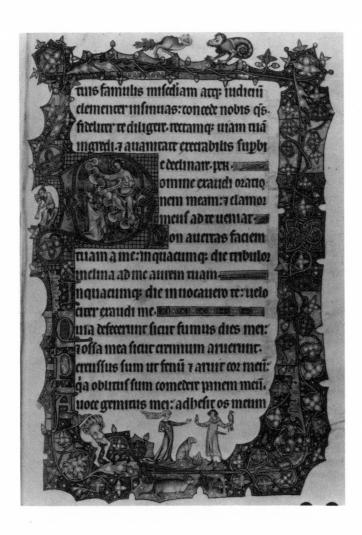

JOHN SKELTON

PRIEST AS POET

SEASONS OF DISCOVERY

*There are few things so astonishing in the history of English
literature as the eclipse of John Skelton.*

IAN A. GORDON

*The learned admired him for his learning, and the people
admired him as one of the most amusing writers of any century:
Skelton, knowing himself to be not only a scholar and a jocular
but a poet, looked to Posterity for nice appreciation . . . and
Posterity has played the jade with him: never quite giving him his
congé, she has kept him dangling. . . . For four centuries he has
lain in his grave, food for the grammarians.*

RICHARD HUGHES

ARTHUR F. KINNEY

*The University of North Carolina Press
Chapel Hill and London*

Both the initial
research and the publication
of this work were made possible in part
through grants from the National Endowment for
the Humanities, a federal agency whose mission is to
award grants to support education, scholarship, media
programming, libraries, and museums, in order to
bring the results of cultural activities to
a broad, general public.

Library of Congress Cataloging-in-Publication Data

Kinney, Arthur F., 1933–
John Skelton, priest as poet.

Includes index.

1. Skelton, John, 1460?–1529—Criticism and interpre-
tation. I. Title.

PR2348.K56   1987   821'.2   86-14595
ISBN 0-8078-1730-9

The hand-carved fifteenth-century
bench ends that appear throughout
this book are from the Church of
the Holy Trinity, Blythburgh, Suffolk,
and were photographed by Arthur F. Kinney.

For F. W. Brownlow,
colleague from the beginning,

Robert S. Kinsman,
dean of Skeltonists,

and the Huntington Library Fellowship

Cumque esset sapientissimus Ecclesiastes,
Docuit populum, et enarravit quae fecerat;
Et investigans composuit parabolas multas.
Quaesivit verba utilia,
Et conscripsit sermones rectissimos ac veritate plenos.
Verba sapientium sicut stimuli,
Et quasi clavi in altum defixi,
Quae per magistrorum consilium data sunt a pastore uno.

And whereas Ecclesiastes was very wise, he taught the people, and declared the things that he had done: and seeking out, he set forth many parables.

He sought profitable words, and wrote words most right, and full of truth.

The words of the wise are as goads, and as nails deeply fastened in, which by the counsel of masters are given from one shepherd.

CONTENTS

KING
Bench end (hand-carved, fifteenth century),
Church of the Holy Trinity, Blythburgh, Suffolk

PREFACE

THE INTERPRETATION of the poetry of John Skelton, "the greatest English poet to have been born in the fifteenth century,"[1] that I put forth here is admittedly a partial one. But it is an essential perspective in appreciating Skelton's particular inventiveness and a necessary modification of the exclusive picture of Skelton as an early Tudor humanist (in the work of William Nelson), a poet chiefly concerned with medieval strategies of satire (as seen by A. R. Heiserman), or a poet who invokes a reader-response through his personal engagements and disengagements with his subjects (as advocated by Stanley Eugene Fish). All of these previous readers of Skelton have given us special insights, but they have not presented the comprehensive evaluation we seek nor even, I think, the basic thrust and aesthetic of Skelton's poems. His primary vocation was that of a priest, not a poet, and it is that which fundamentally informs much of his literary work.

Like Nelson, I had begun this study hoping to see Skelton as a pioneer of the English Renaissance, but my continual reading of his poems kept forcing me in other directions, back to the Catholic Scriptures and to the liturgical services of the Sarum use, which formed the basis of an early Tudor priest's perspectives and prescribed his duties. Whether my chief itinerary was first suggested by F. W. Brownlow or whether he confirmed my thinking at an early stage, I can no longer say, but his own research as well as his advanced seminar on liturgy and literature at Mount Holyoke College have been invaluable. So has the frequent use of the definitive text of Skelton's work, now in its final stages, which the editor, Robert S. Kinsman, has shared with me. Both of these scholars have read drafts of my work, saving me from error and infelicity, and I wish to thank them in particular, as well as several others who helped along the way: Bartlett R. Butler, Horton Davies, Vincent DiMarco, E. Talbot Donaldson, Dan Donno, Ernest Gallo, Gordon Kipling, Thomas McCavera, Leeman L. Perkins, William A. Ringler, Jr., John Steadman, Peter Gram Swing, Kevin Taylor, Retha M. Warnicke, Elizabeth Portges Watson, and Seth Weiner. All of these colleagues assisted me in my pilgrimage; but J. Cecil

Jollands, Chapter Clerk of Lincoln Cathedral, left me behind in the dust as he led the way up stairs, over rafters, and along the high arches at Lincoln so that we might study more closely the stone sculptures of the Angel Choir.

I am also grateful to the National Endowment for the Humanities for a year-long Research Fellowship, to the Henry E. Huntington Library for a senior residential appointment, and to the University of Massachusetts, Amherst, for a Faculty Fellowship Award that relieved me of teaching obligations and other responsibilities and so freed my time for writing. The material presented here was first given as a seminar at the Huntington Library and later, in other forms, as a seminar at the Newberry Library, the New England Renaissance Conference meeting at Wheaton College (in a talk dedicated to Leicester Bradner), the Southeastern Renaissance Conference meeting at Georgia Institute of Technology, the Sixteenth-Century Studies Conference at Ohio State University, the Renaissance Society of America meeting at the University of Pennsylvania, and a special conference on the Tudor court sponsored by the Arizona Center for Medieval and Renaissance Studies housed at Arizona State University in Tempe. In addition, others have heard me propose, at first tentatively, many of the ideas finally formulated here, and subsequently helped me to expand, correct, or refine my thoughts, and I wish to thank my hosts and audiences at the University of Massachusetts at Amherst; the University of Connecticut at Storrs; Bryn Mawr and Haverford Colleges; Yale; Princeton; Cornell; the University of California at Riverside; the University of Michigan at Ann Arbor; the University of North Carolina at Chapel Hill; the University of South Carolina at Columbia; Columbia; Harvard; Brown; Emory; the University of Georgia at Athens; and the University of Illinois at Champaign-Urbana; and, overseas, the Universities of Nottingham and Southampton. At various stages the entire manuscript was read by J. A. Burrow, Melvin J. Tucker, Thorlac Turville-Petre, Laura Youens, and the late Jan van Dorsten, and this book is better because of their knowledge and suggestions. I am also grateful to my editors, Elisabeth P. Smith and Edward Curran, and to the designer, Richard Hendel. Finally, I am indebted to the librarians and staff of the Huntington Library, the Pierpont Morgan Library, the Bodleian Library, the British Library, the Norwich Cathedral Library, the Lincoln Cathedral Library, and the Norfolk County Council; to the librarians of Castle Howard and Arundel Castle; Len Weaver and the Harwich Town Council; Oliver Bernard, Kenninghall; W. Blake, Rector of Roydon, Diss; John Spiers, Diss; the staff of Framlington Castle and the rector of St. Michael the Archangel, Framlingham; J. N. T. Howat, Rector of St. Giles, Skelton, Yorkshire; and Anthony Beck, Honourable Sub-Librarian of the Chapter Library, Norwich Cathedral. I hope that the poet they encounter again in these pages will be one they enjoy and admire, and, above all, recognize.

A. F. K.
Amherst, Massachusetts
Cortland, New York

JOHN SKELTON

PRIEST AS POET

1

STRANGERS AND PILGRIMS

AVARICE
Bench end (hand-carved, fifteenth century),
Church of the Holy Trinity, Blythburgh, Suffolk

S O M E T I M E   I N 1499 John Skelton's first important poem, *The Bowge of Courte*, was issued from the press of Wynkyn de Worde at the Westminster quarters once occupied by William Caxton. This was (so far as we know now) Skelton's first publication, and to Wynkyn, who was less literary but more enterprising than his predecessor, it must have seemed especially appropriate for a printer who concentrated on religious titles: the earliest of Wynkyn's extant works was Mirk's widely used *Liber Festivalis* (1493), followed by *The Golden Legend* with its scores of popular hagiographies, the *Speculum Vitae Christi*, and *Vitas Patrum*; in 1498 he published the first travel guide for pilgrims in English, William Wey's *Informacion for Pylgrymes*. A short time later, just a few months before Skelton's poem was printed at his press, he subcontracted with a neighbor, Julian Notary, to produce with him a new edition of the Sarum Missal, a job too large for his shop alone. And *The Bowge of Courte* must have joined the others as a good investment, too, for in 1510, shortly after he moved to Fleet Street, London, opened a shop in St. Paul's Churchyard, and began printing (almost exclusively) small popular quartos aimed at the widest possible readership, Wynkyn issued a second edition of Skelton's poem. Thus John Skelton's first published work also became his only work printed more than once during his lifetime.

Actually, Wynkyn did not risk much. As John M. Berdan followed by A. R. Heiserman have been pointing out for more than a half century,[1] *The Bowge of Courte* is weighted with tradition. It is a dream-vision with the allegory, the personifications, the rime royal, and even the formulary incipit long established for poems of its kind. If the poem moves the dreaming poet from a garden or hillside into a public house at the Suffolk seaport of Harwich, changes the season from spring to autumn "when the sonne [is] *in Vyrgyne*" and Luna is prominent and "full of mutabylyte,"[2] and renames the protagonist Drede and places him on shipboard with seven tempters but not a single figure of virtue, there are also precedents for each of these putative variations from the norm. Indeed, the poet's dream of Drede is taken up by Favell (flattery), palsied Suspycyon, Hervy Hafter (a rogue), ashen-faced Disdayne, Ryote, Dyssymulation with the two-sided cloak, and Disceyte, each of whom in turn welcomes him, befriends him, and then apparently, alone or conspiratorially, betrays him; it is a distinct variation of William's earlier vision of Envye with his backbiting adder's tongue when, after Matins and Mass, he falls asleep and dreams of a field full of folk with the seven deadly sins in *Piers Plowman 5*. But in Drede's case the accelerating, accumulating meetings with tempters cause his anxiety to grow into an incurable fear. His final reaction, to jump overboard to escape the forces that appear to be growing against him, awakens the poet of *The Bowge of Courte*, who is then inspired to write an instructive (and highly moral) account. At the point of greatest danger to his soul, Drede awakens the drowsing poet and brings him to an active moral statement.

This story of temptation is a simple one and this allegory of man's fall is one that was common. If Skelton makes any significant change, then, it must be by placing the action of the dream on board a ship—by commandeering the basic image of the *Narrenschiff* of Sebastian Brant (1494; translated by Jacob Locher as the Latin *Navis Stultifera*, 1497)—while at the same time fusing all seven traditional tempters into a single, composite portrait of flattery and hypocrisy at court, and thereby drawing on his own observations and experiences as tutor to young Henry, duke of York, at Eltham, an appointment the poet accepted from Henry VII in 1496. Given such a twist, the *tempters* become Drede's peculiar *bowge*—or the daily court ration, which, according to a household ordinance, was supposed to provide daily sustenance through allowances of meat, bread, drink, candles, and faggots, which Henry's servants might place in their large leather wallets each morning. This seems to be the sole early indication of the "inventive" Skelton of later fame. But even this has literary antecedents in the fragmentary Distinction I of *De nugis curialium* by Walter Map, the epistle *De curialium miseriis* by Aeneas Silvius to John Eich in 1444, and the well-known *Book of Vices and Virtues*.[3] Therefore it is little wonder that Heiserman, who likewise cites these earlier texts (pp. 35ff.), can use *The Bowge of Courte* as his first example to argue in an important and impressive study of Skelton published in 1961 that the poet's major works are all constituted of recombinations of literary *topoi* taken with intelligence and creativity from the growing treasury of English and Continental literature.

We must be surprised, then, when another distinguished scholar of early English literature, C. S. Lewis, finds this same poem original and indelible. "I suppose that no reader," Lewis writes, "has forgotten the vividness of its characters or its nightmare crescendo from guilelessness to suspicion, from suspicion to acute nervousness, and thence to panic and awakening." *The poem as nightmare*: Leigh Winser takes up the idea by calling the "plot" of the poem "a nightmarish parade of chaos that reflects Drede's waking fear [in which] he does not know right from wrong," and Paul D. Psilos echoes it too when he sums the poem as "an apocalyptic sinking of the ship of state," and Frances McNeely Leonard when she notes that "Everything about [the poem] is directed toward evoking the sensation of nightmare."[4] Such forceful responses from sympathetic present-day readers cannot be altogether different from observations made during the dawn of the Tudor world, a world governed by a grim, religious ruler clinging to slender Plantagenet claims. Regardless of how the ambitious Wynkyn de Worde read this poem, we ought also to ask how Henry VII's court read it. And what they (like Lewis) must have noted—what they persistently say they noted—were those qualities in *The Bowge of Courte* that make the poem (like the poet) startling and unique. They looked primarily at the ways in which it *departed* from the poems they knew.

In *Piers Plowman*, for example, Envye and his six companions are inspired by Resoun's sermon to confess their sins to Repentaunce. In this patently religious setting, immediately following William's pronouncement of the Creed and the initial mumbling meditations along the beads of his Rosary, the emphasis is analogously on penance, the third of the seven sacraments of the Catholic church and the one which precedes that of the Eucharist. For a moment *The Bowge of Courte* appears to be operating in the same world, for the poet has chosen to take his rest at Powers Key—probably an actual wharf in Harwichport where John Powers operated a tavern but surely a setting meant to highlight Drede's interest in what he senses as a "key" to "power," its royal merchandise (41); and possibly a reference to such wealth as the inversion, or antitype, of keys as the sign of religious wealth and power of the papacy. But only for a moment. We are soon told that Drede is attracted to a ship where such merchants also gather and trade, a ship owned by Dame Saunce-Pere (51) who means to outshine the sun in her surroundings of silk and gold (61; 58–59). While the motto on her throne, "*Garder le fortune que est mavelz et bone*" (67), may indicate the latitude, power, and mystery of divinity, it can also in its doubleness indicate deceit and hypocrisy later figured in Dyssymulation with his two faces and two sleeves hiding two different weapons (428–40) as well as, through the sheer illogic of a statement that says nothing while seeming to say everything, threaten ultimate meaninglessness. That is, *The Bowge of Courte* can be at the farthest remove from the perspective in Langland's poem.

Such equivocation disappears when we acknowledge its proximity to the poet's recognition that this ship's cargo is not merely Favor (that is, material and political gain) but "'Favore-to-stonde-in-her-good-grace'" (55). The easy equation of such favor with goodness and grace suggests an unholy trinity that will invert the apparently traditional poem in which the protagonist ought conventionally to seek and discover salvation. Such a suggestion is confirmed in the final portions of the poem's lengthy prologue, when Drede, determined not to lag behind other merchants (43–44), goes aboard but, almost at once, finds no acquaintance, finds himself isolated. In this context, Desyre tells him (106ff.) that "'Fortune gydeth and ruleth all oure shyppe'" (111). Fortune's despotism (similar to that of Elynour Rummyng in a much later poem) breeds self-indulgence and lust and (dissimilar to Elynour) hatred, vengeance, and eternal conflict (112–21). But, again, this view of Fortune is not quite like any of its predecessors. Queen Fortune's palace in the prototype of the *Roman de la Rose*, for instance, allows for the absolute placement of people in the wings of prosperity or adversity. In a second tradition, employed by Boethius, she serves as a ship's guide, leading the vessel to a safe or unsafe harbor; a third, allied tradition makes her constant inconstancy comparable to Luna, while in a fourth tradition she is likened to Our Blessed Lady.[5] In each appearance she is a known force and assigned a clear position. In *The Bowge of Courte* this would also seem to be the case with its opening allusion to Luna (3), but what occurs unexpectedly, what divorces Skelton's Fortune from all these apparent progenitors, is the unusual vagueness by which she is portrayed. While she *seems* to take form in Desyre's summary description (107–17), she actually remains shrouded in mystery, especially when we compare later descriptions, say, of Hervy Hafter (231–38), Ryote (351–64), or Dyssymulation (428–40). Even when Drede tries to describe or evaluate Fortune's actions (or both)—when "we asked favoure, and favour she us gave" (126)—the word *favour* is teasingly ambiguous and his subsequent attempt to elaborate on *favour* (129–30) slides without warning into the slow-building obsession with the tempters, the "Full subtyll persones in nombre foure and thre" (133).

The reason for this is that Skelton is calling on still a fifth tradition for his portrayal of Fortune, a tradition considerably less familiar to us but by far the most familiar to the early Tudors at the turn of the century. He means her to be mysterious because she has no actual existence; like her works, she is illusory. This is precisely the way the Church Fathers from Lactantius and Augustine to Thomas Aquinas defined Fortune. In this sense she was attacked both as a queen and as a guide at sea by Jerome. Just *because* she was illusory, she tempted Christians away from the Church; in this we have both the *donnée* of Skelton's poem and the reason why Drede will see only *evil* temptation in the poet's *dream*. This is also why, when Wynkyn de Worde's customers chose from Macrobius's well-known definitions the kind of dream that might best characterize (and so explain) the eerie quality of Drede's vision and the poet's dream, they would have selected *insomnium*, which, Macrobius reports, "may be caused by mental or physical distress, or anxiety about the future. . . . As examples of the mental variety, we might mention the man who fears the plots or might of an enemy, or is confronted with him in his dream or seems to be fleeing him. . . . Anxiety about the future would cause a man to dream that he is gaining a prominent position or office as he had hoped, or that he is being deprived of it as he feared. . . . [The dreams] flee when he awakes and . . . are noteworthy only during their course and afterwards have no importance or meaning."[6] Like any wholly evil view of the world as not only fallen but also irredeemable, such a dream as we find in *The Bowge of Courte* would be, to the Catholic Tudors under Henry VII, blasphemous.

The theme of unholy parody is reiterated throughout much of Skelton's poem. Favell's instant appreciation of Drede (and to Drede) as one who has spent his days virtuously (151) and therefore observes "'my ladyes grace'" (156; cf. 152) shows his own delusion in his blasphemous comparison of his blessed Fortune to the Tudors' Blessed Lady. His vow "'By Chryste'" (187), Suspycyon's subsequent swearing by taking God's name in vain (199), Hervy Hafter's vows "'By Goddis soule,'" and "'By God,'" (262, 306), Dysdayne's "'By Cryste,'" "'By Goddis bones,'" and "'By him that me boughte'" (300, 304, 309; cf. 325, 332), Ryote's "'in fayth'" and "'by Saynte Thomas of Kente'" (379, 348; cf. 378), and even Disceyte's simple "'by God,'" (514, 522) keep placing a particular dimension on the tempters' speeches. They continually show us how values corrupted by blasphemy can, as patristic writing and commentary insisted, lead to the kind of illusion that converts what action there is in the poem into the innuendo, intimidation, and strangely coded messages that are the natural outgrowths of sinful, self-destructive dreams. "The extent of the evil," Paul D. Psilos reminds us, "is most readily seen in the speeches of Favell, Suspycyon, and Dyssymulation, who approach Drede to offer a parody salvation from fear. They set themselves up as parodies of Christ—preaching the gospel of Fortune while holding out the promise of a private, paranoid salvation with strings attached" (p. 315). So there is even "The note of pathos, of tragedy, in Riot's high spirits and gay tatters," according to John Holloway, which is "not the mere interpolation of a modern mind. 'Counter he coude *O lux* vpon a potte,' Skelton writes; it is the medieval hymn *O lux beata trinitas* that Riot counters. We are never . . . throughout this poem . . . allowed to forget the religious dimension in which all these essentially human and mortal figures have their being. . . . All [such references] illustrate something which is sustained so much without intermission through the poem, that in the end it is quite inescapable."[7] Such self-delusions come to a stunning climax when Dyssymulation, whose motto is *"A false abstracte cometh from a fals concrete"* (439), argues by the authority of "'Saynte Fraunceys, that holy man and frere'" (470) and by Holy Scripture (448). "Spiritual aridity," claims Stanley Eugene Fish, "is the central problem of the poem."[8]

Drede's instinctive response—that he is being robbed of all his wealth (236, 238, 504)—metaphorically reveals his consequent state of fear and trembling in adversity (*trepidus et pusillanimus in adversis*). This state of being is the third of St. Bernard's spiritual ages of man, the state man arrives at when his undirected wandering takes him into a land of unlikenesses (from the viewpoint of God's eternity), a state, that is, where evil men swear by Christ's Passion and by Holy Writ. This is the land where Lydgate places Pilgrim in his translation of Guillaume de Deguileville's *Pilgrimage of the Life of Man* (1426), the same poem Skelton claims to have translated. There too the sense of alienation produces the sense of nightmare—nightmare in Bernard's sense of the word. For de Deguileville such a nightmare was inevitable in any secular life (as it may also have been for John Lydgate, the monk from Bury St. Edmunds); it was part of his argument for taking monastic vows. For Lydgate's successor Skelton—who seems never to have entertained thoughts of a conventual life—it is the more pervasive and dangerous kind of secularism that divides man from Holy Mother Church. It is the state of forgetfulness or perversion that leads to temptation and doom.

Such classifications of dreams as we find in the Church Fathers were also popular among Tudor theologians and preachers, who insisted that the mind was influenced by either divine or demonic impulses. Gregory the Great, author of the *Regula pastoralis*, later translated by King Alfred, and putative originator of plainsong ("Gregorian chant"), which formed the roots of the services in Skelton's day, identified six classes of dreams. Two classes of dreams were caused physically, one (which was illusory) caused by the devil, one caused by an unholy mix of thought and illusion, one from revelation, and one from mixing thought and revelation. Only the devout, Gregory writes, can distinguish between demonic and divine revelation, and even the holiest of men must maintain strict and unceasing vigilance. Clearly this sense of ongoing circumspection becomes the subject of *The Bowge of Courte* when, after the framing prologue describing Fortune and her ship, Drede enters into a series of graduated colloquies with seven tempters who, ostensibly mocking the confessional in their varying pretenses to self-revelation, actually catechize Drede into a position of faithlessness, a psychological state of denying God to save himself. On board a ship no longer guided by Christ but instead by an antitype of the Holy Virgin, where favor and success are to be measured by power and material gain, other practices and sacraments of the Church are burlesqued by inversion. What might have been an instructive pilgrimage for Drede becomes the slow but awful realization that he is not a pilgrim at all but a stranger in exile from Eden (Genesis 15:13, 17:8, 28:4) or from Heaven (Hebrews 11:13–16; 1 Peter 2:11).[9] Nor was such an idea in any way unfamiliar to Wynkyn de Worde's readers. Man's condition as an exile, necessitating life as a pilgrimage, was the basis for the entire exegetical tradition of the early Fathers, confirmed and extended by Ambrose, who condensed biblical history into a three-stage journey from an initial desert-like existence through a garden reminiscent of Canticle of Canticles to the final admission into Paradise at the hands of Christ; such a sense of pilgrimage was also the favorite exegetical topic of the priests at Paul's Cross each day and of the priests in countless parish churches throughout Tudor England each Sabbath.[10] Such an interpretation of the human condition and of man's response was often the context of those Psalms (particularly 38 and 119) which formed the basis of Church liturgy, and served as the source of many of the responsorial chants of the Mass and the Offices according to the Sarum use that Skelton and his readers observed. So commonplace was the idea of exile and pilgrimage to Tudor ears and to the Tudor imagination before the Reformation, in fact, that they found no difficulty in understanding even Christ's visit to Emmaus, during which He appeared as a stranger to two of His disciples (Luke 24:13–35), as another pilgrimage; throughout the medieval and early Tudor period Emmaus remained a central point of reference for liturgical, homiletic, and dramatic commentaries on the meaning of pilgrimage.[11] By naming his poem *The Bowge of Courte* after *the name of Fortune's ship*, Skelton subordinates everything, including the apprehensive Drede and the dreaming poet, to that stark meaning of sailing forth in exile.

To change contexts (but not meaning), the poem charts Drede confronting a *psychomachia* in which there are good forces to do battle with evil ones.[12] "No poet has ever caught this horrible atmosphere with greater skill," Peter Green writes, "the filed tongues, the soft gabble of scandal, the nods and hints and smooth insinuations, the sexual boasting, the social snobs, the hearty gallants with their dice and fashionable songs, the vulgar exhibitionists such as Riot . . . or slippery Dissimulation."[13] To Drede the world seems wholly antagonistic and the odds overwhelming because the seven tempters, even as courtiers, display not only the frag-

menting and pervasive forces of Fortune but also realize and dramatize the
seven deadly sins as they are defined in Chaucer's *Pardoner's Tale*, in *The
Book of Vices and Virtues*, and in contemporary popular religious teaching:
individually and collectively they form a natural passenger list for Dame
Fortune as they spread her effects throughout the damned ship. Thus
Favell displays pride and vainglory (*scientia*); Suspycyon embodies envy
and jealousy (*invidia*); Hervy Hafter, ostensibly a thief, depicts wrath;
Disdayne combines envy and wrath to produce sloth (*accidia*); Ryote,
gambler and panderer, portrays avarice and lechery; and Dyssymulation,
most nearly the icon of Fortune because he has two faces, one lean and the
other threatening, shows Drede, the poet, and us the two sides of *gula*—
gluttony and adversity. The last of all, the most terrifying because the most
mysterious, is Disceyte, who confronts Drede (through coded, nearly im-
penetrable language) with the generalized forces of temptation and sin, of
intimidation and death.[14] For these are more than nominal figures—they
become quite literally deadly temptations and sins because they drive their
victim toward the greatest of mortal sins, toward suicide. Thus upon
examination there is no reason for us to be surprised at the nightmarish
quality of *The Bowge of Courte*, nor can there be any doubt about how
Henry VII's subjects read the poem through in two separate editions over
the course of a decade; it provided yet another testimonial to the felt need
for survival through salvation. While the events of the poem were puta-
tively set by astrological dating in the court of Edward IV, it was written
and published in the time of Henry VII;[15] if it never cut close enough to
the bones of any one particularized individual to risk being misconceived
as satire, it was true enough to the conditions at court and the human
condition of life to work well at the deeper, more profound, more spiritual
level. The poem is actually a sermon without sermonizing, serving the
Tudor court, as well as the citizens of Westminster and the customers in
the bookstalls of St. Paul's Churchyard itself, as a contemporary *parable*. It
figures forth its meaning within image and drama, revitalizing the tradition
of the dream vision employed by a predecessor like Langland.

If this reorientation to *The Bowge of Courte* is considerably more theo-
logical than customary, we must remember that besides being Skelton's
earliest (or one of his earliest) and most popular (or one of his most
popular) publications, the poem frequently refers to the ship, a popular
homiletic figure. Jerome expands on this use of the ship on the sea of life
in *Navis per maria, antenna cruci similata sufflatus* and G. R. Owst has
traced the use back to Ambrose but also forward to Master Achard, abbot

of St. Victor, who compared the sea to the world in his own day. "To cross that sea, we must have a ship, mast, sail," he writes; "The Ship signifies the Faith; the sentences of Holy Scripture are its planks, and the authorities of the Holy Doctors its rudder. The ship is narrow in prow and stern, and broad in the middle; so is the Faith."[16] Contemporary English homilies, too, demonstrate how *The Bowge of Courte* uses the dreamer's central image to burlesque the condition of both Drede and his tempters. For here the ship represents by turn Holy Church and the Good Man— "good," in John Bromyard's words, "not because it is painted with gay colours" like Ryote, "not because its prow is silvery or golden" like Fortune's throne in Skelton's poem, "but because it is steady and firm, compact and watertight, solid and swift, to meet the oncoming sea" (pp. 68– 69). Unlike the passive, impotent Drede, the Good Christian marches forth to fight his evil foes—like St. John, who was associated with a boat, usually (as in a 1465 German block book now housed at the Harvard College Library) about to set out for Patmos where, like Drede's antitype, he will have his apocalyptic dream.

In a related homiletic tradition shared by the early Tudors, the ship itself could also, as in *The Bowge of Courte*, represent Danger and Death. Derived from Ecclesiasticus 43:26—"Let them that sail on the sea, tell the dangers thereof"—one sermon cited by Owst develops an amplified description of the "two arms" of this great sea, one "welth and prosperite," the other "woo and adversite" (p. 71). Like the tempters and Drede, one peril leads to pride and ambition, the other to grief and despair. We have lost much of the force of this Tudor commonplace, however, just as we have lost the Tudor pun then current, which is at the root of the poem: *bouge* in Skelton's day meant not only "court rations" and the leather wallet they were packed in but "to stove in the sides of a ship" in adverse seas. Men (and courts) not stout in the Christian faith, Skelton is saying, are doomed in their voyage on the sea of life.

Nor is Ecclesiasticus the only scriptural reference that might come to the mind of a priest like Skelton when writing a poem about alienation, pilgrimage, and the hope for salvation. Drede falls, like Adam before him, because he is tempted and intimidated by the speeches of others. References to this as the cause of evil in man are found in numerous biblical passages, such as Psalm 13, excerpted for the Proper of the Mass for the first Sunday after Trinity for the Sarum rite and employed in associated antiphons:

The fool hath said in his heart: There is no God.

They are corrupt, and are become abominable in their ways: there is none that doth good, no not one.

The Lord hath looked down from heaven upon the children of men, to see if there be any that understand and seek God.

They are all gone aside, they are become unprofitable together: there is none that doth good, no not one.

Their throat is an open sepulchre; with their tongues they acted deceitfully; the poison of asps *is* under their lips.

Their mouth is full of cursing and bitterness; their feet are swift to shed blood.

Destruction and unhappiness in their ways: and the way of peace they have not known: there is no fear of God before their eyes (1–3).

1 Timothy 6 is another of many passages that Tudor audiences of *The Bowge of Courte* might recall because it describes so exactly the allegorical situation that unfolds in the poem. If any man "consent not to the sound words of our Lord Jesus Christ," Paul writes the bishop of Ephesus to instruct him in his duties,

He is proud, knowing nothing, but sick about questions and strifes of words; from which arise envies, contentions, blasphemies, evil suspicions,

Conflicts of men corrupted in mind, and who are destitute of the truth, supposing gain to be godliness.

But godliness with contentment is great gain.

For we brought nothing into this world: and certainly we can carry nothing out.

But having food, and wherewith to be covered, with these we are content.

For they that will become rich, fall into temptation, and into the snare of the devil, and into many unprofitable and hurtful desires, which drown men into destruction and perdition.

For the desire of money is the root of all evils; which some coveting have erred from the faith, and have entangled themselves in many sorrows.

But thou, O man of God, fly these things: and pursue justice, godliness, faith, charity, patience, mildness.

Fight the good fight of faith; lay hold on eternal life, whereunto thou art called, and hast confessed a good confession before many witnesses (4–12).

But the Bible, unlike the poem, also teaches how the force of God can overcome the mortal sin of despair.

Acknowledging the seven temptations of the seven deadly sins, the Church also encouraged the practice of penance by the service of Penitential Psalms; in response to the antiphon "Remember not, Lord, our offences, nor the offences of our forefathers; neither take thou vengeance of our sins," the communicant was asked to meditate against anger, pride, gluttony, lust, avarice, envy, and sloth by reflecting in turn on Psalms 6, 32, 38, 51, 102, 130, and 143. Poems of visionary quests originating in thirteenth-century France and coming somewhat later into England were structured in seven parts (or *passus*) to suggest the Penitential Psalms and were intended to serve as guidebooks for the sinning Christian as he purified himself through the Lenten season for his customary annual communion at Easter, in celebration of Christ's Resurrection and man's redemption. In these handbooks a dreaming narrator often would encounter the seven deadly sins before arriving at last at the throne of the Lamb in the New Jerusalem. As Barbara Nolan has shown, *Piers Plowman* was written in just such a series of seven meditations,[17] while Drede's seven encounters are an inversion, an antitype that becomes a handbook on the road to self-destruction. Again, in cataloguing the seven stages of Christ's life, the Creed was thought to recall to the worshipper the seven temptations that He overcame. Recalling this early Tudor ritual, we understand why William is made to recite the Creed just before he dreams of the seven deadly sins it evokes in his mind in *Piers Plowman 5*, while the absence of any such saving ritual establishes at once the state of Drede's soul as he is attracted to Dame Fortune's ship.

In his major poems Skelton frequently incorporates scraps of Church liturgy to signal perspective and meaning elsewhere, which a full appreciation of his poem demands. We recall, for instance, Drede's observation about Ryote that "Counter he coude *O lux* upon a potte" (365). Accompanying himself by beating on his drinking pot, Ryote could sing *O lux beata Trinitas*, ordinarily sung at Saturday Vespers. The reference is ironic. As the sixth canonical hour of the day, Vespers (or evening prayer) was meant to celebrate at dusk the idea of Eternal Day when the elect would be reborn into a new life overcoming the end of darkness experienced on earth. Consequently, the Psalms chosen for this service and inscribed in the priest's breviary were "joyful chants, full of admiration and thanksgiving," as M. L'Abbe Bacquez has it.[18] But the Song of Thanks in the service, to which Skelton particularly directs us, is taken from Psalm 143 ("Deliver me, And rescue me out of the hand of strange children; whose mouth hath spoken vanity: and their right hand is the right hand of iniquity") and Psalm 144 ("The Lord keepeth all them that love him; but all the wicked he will destroy. / My mouth shall speak the praise of the Lord: and let all flesh bless his holy name for ever; yea, for ever and ever"). Together the Psalms of this service (outside Paschaltide) figure *The Bowge of Courte* in miniature. But there may be additional reasons why Skelton has caused us to be concerned with Saturday Vespers. In the many Books of Hours (such as the one belonging to Lord Hastings), the offices were associated with events in the life of the Blessed Virgin; in such books, Vespers is the Hour during which we are invited to consider the Slaughter of the Innocents. On the one hand, this suggests Drede, characterized as he is by guilelessness and simplicity; on the other, we are meant to be reminded of Childermass, or Holy Innocents' Day, 28 December, which the Tudors celebrated with a Mock Mass featuring the sort of obscene dancing, singing, and gaming that characterize the tempters of *The Bowge of Courte*, especially Hervy Hafter and Ryote. The other significance of the sixth hour of the Virgin is likewise apposite to the poem: the Flight into Egypt, when Mary, Joseph, and the Christ Child found themselves strangers in exile.

Just which of these commonplace contexts Skelton meant his readers to recall first we can no longer determine, but in a period when religious poetry was apt to have several references concurrently, he probably meant to suggest most or all of them as shaping forces behind the structure and events of *The Bowge of Courte*; this may also explain the poem's special attractiveness for Wynkyn, whose other books (like *The Golden Legend*) often elaborated many of the same motifs. The conclusion of Skelton's poem continues the irony to the end of the parable: in attempting to jump overboard, Drede himself completes the design of the conspirators—rather than frustrating their plans, he seems to fulfill them, awakening us to his danger and saving the poet, and us, in his representational, his figural, commentary on sin and its consequences. The narrative of the poem, then, leads to a kind of nightmarish vision not unlike the Doomsday paintings of the Last Judgment, which decorated many of the parish churches throughout England—churches where Skelton must have worshipped before taking orders. There he doubtless noted that the parishioners, seated in the *navis* of their church, would watch the priest celebrate the Last Supper before the altar, surrounded, in their field of vision, by the picture of Doom commonly painted on the tympanum of the chancel arch that separated them. Thus *The Bowge of Courte*, with its idea of exile and its need for salvation, was continually, daily, being reborn before the living. It is *forever figural*, like Holy Scripture, in which the Word is made flesh.

In many important ways, then, "Skelton presents himself as the Christian moralist whose claim to prophetic authority is also a function of his status as poet, and a powerful one," as A. J. Smith comments,[19] giving renewed force to Heiserman's earlier statement that Skelton was the most learned poet of his time (p. 7). And Skelton does not limit the complex use of Scripture and liturgy as the basis of his work to his early period. He uses the same basis for late poems such as *Speke, Parrot* (1521). Since the earliest serious study of Skelton (that by Dyce in 1843) this has been the poet's most recalcitrant work, and for obvious reasons: it exists in two separate, partial versions (one in manuscript) that must somehow be conflated to establish a full text; it was written at discrete periods and, especially in sequentially dated envoys, seems layered in its presentation; and even in the opening section, which like *The Bowge of Courte* declares the situation on which the poem elaborates, the persona Parrot feels it necessary to speak figuratively rather than directly, by what he describes as "*Confuse distrybutyve*" (198)—that is, a poem that seems confusing because it scatters or distributes its meaning throughout the poem so that the significance grows in the mind of the reader as he progresses through it (as often with Scripture).

But it is hardly the "cryptogram of which we have lost the key" that C. S. Lewis thought it,[20] for it works in ways *identical* to the earlier Skelton poem we have just examined. The difference is a simple one: *The Bowge of Courte* is a *dramatic* poem in which we are to understand that Drede, having neglected his Creed, is so open to temptation that he contemplates leaping from the church (ship) altogether. *Speke, Parrot* is instead a poem of *commentary* and instruction in which Parrot does not warn us what will happen to us so much as *tell* us what we are to know and how we are to interpret it. About this Parrot could not be plainer:

> But of that supposicyon that callyd is arte,
> *Confuse distrybutyve*, as Parrot hath devysed,
> Let every man after his merit take his parte;
> For in this processe, Parrot nothing hath surmysed,
> No matter pretendyd, nor nothyng enterprysed,

> But that *metaphora, alegoria* withall,
> Shall be his protectyon, his pavys and his wall (197–203).

In constructing a proposition (*supposicyon*) that one would consider well arranged (*arte*), Parrot has jumbled together scattered bits of truth (*Confuse distrybutyve*) in a way that will allow readers to determine their meaning, each according to his merit. "Every man shall receive his own reward, according to his own labour" (1 Corinthians 3:8). But the *arte* is in the *supposicyon*, the *donnée* and the selection, not in the material itself which is *never* created (*No matter pretendyd*) nor unusually arranged (*nor nothyng enterprysed*). True, Parrot employs signs and figures (*metaphora, alegoria*) as his shield (*pavys*). Moreover, he will use the mirror in his cage to see prismatically, as if through a glass darkly—"The myrrour that I tote in, *quasi diaphanum, / Vel quasi speculum in enigmate*" (190–91), from 1 Corinthians 13:12. But this is not because what he will say is politically dangerous. He is only a parrot, after all, and he will not flinch, in his envoys, from exposing Thomas Cardinal Wolsey. Rather, *metaphora* and *alegoria* are necessary because God's truth is so dazzling. Parrot's truth, like St. Paul's, *must* be comprehended indirectly on earth; only in Paradise—from where Parrot came and gained his insight—would we be able to see it directly, in all its brilliant glory. There, it would be splendidly lucid, neither divided in its grand design nor distributed across human history. And such a poetic was not at all new to those pre-Reformists like Skelton, who thought of truth as both biblical and figurative. Nor should it now be at all surprising to us who, as readers of *The Bowge of Courte*, know that the shadows of typological truth make the Bowge of Courte a fallen church where passengers interested only in favor will sail into exile and doom. If we convert our attitudes into the pre-Reformist, Catholic attitudes taught by Holy Mother Church, *Speke, Parrot* is as plainspoken as any prophecy of the Old Testament or as any parable of the New.

Because the primary prism in *Speke, Parrot* is Parrot himself, he is careful at the outset to tell us just what *he* signifies. But as if he were a prophet or Christ, he tells us in an accommodating narrative:

> My name is Parrot, a byrd of paradyse,
> By nature devysed of a wonderous kynde,
> Dyentely dyeted with dyvers dylycate spyce,
> Tyl Euphrates, that flode, dryveth me into Inde,
> Where men of that countrey by fortune me fynd,
> And send me to greate ladyes of estate;
> Then parot must have an almon or a date (1–7).

This seems plainer than some denser verses we shall be encountering in a moment, but it nevertheless invites the kind of figural speculation in which Parrot wishes to train us because, as a citizen from Paradise, he wants to elevate us in time to the perspective (or truth) he learned there. He must, because that is the only truth he knows, and his poem will have, we remember, "*No matter pretendyd.*" If we read these opening lines as *alegoria*, as Parrot tells us to do (surprisingly few have done so), then Parrot aligns himself with Adam, Abraham, Moses, or Christ: he is *wonderous* by *nature* because he is from *paradyse*, where as in Canticles he has been fed sweets (*dylycate spyce*). But then he somehow fell to earth (like his scriptural counterparts) where a flood as dreadful as Noah's drove him into our fallen world. Luckily found (like Moses) or revealed (like Christ) he was sent to the best home possible (*ladyes of estate*), but even this was so harsh for one who had seen the face of God that he must repeatedly ask for anodynes (*an almon or a date*) to soothe his pain of remembering. In subsequent stanzas, these women, who are more sinful than they realize (Eve, perhaps, or Delilah, or Salomé) entice Parrot to worldly pleasures and from time to time he succumbs ("With ladyes I lerne, and go with them to scole," 21). He learns their languages (French, Flemish, Castilian—in addition to the biblical languages of Latin, Hebrew, Arabic, Chaldaic, and Greek, 25–26), their pat slogans " 'Cryst save Kyng Henry the .viii., our royall kyng,' " 34), and even their tricks of rhetoric (43). Therefore he must pull himself back from a fallen state from time to time by calling first for an electuary (48) and then, when that is insufficient, on the liturgy of salvation itself, such as a popular hymn of the Church, *Salve festa dies* (49).

As we might expect from a man of Skelton's learning—self-proclaimed as England's first and then England's only triple laureate, with honors from Oxford, Louvain, and Cambridge—the poet conflates here several traditions. Following the current bestiaries (which claimed India as Parrot's birthplace), Parrot (or Psittacus) was known for his skill at language and his quick ability to mimic others. In time he was made "roughly comparable to the court jester who offers garbled scraps of wisdom in snatches of foreign tongues, an outspoken revealer of confidences, indulged because he is not responsible for his sometimes telling juxtaposition of random phrases," as Fish has it (p. 135). But this wise fool has a dual nature; if fallen now (or apparently falling) he still trails his clouds of Paradisiacal glory and so will occasionally speak in (what seems to us) tongues reminiscent of Pentecost or Whitsunday. He has credentials for this, too: a second pedigree, which the Tudors received from Boccaccio

(*Genealogia Deorum*, 2, xlix), assigned the parrot divinity as a descendant from Prometheus (who breathed the breath of life into clay, like God) and who, as the son of Deucalion, barely escaped the flood, the eschatological memory of which will nearly overcome Parrot at the end of his poem (449–518). For Parrot cannot obliterate historical matters of figural significance no matter how many anodynes he consumes. Finally, Parrot is blessed in his cage with a mirror that refracts light and so throws into relief much that is around him. In medieval homiletic literature, the mirror was a figure for the Host, its broken pieces the various communicants who wished to unite their bodies with Christ's. The scriptural authority for this was again St. Paul (1 Corinthians 12:3–8, 11–13). Owst has located a representative sermon on the Feast of Corpus Christi in which the mystery of Transubstantiation is explained by likening it to the splinters of a broken glass mirror, where a separate face is seen in each piece:

> And that loke by skile. Lo! here:
> Bihold thi-self in a schewere [mirror].
> Thou ne sest but onliche thi faas,
> The while all hol is the glass.
> And brek the glas in two or thre,
> And so moni formes thou miht se.
> Beo the makyng of the oblee
> Wel and skilfoliche me may se
> Of wȝuche we make Godus fflesch,
> This is the saumple whose wol esch (p. 195).

Before Skelton's day, John Wyclif had made the figure famous by discussing it in one of his best-known sermons attacking the doctrine of the Eucharist based on the notion of Christ's broken body (*Hoc est corpus meum*, Matthew 26:26). Parrot is thus always reminded of Christ's Passion and of man's fallen nature.

Such driving awareness as his nature and situation provide him, then, forces Parrot to interrupt his mimicking in English and foreign tongues—his "gibberish"—to talk prophetically (*quasi speculum, in enigmate*). Parrot's overt reference directs us once more to Corinthians where (1 Corinthians 12–14) St. Paul makes the oblique telling of such prophetic truths synonymous with speaking in tongues:

> Now concerning spiritual things, my brethren, I would not have you ignorant.

You know that when you were heathens, you went to dumb idols, according as you were led.
Wherefore I give you to understand, that no man, speaking by the Spirit of God, saith Anathema to Jesus. And no man can say the Lord Jesus, but by the Holy Ghost (12:1–3).

It is when Parrot speaks like the world of ladies and estates—speaks *our* language and thoughts—that *he* feels he is speaking gibberish, when he is "as sounding brass, or a tinkling cymbal" (1 Corinthians 13:1). Contrarily, he must speak such gibberish because he must share his burden of knowledge. "And if I should have prophecy and should know all mysteries, and all knowledge, and if I should have all faith, so that I could remove mountains, and have not charity, I am nothing" (1 Corinthians 13:2). Thus Parrot's figural cage: his knowledge separates him from the fallen world he inhabits while Paul's (and Christ's) demand for charity requires him to operate within it. So he finds a language—the *Confuse distrybutyve*—which will allow him to prophesy the future by recalling splintered but appropriate typological events from man's biblical past and then reuniting them to make his own dark mirror whole. He will fulfill God's purpose by using God's own means.

Far from being a cryptogram, then, *Speke, Parrot* begins by announcing its method and its end, and it follows precisely its own prescription: when it talks to its Tudor audience in contemporary language of contemporary events, it provides merely fleeting exempla from a fallen world for the figural truths always presented by scriptural references. In juxtaposing (or mixing) the two, Parrot means only to display (and insist on) the relevance of current events to God's plan of history. This is central (and crucial) to the meaning of each of the four parts into which critics have for some time been dividing the poem for convenience (although Parrot would, of course, say this is again a matter of accommodation by a fallen world struggling to understand the design of God's scheme).

In Part 1, Parrot first tries to keep things as whole as possible. He injects whole stanzas to demonstrate that in Tudor England (where he is presently caged) Henry VIII and Thomas Cardinal Wolsey are reenacting typological roles already forewarned in the Old Testament. To this end— he seems to give up on us rather quickly—there are only two really puzzling passages. The first one is this:

"Besy, besy, besy, and besynes agayne!
"*Que pensez-voz*, Parrot, what meneth this besynes?"

> *Vitulus* in Oreb troubled Arons brayne;
> Melchisedeck mercyfull made Moloc mercyles:
> To wyse is no vertue, to medlyng, to restles;
> In mesure is tresure, *cum sensu maturato*:
> *Ne tropo sanno, ne tropo mato.*
>
> Aram was fyred with Caldies fyer called Ur;
> Jobab was brought up in the lande of Hus;
> The lynage of Lot toke supporte of Assur;
> Jereboseth in Ebrue, who lyst the cause dyscus.
> Peace, Parrot, ye prate as ye were *ebrius*!
> Howst the, *lyuer god van hemrick, ic seg*;
> In Popering grew peres, whan Parrot was an eg (57–70).

Besynes is a sign of our fallen world (as *business* is a chief word in our vocabulary); to understand it we need to call on Parrot to explain. He sees it as a distraction to things of this world and an avoidance of the truths of God. He tells us this figurally, by referring us to Exodus 32 where Aaron forges a calf (*vitulus*) from the golden earrings of wives, sons, and daughters, dabbling in material wealth to make a false idol (2–4). When Moses comes down from Sinai with the tablets of God's Law, he confronts such sacrilege, but Aaron says it just happened: "I cast it [the gold trinkets] into the fire, and this calf came out" (24). A. R. Heiserman was the first to decipher this: "Wolsey, the son of a butcher, and thus a calf, must have appeared simply to have 'come out' of the gold Henry cast about him, and Henry's reaction to the phenomenon seemed to the [poet] as weak as Aaron's" (p. 137). In the next line, Parrot tells us that Henry VIII's indulgence of Wolsey (*Melchisedeck mercyfull*) encouraged him to even greater wrongs (*Moloc mercyles*), setting up the poem's figure for Tudor times in the conflict between Melchisedech, the priest-king of Genesis 14:18–24, and Moloch, the Antichrist, the "idol of the children of Ammon" (3 Kings 11:5–7). Such an indulgence by Henry is dangerous, as the Old Testament tells us throughout, just as bowing down to a false god (the golden calf or Moloch) is dangerous—witness the death of *Aram* (rightly Aran, Genesis 11:28) by fire and the sufferings of *Jobab* (Job). It enlists one with such enemies of the Jews as the Moabites (Judges 3:28) and the Amorrhites (Judges 1:34), *the lynage of Lot*, and the Assyrians (4 Kings 19:35; cf. Isaias 37:36), descendants of *Assur*. What is needed in a time of gathering evil forces is another *Jereboseth* (2 Kings 11:21), a homonym for Jerobaal and a common name for Gideon, Hebrew for "contender with the idol," as the multilingual Parrot knows. Without a proper leader (Melchisedech, Gideon, Christ), the world will be filled with the chaos of sin. Parrot may be thought drunk in such a prophecy (*ebrius*), but it is actually the world that is intoxicated, as the colloquial Flemish (and so gibberish) tag-line and the reference to Wolsey's selfish negotiations at Calais (indicated by its neighbor Poperinghe) mean, through the dark glass, to confirm.

We can simplify Parrot's history lessons, then, by concentrating on three people who serve as biblical types of behavior to which he refers us as illustrative of the choices that are open: Melchisedech, Moloch, and Gideon. In Genesis 14:18, Melchisedech offered Abraham bread and wine, prefiguring the Eucharist, and in time he came (in Hebrews 6:20) to prefigure Christ. He prefigures Christ more particularly, St. Paul goes on, because he was also a Prince of Peace:

> For this Melchisedech *was* king of Salem, priest of the most high God, who met Abraham returning from the slaughter of the kings, and blessed him:
> To whom also Abraham divided the tithes of all: who first indeed by interpretation, is king of justice; and then also king of Salem, that is, king of peace:
> Without father, without mother, without genealogy, having neither beginning of days nor end of life, but likened unto the Son of God, continueth a priest for ever (Hebrews 7:1–3).[21]

His law, "the order of Melchisedech" (Psalm 109:4), is "according to the power of an indissoluble life" (Hebrews 7:16). Indeed, Melchisedech was far more important in Skelton's time than he is in our own. The Church Fathers—Clement, Cyprian, Ambrose, Eusebius of Cesarea—made him a part of the common catechesis, using him as the prefigurement of Christ again and again and his sacrifice as the forerunner of Holy Communion; "Who is more a priest of God Most High," asks Cyprian of Cecilius, "than our Lord Jesus Christ, Who offered to the Father the same offering as Melchisedech, that is, bread and wine, which is to say, His Body and His Blood?" (*Epistles* 63:4). Even more importantly, Melchisedech would have been a central figure of the Church to any Tudor because his name was intoned in each and every Mass of the land as part of the Canon according to the Sarum rite when the celebrant passed for the fifth time over the chalice: "Upon which do thou vouchsafe to look with a favourable and gracious countenance, and to accept them as thou didst vouchsafe to accept the gifts of thy righteous servant Abel, the sacrifice of our patriarch Abraham, and the holy sacrifice, the pure oblation, which thy high priest Melchisedech offered unto thee."[22] (Douglas Gray has recently reported

an altar mosaic from Ravenna picturing this [p. 8].)²³ But it is important
for Parrot to direct his Tudor congregation back through the Mass to
church history because Melchisedech's law was the continuity of a cove-
nant with Noah and, as we have seen, Parrot has identified his own history
with the time of Noah's flood. Parrot is thus speaking of his *own* law, the
covenant to which *he* has agreed. Furthermore, beginning in the time of
Pope Demasus, Melchisedech became identified with the Holy Spirit (be-
cause he was conceived without known parents; Ambrose has a consider-
able discussion of this) and thus becomes a shadow—as the Holy Spirit,
redefined by St. Paul—of Parrot himself! Within the "history" of the
poem, Parrot, speaking in tongues, joins with Henry VIII, as King of
Peace, in eternal contest with Moloch/Wolsey, the Antichrist (Leviticus
18:21). For Moloch, or a follower of Moloch, God allows no concessions:
"the people of the land shall stone him" (Leviticus 20:2). Moloch's New
Testament fulfillment was believed by Skelton's readers to be Herod (Mat-
thew 2:13), a point underlined at least once a year by the cycles of mystery
plays, such as the one in Wakefield, which contrasted a play of Melchised-
ech (now lost) with the play of Herod. We shall get to the third of Parrot's
sacred trinity, Gideon, shortly.

The second puzzling passage in *Speke, Parrot* returns to the subject of
the Antichrist, again by figural scriptural history:

> *Ulula*, Esebon, for Jeromy doth wepe!
> Sion is in sadnes, Rachell ruly doth loke;
> Madionita Jetro, our Moyses kepyth his shepe;
> Gedeon is gon, that Zalmane undertoke,
> Oreb *et* Zeb, or *Judicum* rede the boke.
> Now Geball, Amon and Amaloch—"Harke, harke,
> Parrot pretendith to be a bybyll clarke!"
>
> O Esebon, Esebon, to the is cum agayne
> Seon, the regent *Amorreorum*,
> And Og, that fat hog of Basan, doth retayne
> The crafty *coistronus Cananeorum*;
> And *assilum*, whilom *refugium miserorum*,
> *Non phanum, sed prophanum*, standyth in lyttyll sted:
> *Ulula*, Esebon, for Jepte is starke ded! (113–26).

King Sehon, of the Amorite city of Hesebon, was defeated by Moses
when he refused the Jewish leader peaceable passage in his long desert
journey to the plains of Moab (Numbers 21:29–31), but this defeat causes

Parrot to weep for Hesebon as Jeremiah did for Jerusalem and Rachel for Zion. Tropologically, the contest recurs (Judges 11), just as it shadows Gideon's defeat of the Madianites and his execution of their king, Salmana, and their princes, Oreb and Zeb (Judges 7,8). For Moses (to whom the Tudors attributed authorship of the Pentateuch) it became proverbial: "Therefore it is said in the proverb: Come into Hesebon, let the city of Sehon be built and set up" (Numbers 21:27). For patristic commentators preceding Skelton each of these struggles prefigured the eternal struggle between Christ and Antichrist and so foreshadows the Last Judgment. All of these battles, in fact, so haunted the Jewish imagination of the Old Testament that they are brought together again in Psalm 82, a song for Asaph, subtitled in the Vulgate "*A prayer against the enemies of God's church.*"

O God, who shall be like to thee? hold not thy peace, neither be thou still, O God.
For lo, thy enemies have made a noise: and they that hate thee have lifted up the head.
They have taken a malicious counsel against thy people, and have consulted against thy saints.
They have said: Come and let us destroy them, so that they be not a nation: and let the name of Israel be remembered no more.
For they have contrived with one consent: they have made a covenant together against thee, the tabernacles of the Edomites, and the Ismahelites;
Moab, and the Agarens, Gebal, and Ammon and Amalec: the Philistines, with the inhabitants of Tyre.
Yea, and the Assyrian also is joined with them: they are come to the aid of the sons of Lot.
Do to them as thou didst to Madian and to Sisara: as to Jabin at the brook of Cisson.
Who perished at Endor: and became as dung for the earth.
Make their princes like Oreb, and Zeb, and Zebee, and Salmana.
All their princes, who have said: Let us possess the sanctuary of God for an inheritance.
O my God, make them like a wheel; and as stubble before the wind.
As fire which burneth the wood: and as a flame burning mountains:
So shalt thou pursue them with thy tempest: and shalt trouble them in thy wrath.
Fill their faces with shame; and they shall seek thy name, O Lord.

Let them be ashamed and troubled for ever and ever: and let them
be confounded and perish.
And let them know that the Lord is thy name: thou alone art the
most High over all the earth.

This Psalm explains the causes of Hesebon's fall, and so provides the
necessary gloss to Parrot's final references in our second extract. In his
Enarrationes in Psalmos, Augustine tells us that Asaph signifies the congre-
gation of the Church which appeals in Psalm 82 to Christ (because he was
in their likeness as a man) to save them against the enemy, "that head
which is *exalted above all that is called God, and that is worshipped.*" Various
Augustinian etymologies for the names in Psalm 82 (perhaps joined with
other *scholia* in various medieval texts) join them all into "the head" which
is Moloch/Antichrist.[24] But the Psalm is itself so dreadful that it is one of a
very few omitted altogether from the Sarum Missal (and from the Propers
of the Mass). Skelton would have known it, however, for it would have
been in the psalters and primers of his day and, as a priest, he was required
to recite it weekly in connection with the offices. But that Parrot would
think of a vision of Scripture so horrible in its destructiveness shows us
that he is meant to be characterized as a seer whose prophecies, springing
from his surroundings, can only be riddled with eschatological thoughts.
Thus from the viewpoint of the Church Fathers Parrot is exactly right in
choosing a Psalm as his text of reference in this poem as lectionary; from
the days of the primitive Christian community (and with the later patristic
commentary) the importance of Psalms lay in their messianic significance,
and that was derived from the eschatological need, demonstrated in the
Psalms in a variety of ways, for the Second Coming. Parrot's denunciation
of the figure of Moloch now leads him to a stunning climax: "*Quod
magnus est dominus Judas Scarioth*" (133).

It is this amassing of forces against Melchisedech/Christ that makes
Parrot so anxious—a far more sweeping and profound anxiety than that
conceived by the selfish Drede—and it guides us through the rest of *Speke,
Parrot*. As Part 1 progresses, Parrot grows more urgent, even more plain-
spoken. He first condenses his fears into a single line, "But *moveatur terra,
let the world wag*" (88), recalling both Psalm 98 ("The Lord hath reigned,
let the people be angry: he that sitteth on the cherubims: let the earth be
moved," 1) and the *Libera me* from the Office for the Dead ("In that
dreadful day, when the heavens and the earth are shaken").[25] "That dread-
ful day," the Doomsday which this poem keeps announcing, is brought
closer to home in Part 2 of the poem. Here the apparent digression con-

cerning the "Grammarians' War" of 1519–21 testifies to the advancing forces of Moloch, because the referential texts are no longer so ancient as the Psalms. Rather, they are as current as the revolutionary *Vulgaria* of William Horman and John Stanbridge (which break with the Church's centuries-old method of teaching Latin) and the present-day acts of Wolsey who, setting himself up as a patron of the New Learning by founding a Greek professorship at Oxford, once more showed his opposition to the traditions of Holy Mother Church. On one hand, Parrot's absurdly extended use of "Suche shredis of sentence, strowed in the shop / Of auncyent Aristippus and such other mo" (92–93) rather than the Scriptures and liturgy (97) leads him into rhetorical nonsense that easily accommodates the "gibberish" he has found in the fallen world (134–82). On the other hand, this sort of grammatical nonsense—the antithesis of typological citation—reminds him of the Tower of Babel, that precise moment when evil in the world dispensed itself beyond any reckoning: "there the language of the whole earth was confounded: and from thence the Lord scattered them abroad upon the face of all countries" (Genesis 11:9). Now, imprisoned on earth, exiled as he is from home, Parrot (whose name, etymologically, is "Little Peter") has tried by scriptural authority to rescue language long enough to warn of Doomsday. Exhausted, he stops, asks for another painkiller, and recommends himself to St. Nicholas, patron saint of captives.

> Now a nutmeg, a nutmeg, *cum gariopholo*,
> For Parrot to pyke upon, his brayne for to stable,
> Swete synamum styckis and *pleris cum musco*!
> In Paradyce, that place of pleasure perdurable,
> The progeny of Parrottis were fayre and favorable;
> Nowe *in valle* Ebron Parrot is fayne to fede—
> "Cristecrosse and Saynt Nycholas, Parrot, be your good spede!" (183–89).

As Parrot repeats his means of writing poetry, the first version of *Speke, Parrot*, the public one printed by Richard Lant for Henry Tab (c. 1545), comes to an end.

Part 3, in its fullest form in the later manuscript once belonging to the London mercer John Colyn (British Library MS Harleian 2252, fols. 133v–40v), is a single brief interlude in a markedly different tone. The women about Parrot's cage have been replaced by Galathea who "pray[s]" that Parrot, "for Maryes saake," will sing her a love song (233–34). Parrot responds in kind, with a song at once erotic and again so general that it

would seem to be a song of intercession for mankind delivered by Parrot,
now speaking as Christ.

> My propire Besse,
> My praty Besse,
> Turns ons agayne to me;
> For slepyste thou, Besse,
> Or wakeste thow, Besse,
> Myne herte hyt ys with the (235–40).

Some years ago H. L. R. Edwards recognized that the reference came
from Skelton's own time, from a popular Tudor ballad that begins,

> "*Come over the burn, Besse,*
> *Thou little pretty Besse,*
> *Come over the burn, Besse, to me!*"
> The burn is this world blind
> And Besse is mankind,
> So proper I can none find as she;
> She dances and leapes,
> And Christ stands and clepes:
> "Come over the burn, Besse, to me!" (p. 193).

Had he followed the song to its conclusion, he would have found it, like
so much else Parrot has spoken, apocalyptic.

> Nowe, Besse, redresse the,
> And shortly confess the
> Of synnes that opres the, let see;
> The water hit fallyth,
> And Crist stondyth and callyth,
> Come over the burne, Besse to me.[26]

It is one, that is, of a number of eschatological poems that appeared
around 1500, around the time of *The Bowge of Courte*. Here is part of
another:

> Com home againe!
> Com home againe!
> Mine owene swet hart, com home againe!
> Ye are gone astray
> Out of youer way,
> Therefore, com home againe!

Mankend I cale
Which lyeth in thrale:
For love I mad thee fre.
To pay the det,
The prise was gret,
From hell that I ransomed thee.[27]

Parrot's song and Galathea's gratitude—"Goddis blissyng lyght on thy lytyll swete musse!" (266)—conclude in the rubric *"Vita et Anima, / Zoe Ke Psiche"* (267–68). Combining the old Latin and the newly-fashionable Greek for "Body and Soul," it suggests that this "dialogue" is merely Parrot's fresh way of renewing his urgent sense of the imminence of the Last Judgment by bringing history into his own times (an equivalent extension of Psalm 82) and by focusing attention on a single listener, the reader. "For whoo lokythe wyselye in your warkys may fynde / Muche frutefulle mater" (296–97). The subsequent Part 4 is a series of four unusually long envoys, sequentially dated by an internal system beginning with the year of Skelton's laureateship at Oxford, which detail Wolsey's increasing failure at Calais as an index (as Moloch/Wolsey) to his increasingly futile but dangerous power.[28] Whether the envoys were independently written as an ongoing series of confirmations of Parrot's accurate sense of approaching doom, or whether they are fictionally dated to suggest a world whirling madly toward its own destruction, we can no longer say, but so frightened is Parrot now that he breaks away from tongues and from scriptural and liturgical references altogether, ending with a most extraordinary catechism of the new Moloch's sins, which in the aggregate will assure God's wrathful punishment equal to the flood of Noah (or Deucalion) which he had experienced early in his life.

So braynles calvys hedes, so many shepis taylys;
So bolde a braggyng bocher, and flesshe sold so dere;
So many plucte partryches, and so fatte quaylles;
So mangye a mastyfe curre, the grete greyhoundes pere;
So bygge a bulke of brow-auntleres cabagyde that yere;
So many swannes dede, and so small revelle—
Syns Dewcalyons floodde, I trow, no man can telle (484–90).

So many swannes dede: Parrot refers to the Duke of Buckingham (whose crest had featured a swan), executed on trumped-up charges of treason by Wolsey who used this event to ruin the spirit of Thomas Howard, duke of Norfolk, and so effectively end the power of the older aristocracy, which had constituted the rival faction at Henry's court. Thus this butcher's son, who would make his living too by the carnage of all about him, had his way clear as ruler of the King himself (*the grete greyhoundes pere*, referring to the Tudor badge). In the epistle which Parrot had earlier taken for his text, Paul's first letter to Corinth, Parrot had been told that

> if I should have prophecy and should know all mysteries, and all knowledge, and if I should have all faith, so that I could remove mountains, and have not charity, I am nothing.
>
> And if I should distribute all my goods to feed the poor, and if I should deliver my body to be burned, and not have charity, it profiteth me nothing (13:2–3),

and he has done his best by telling us all that he knows and warning us for the sake of our own salvation. Alas, Wolsey and the times have outdone him.

> So many vacabondes, so many beggers bolde;
> So myche decay of monesteries and of relygious places:
> So hote haterede agaynste the Chyrche, and cheryte so colde;
> So myche of my lordes grace, and in hym no grace ys;
> So many holow hartes, and so dowbylle faces;
> So myche sayntuary brekyng, and prevylegidde barrydde—
> Syns Dewcalyons flodde was nevyr sene nor lyerde (498–504).

On 1 April 1521 Wolsey was given papal powers to legitimatize bastards, to reform secular clergy no matter how eminent, to dispense with canonical impediments to holy orders, to appoint to ecclesiastical benefices at will, and to absolve men from all ecclesiastical penalties including excommunication. He had in effect, Parrot implies, destroyed Holy Mother Church; and with such a fall of the Church would come Doomsday itself. Parrot still gathers about himself, as he has throughout the poem, classical Latin tags, but they are secular and of little real use even for consolation. No real rhetorical *pavis* is left, although Parrot's spirit remains undefeated.

Yet early in the poem there were dark hints of such an outcome: if we review the work in light of the original trinity with which Parrot began, we will see an increasingly powerful Moloch set against a progressively weaker Melchisedech. As for Gideon, whom the Tudors desperately need, Parrot has tried his best and failed. Perhaps that is because he pinned some slight hope on the ladies of great estate that they might, with him, rest their faith in Christ's ability to save good men and women on Judgment Day as He had saved them earlier by harrowing Hell. This at least occurs

to Parrot at line 49 where, citing the Easter hymn *Salve festa dies* that
begins with that fact, he points past it to the Sequence in the Proper of the
Mass for Easter Sunday.

> Prince of evil, wicked fiend,
> What avails thy impious lie?
> In fiery chains thou art confined
> By Christ's glorious victory.
> Ye peoples! marvel at the tale!
> Whoe'er such miracles hath heard?
> That death o'er death should so prevail,
> Such grace on sinners be conferr'd!
> Judea, unbelieving land,
> Look forth, and on the Christians gaze.

He was mistaken; the women ignored such guideposts, such solace. With-
out disturbing his sense of scriptural history and Old Testament prophecy,
he signals his dreadful despair at the close of Part 2 with the reference to
St. Nicholas, whose feast day the early Tudors celebrated on 6 December.
Nicholas was (after Mary) the most popular saint with the Tudors—even
Skelton's parish town of Diss had built a special guild chapel dedicated to
him—and it is to the Sequence of the Proper of *his* Mass that Parrot finds
his sorrow echoed, his only hope before the coming flood.

> O Nicholas, thou blessed saint!
> in bitterness of death we faint,
> > us to some harbour lead;
> Lead us to some safe sheltering place,
> thou who dost by thy kindly grace
> > so many help in need; . . . .
> We who in this sad world abide,
> already shipwrecked in the tide
> > of guilt and sin and pain,
> Thee, glorious Nicholas, we pray
> to that safe harbour shew the way,
> > Where peace and glory reign.

Thus Christ in Part 1 and Nicholas in Part 2 are suggested by Parrot as new
possibilities for Gideon; Skelton himself serves as a kind of Gideon too,
the priest and poet as teacher. But such suggestions fall on deaf ears, and
the poem pushes them away, as it has pushed out so much that was good,
to conclude in Part 4 with the hulking body of Wolsey. The portrait of

England's chief prelate with which we are left in the poem's penultimate line—Wolsey riding his mule in trappings of gold (517)—pointedly parodies Jesus on his way to Jerusalem where His trial and crucifixion will allow Him at least to harrow Hell, while the gold reminds us, at the end, of Aaron's golden calf with which Parrot's (and Skelton's) history of man's fall began. *Speke, Parrot* like *The Bowge of Courte* depicts events on the tangent of eternity and takes them to the edge of doom.

In both these major works, then, one early and one late, Skelton writes a poetry that continually points beyond itself. It was the sort of poetry he knew best. D. W. Robertson, Jr., has shown in some detail in his illuminating and influential *Preface to Chaucer*, subtitled "Studies in Medieval Perspective," how the continuing study of Scripture that Skelton inherited led to habits of reading and preaching that were allegorical, figural, referential. Like Scripture, poetry became a matter of signs. Such a poetics also came from the Church Fathers—specifically from Augustine's *De Doctrina Christiana*. There Bernard F. Huppé sums, "Aesthetic pleasure derives . . . from the very discovery of hidden meanings; the quality of the pleasure has a direct relation to the difficulty of the ambiguities to be resolved. As the mind is exercised it is prepared to receive with warmth and delight the dogmatic truth which stated plainly might be accompanied by no pleasurable movement of the mind."[29] As a priest, Skelton added references to the well-known portions of Catholic liturgy. True to the Church he served as priest, the poet Skelton wrote poems that become their own lectionaries; we as readers become, while reading them, communicants with him. We are not surprised to find Drede's vision (however traditional its poetic form) to be nightmarish, nor should we be confused by Parrot's use of figural history. And we shall not be surprised either when we turn to Skelton's other works to find that the hawking curate of Diss is far more to Skelton than a curate; that Jane Scrope is no mere novice of Carrow to him, but much more; and that Elynour Rummyng is not simply an alewife in Leatherhead, either. But to understand Skelton's particular artistry we must first look further at his resources. Let us stop momentarily to examine the poetics available to a priest in England in those days just preceding the Reformation.

2

A PRIEST'S POETICS

PRIDE
Bench end (hand-carved, fifteenth century),
Church of the Holy Trinity, Blythburgh, Suffolk

THE WIDELY DIVERGENT VIEWS of Skelton now current result from the temptation to fill large gaps in our information about the man: he invites conjecture. Even after decades of research, so assiduous a scholar as H. L. R. Edwards published a biography in 1949 that is largely speculative. There are, to be sure, a number of indirect references that allow us to fashion interpretations—such as the dedication of his first poem to "that excellent doctor of theology, Master Ruckshaw" of Peterhouse, Cambridge—and a number of comments by contemporaries—such as Erasmus's lavish praise, when he once found Skelton tutoring Prince Henry, and Caxton's admiration for his scholarship. These reflect Skelton's learning. But we can also pretty safely infer Skelton's staunch faith by quoting the Venetian ambassador concerning Skelton's pupil, Henry VIII, as Lacey Baldwin Smith does. This Italian diplomat tells us that Henry was "very religious; heard three masses daily when he hunted, and sometimes five on other days," while Smith attributes the fact that the prince was "thoroughly inculcated with orthodox habits" and even "the works of Thomas Aquinas" to Skelton who "drilled" him "in healthy respect for stern piety and a fear of the seven deadly sins which no amount of humanistic laughter or Renaissance anticlericalism could dispel."[1] Moreover, Henry VIII's grandmother, the devout Lady Margaret Beaufort, awarded Skelton his living at Diss. But still other judgments have been built on inferences that may rely on no facts at all, but on Skelton's own self-allusions, often slanted by the *persona* of a poem, or on conventions of extravagant fiction as in his flytings against Christopher Garnesche (around 1514), or even on irreverent or light-hearted jests that circulated about him some time after his death (save one), jests which, as we shall discover, may well have been colored by post-Reformationist wit.

When we turn to primary documents, though, a clear pattern emerges: most of them record Skelton's association with the Catholic Church. (The exceptions are his foreign laureation noted in the Cambridge University Registers in 1493; his dismissal from court as Prince Henry's tutor on the death of Prince Arthur, 29 April 1502; his taking meals in Westminster and Cambridge with members of the University; and his lease of residence in later years in Westminster.) The first three extant documents set down his admission to the major clerical orders, while a fourth notes the King's payment to him for celebrating Mass, as we have seen. Two new citations, recently discovered by Gordon Kipling and unpublished until now, show that Skelton was serving young Henry, the son of Henry VII, as chaplain in 1500. PRO LC2/1 is a series of Tudor funeral accounts; an entry for Prince Edmund (1500) notes:

for ther gown*es* & hod*es*
Mr. Geffrey chapleyn to my lorde of york——iiij yardes
Mr Skelton chaplayne to my lorde of york——iiij yard*es*
at iij s vii d yee yarde (fol. 4).

In 1503 Skelton was again present for the funeral of Queen Elizabeth; a
"M*r* holt" drew mourning cloth for "my lorde prync*es* houshold ser-
u*a*ntes" where Skelton is described as a "scolmaiste*r*" (fol. 72v). Addi-
tional records, in the archives of the episcopal court at Norwich, record to
a slight degree his activities after he took up his position as rector of Diss,
a prosperous market town on the banks of the Waveney River in southern
Norfolk. On 10 April 1504, for instance, Skelton witnessed the will of his
parishioner Margery Cowper: "Theise beyng witnesse M*aster* John Skel-
ton laureat p*ar*son of disse and S*ir* John Clarke sowle preest of the same
towne" (Register "Rix," 1504–07, fol. 112). On 3 December 1509 one John
Chapman certified before the Consistory Court that Thomas Pykerell of
Diss had been cited to appear to answer certain interrogatories concerning
the health of his soul; Skelton was the complainant. Although Pykerell
was absolved on 4 January, he did not appear in court on 14 January as
ordered, and so on 4 February he was "suspended"—that is, he was for-
bidden to enter Skelton's church. Another ecclesiastical suit occurred on 6
November 1511, when Master William Dale, who had succeeded Thomas
Wolsey as rector of Redgrave in March 1506, denied charges made against
him; when he reappeared with one Thomas Revet, presumably his ac-
cuser, Bishop Richard Nikke (occasionally spelled *Nikkes* and surely pro-
nounced "Nix") appointed as arbiters Master Simon Dryver, Doctor of
Decrees, and John Skelton, rector of Diss. Apparently they brought about
a reconciliation (Institution Book XIV, fols. 60k[r], 60k[v], 60l[v],
600[r])[2] that was acceptable to a stern and authoritative man like Nikke.[3]

In 1512 or 1513 Skelton began signing his poems "orator regius," suggest-
ing he had moved to Westminster—the lease mentioning him is dated
1518—but he still was thought of as a member of the Church, as a com-
mendation of him in a *Life of St. Werburge* (1513) by Henry Bradshaw, a
monk of Chester, makes clear.[4] Late in Skelton's life, the conservative
Bishop Nikke—by then active in his attempts to suppress heresy, deter-
mined to prevent distribution of Tyndale's translation of the Bible, and
the leader in the prosecution of such men as Thomas Bilney, who would
be burnt in 1531—called on him once again. On 4 May 1528 he was present
as a witness at the abjuration of Thomas Bowgas, a fuller of Colchester
who supported the Reformers, in the Norwich Inn, the bishop's residence

in Charing Cross, London.[5] Finally, there is recorded his own Requiem Mass at St. Margaret's Church, Westminster, when, on 21 June 1529, bells pealed and candles burned for the priest John Skelton's soul ("Master" then designating "learned priest"):

> Receiptis by the sayde Wardens Receyuyd in the second yere of this ther accompte for buryalles obittes and lyghtis as perticuler[l]y folowyth
>> Item of *Master* skelton for iiij tapers ij^{s}viiij^d
>> Item of hym for iiij torches iiij^s
> Receptys of the belles for kynlles and peales This second yere
>> Item of *Master* Iohn skelton for knyll and peales vj^{s}viij^d
> Paymentes leide oute by the saide accomptantes this second yere ffor Ryngyng off knylles and pealles
>> Item paid to *our* lady brotherhed for *Master* skelton xx^d
>> Item paid for Ringyng of his knyll and peales xij^d (Churchwarden's Accounts, Vol. E2, n.p.).[6]

But there remains no shred of evidence concerning his birth (thought to be around 1460) or his lineage (perhaps from the numerous Skeltons in Yorkshire and Cumberland).

The best we can do with such meager data is to note that for most of the time during which he was writing poetry—for all of it, in fact, except for a half-dozen years represented by the Northumberland elegy and a handful of secular court songs—Skelton was an ordained priest in a Church resplendent with liturgy and thick with duties and rituals to be performed by the priesthood. And for this there is, conversely, abundant evidence. From *The Bowge of Courte* onward, his poems feature references (such as that to the *Salve festa dies*), images (such as the ship), themes (such as Doomsday), *personae* (such as Drede), meter (as in the Skeltonics), a mixture of tones (including the dramatic, lyric, prophetic, and grotesque), macaronic writing, and nuances of all sorts that are directly related to Holy Mother Church. The Church, in short, inspired Skelton and profoundly shaped his imagination. Living just prior to what R. W. Chambers has labelled "the great dividing days of English history," the summer days of the Act of Supremacy (1534),[7] Skelton wrote to the Tudor laity in the terms and images they had all learned from childhood and held to all their lives. To understand Skelton and his age as he did, then, and as his readers understood them, we must understand their Church.

By our reckoning early Tudor England appears to have been confident in its faith and loyal in its devotion. We still have, for instance, numerous accounts for the building of a superb steeple at Louth, in eastern Lincolnshire. "Its three hundred feet of soaring grace still bears witness to the devotion and pride of a little town standing somewhat apart from the mainstreams of Tudor England," A. G. Dickens writes. Begun about the time of *The Bowge of Courte*, in 1501, it took fourteen years and a staggering £305 to complete. "At last, on the eve of Holy Rood Day 1515 the weathercock was erected, 'there being Will Ayleby, parish priest, with many of his brother-priests there present, hallowing the said weather-cock and the stone that it stands upon, and so conveyed upon the said broach; and then the said priests singing *Te Deum laudamus* with organs; and then the kirkwardens garte [made] ring all the bells, and caused all the people there being to have bread and ale, and all to the loving of God, Our Lady and All Saints.'"[8] This simple slice of life in a remote Tudor parish is an accurate representation of what was going on every day of Skelton's life from one end of England to the other. Because of the Reformation we have lost now nearly all of the sense of the power and glory that the Catholic Church provided during the reigns of Henry VII and Henry VIII when "the country was dotted with hermitages, monasteries, crosses, wayside chapels, and holy wells," as the Rev. Leonard E. Whatmore reminds us.[9] But we must reconstruct those times if we are ever to understand Skelton's poetry, or appreciate his contribution to that culture. We must envision a time when it was the Church alone that tied England into powerful alliances with other countries, when the Church owned at least a fifth of the land, and when the Church received a large portion of the private wealth as it poured into founding, expanding, and endowing chapels and chantries. The Church was central to Henry VII as he planned his splendid chapel in Westminster Abbey, and to Wolsey when he founded Cardinal College, Oxford, but it touched the lives of every merchant, artisan, and farmer, too.

> Men still kissed the pax at Mass, still lit candles to their patron saints, still obtained indulgences for their sins, still went on pilgrimage, especially to the shrine of Our Lady of Walsingham or of St Thomas of Canterbury. Congregations still carried candles round the church at Candlemas, received ashes on Ash Wednesday, crept to the Cross on Good Friday, kindled their fires from the Easter Candle, watched the dove descending from the roof of the church at Whitsuntide, joined in processions at Corpus Christi, offered loaves at Lammas, remembered the dead at All Hallows, and listened to the

sermon of the Boy Bishop on St Nicholas' or Holy Innocents' Day. A Venetian who visited England at the end of the fifteenth century was struck, not only by the wealth of the churches, but by the devotion of the people. Parish churches were the centres of the social life, of the community, and the clergy controlled education, hospitals, and poor relief. Economic organizations, such as the gilds, participated in a variety of religious activities, from masses to miracle plays. The towns were dominated, not by factories and warehouses, shops and civic buildings, but by a forest of church towers and steeples. Their bells were constantly tolling to call men to devotions within the churches, and friars frequently harangued the people outside. In short, the Church was everywhere in evidence and seemed to be all-powerful.[10]

Even at Court it was the clergy who, for the most part, advised Henry VII and Henry VIII on the King's Council and who carried out the chief administrative tasks, while all the great houses had their chapels, often quite elaborate ones, each noble household its staff of chaplains, and every gild its patron saint. Crosses and crucifixes displaying Christ's Passion were everywhere—in court, in churchyards, and in the streets, while inside the churches altars and chantries were forever multiplying. At the time of Skelton's death, Durham Cathedral had more than twenty altars, York Minster had fifty-six perpetual chantries, and even a single, fairly small parish like Great Hale had four chantries besides the church, all requiring daily Masses to be said. Naves of such parish churches, large and small, served as public markets, social gathering places, and even centers for conducting local government; from church to church, beadrolls circulated inviting intercessory prayer on which the state of the next life rested. (Jane Scrope has a beadroll in "Phyllyp Sparowe.")[11] Much of the music of the time was sacred music, perpetuated in city and village choirschools, and so was much of the art—the architecture, sculpture, statuary, paintings, mosaics, and tapestries, such as the Wilton diptych, which showed a youthful Richard II presented to the Virgin and Child by his patron saints.[12] Manuscripts and books were more common than we might think, too—gospel books, epistle books, Graduales, prosers, tropers, sequentiaries, versaries, kyriales, missals, psalters, breviaries, portos, diurnals, processionals, tonales, ordinals, customaries, ceremonials, and books of hours—as an exhibition catalogue from the Bodleian Library amply demonstrates.[13] So pervasive was the practice of Christianity, in fact, that a number of stories are legion, such as that of the shepherds in the Wakefield Nativity play who, wanting to make a gesture, made the sign of the Cross. By Skelton's time England had two archbishoprics, nineteen bishops, 600 religious houses, and just under 9,000 parish churches. York itself, near which Skelton resided at the start of his career, had 40 churches, 36 within the city walls, besides the massive minster; Norwich and London each had an even greater number. Therefore it follows that when Henry VIII marched into battle in France in 1513, banners displaying Our Lady and the Trinity preceded banners displaying the royal arms, according to the Tudor Edward Hall's chronicle,[14] while at home Queen Catherine stitched more banners of religious emblems and at Flodden Field Thomas Ruthal was attributing Surrey's surprising victory over the Scots to St. Cuthbert. But Katherine had already been formally welcomed into England in 1501 with a pageant at London Bridge where she was greeted by St. Catherine and St. Ursula; in later pageantry at Leadenhall, the Zodiac was presided over by Raphael the Archangel; and at the Standard at Cheap she saw the Temple of God. And in 1509, at the time of his death her father-in-law Henry VII with "singular devotion"[15] made as his own bequest—literally—ten thousand Masses for the safety of his soul at the rate of sixpence each, at least half again the standard fee.[16] For we are still in that age when the King was called not "His Majesty" but "His Grace."

And Skelton was in the center of this: if we cannot reconstruct his biography with much assurance, we can still determine what, as a priest of the Church, much of his life must have been like. We can still determine with considerable authority what he must have undergone and what he must have done much of the time. In her concise but impressive study of the church until 1500, for instance, Margaret Deanesly describes the customary ordination in Tudor England.

> Ordination to the higher [order of priest, which must be conferred by a bishop] was given four times a year, in the Ember weeks, generally in the cathedral, but also at other important churches. Candidates were summoned to present themselves the Wednesday before, to be examined for three days orally by the archdeacon, as to their character, learning, and whether "they firmly grasped the catholic faith, and could express it in simple language." . . . The actual ceremony of ordination was long: it might last from nine in the morning till three or four in the afternoon, while bishop and ordinands were all fasting. The candidates for each of the seven orders were presented by the archdeacon, instructed in the peculiar functions of the order, received its symbol, and were blessed by the bishop with

appropriate prayers. All the different orders were conferred at the
beginning or in the course of the mass, at which all communicated.[17]

From that day in 1498 Skelton would have celebrated the feast of Our
Lord on Sundays as well as on the 35 or 40 important major and minor
feasts (some listed as movable feasts in the temporale) and the feasts of the
Virgin and saints (from the Propers in the sanctorale), according to the
Sarum rite then in use, as well as daily morning Mass which he might have
indicated on the "Mass-dial" outside his church. The great community of
believers past and present—297 groups of medieval figures still remain
carved in the magnificent west front of the cathedral at Wells—realized
with the priest at matins or lauds the Te Deum: "The glorious company of
the Apostles praise thee. / The goodly fellowship of the Prophets praise
thee. / The noble army of the Martyrs praise thee. / The holy Church
throughout the world doth acknowledge thee. / Thou art the King of
glory, O Christ." Alongside such joyful lauds, the Catholic Church in the
decades preceding Skelton's ordination was becoming increasingly serious
and Marian in its ritual; according to Donald L. Edwards, "The most
popular devotions of the fifteenth century centred on the suffering of the
incarnate Christ (this was the time when the devotion of 'the stations of
the cross' developed); and on the humble purity of the mother of Christ
(this was the century in which it became customary to recite the *Angelus*
and rosary prayers in honour of Our Lady). Above all, there was the
emphasis on the power of the sacrifice of Christ, and of the intercession of
his mother, to free the souls of the living and the dead from the pains of
purgatory."[18]

Their Mass was participatory then as now, with the congregation
kneeling, standing, genuflecting, responding, and even on occasion chant-
ing; they might follow the service in their missals or Mass Books. (Four
texts of the *Lay Folks Mass Book* from the fifteenth and sixteenth centuries
were edited for the Early English Text Society in 1879; it is this habit that
causes Jane Scrope to follow her own text independently of the others at
the prayer service in "Phyllyp Sparowe.") Priests such as Skelton were
supposed to preach sermons at the parish Mass on Sundays, taking their
texts from the set gospels or epistles in the Proper, but by the time of
Henry VII, the use of biblical narrative for preaching had been displaced
by a concern with the fourfold meaning of Scripture, and the Tudors'
handbooks on the art of preaching, the *artes praedicandi*, stressed extend-
ing the literal meaning or eliminating it altogether for *dilatio* on the
anagogical, allegorical, and especially the moral meanings of biblical

events—precisely the sort of approach we have seen Parrot take on texts from the Pentateuch and Psalms. Such an explosion of the precise text into various levels of significance and forms of application "decentralize" it, according to Marianne G. Briscoe,[19] so that emphasis is placed on abstraction and commentary. (We shall see Skelton make use of this, too, in various scriptural, liturgical, and iconic references behind "Ware the Hauke," "Collyn Clout," and "Why Come Ye Nat to Courte?") Such sermons were delivered in both the aureate and plain styles—the two styles which Parrot untraditionally mixes in his urgency—and, as we might further expect from *Speke, Parrot*, they often concerned bad priests as well as the sins of the laity. "In these days the clergy so misbehave themselves that their life is vastly inferior and more despised then that of the laity," John Alcock, bishop of Ely, preached in a sermon quoted by J. W. Blench, "For today, as Jerome says, the lay people are as saints compared to the clergy."[20] Holy John Fisher was also a forerunner to Skelton's sermon-like attacks on Wolsey.

> Truly it was a more glorious sight to se saynt Poule whiche gate his lyuynge by his owne grete labour in hungre, thurst, watchynge, in colde, goynge wolward, & berynge aboute the gospell & lawe of cryst bothe vpone the see & on the londe than to beholde nowe tharchebysshoppes & byshoppes in theyr apparayle be it neuer so ryche. In that tyme were no chalyses of golde, but than was many golden prestes, now be many chalyses of golde, & almoost no golden prestes, truly neyther golde precyous stones, nor gloryous bodyly garments be not the cause wherfore kynges & prynces of the worlde sholde drede god & his chyrche, for doubtles they haue ferre more worldly rychesse than we haue, but holy doctryne, good lyfe & example of honest conuersacion be the occasyons wherby good & holy men, also wycked & cruel people are moued to loue & fere almighty god.[21]

Fisher, too, delivered many sermons denouncing political and social actions whenever he saw them as related to the texts designated in the Proper—as in his sermon against Luther in 1521, using the day's gospel (John 15:26), and in his attack on heretics on Quinquagesima Sunday 1526 (preaching on Luke 18:31–43, the story of the blind man). Skelton uses this same means; we shall soon see that most of his poems that seem strange or inventive to us would have seemed nearly commonplace to his earliest readers.

But celebrating Mass and preaching were only a part of Skelton's function as rector at Diss. He was also responsible for instructing his parish in the Creed, the commandments, the sacraments, the seven works of mercy, the seven virtues, and the seven deadly sins—upon which the fates of their very souls rested—and for performing the sacraments. Such responsibilities can hardly be overestimated. A popular early English translation of Archbishop Thoresby's widely circulated *Catechism* requires that "als prelates and persons, vicars and prestes opynly, one ynglysche, apone sonnondayes, preche and teche þaym þat þay hase cure off, þe lawe and þe lare to knawe God Almyghty, þat principally may be schewede in theis sexe thynges—in þe fourtene poyntes þat fallis to þe trowthe [the Creed]—in þe ten commandementes þat Gode hase gyfene vs—in þe seuene sacramentes þat er in Haly Kyrke—in þe seuene werkes of mercy vntill oure euene cristyne—in þe seuene vertus þat ilke mane sall vse—and in þe seuene dedly synnes þat ilke man sall refuse" (EETS [London, 1976], p. 2). As for the sacraments, the priest on Shrove Tuesday or in Lent heard all his people confess, at which time it was his duty to hear them recite these beliefs of the Church, to examine them about their sins under the headings of pride, wrath, envy, sloth, avarice, gluttony, and lechery, and then to give them penance and absolution. (This was done in the open chancel where carvings, paintings, and statuary gave ready images of sins and sinners and may suggest still another source behind *The Bowge of Courte*—another point of reference for Skelton's early readers.) The priest must also baptize all the children of his parishioners and later confirm them in the faith by use of the catechism, perform marriages (followed by Bride-ales, a feast pertinent to "The Tunnyng of Elynour Rummyng"), visit the sick, administer wills, anoint the dying with the holy chrism in the sacrament of extreme unction, and commemorate the dead with Requiem Masses and prayers for the dead (especially on All Souls Day), encouraging an ongoing reciprocity between the living and the dead that caused the Christian community to know no boundaries of time or place —something else that profoundly moves Jane Scrope. Treatises on Christian sacraments and the priest's duties were easily available; indeed, "'þer beþ so manye bokes & tretees of vyces and vertues & of dyuerse doctrynes,' complained one writer in the fifteenth century, 'þat þis schort lyfe schalle raþere haue anende of anye manne þanne he maye owþers studye hem or rede him.'"[22]

All these matters concerned all communicants, literate or not; strictly speaking, the daily canonical offices did not affect all communicants, although fifteenth-century manuals began to urge their attendance at Sunday matins and vespers. The idea underlying the divine office was that of

the vigil, the primitive Christian sentiment, still very much alive, of the
watch kept for the Lord's coming—"Take ye heed, watch and pray. For ye
know not when the time is. . . . / Watch ye therefore, (for you know not
when the Lord of the house cometh: at even, or at midnight, or at the
cockcrowing, or in the morning,) / Lest coming on a sudden, he find you
sleeping" (Mark 13:33, 35–36)—the very duty, in short, that motivates Par-
rot but which Drede so fatally ignores. The offices provided priests (as
well as monks) with seven daily occasions for prayer and reflection. They
include the major night offices of matins (at midnight or first dawn) and
lauds (a service of praise) and, at day's end, vespers (at sunset) and com-
pline (before retiring). In between come the lesser hours of prime (dawn),
tierce (about 9 A.M.), sext (noon), and none (3 P.M.). Each service in-
volved singing Psalms (to Psalm Tones) and antiphons, and reciting lec-
tions (short scriptural readings); some involved singing responsories (sen-
tences called versicles), canticles (biblical passages of especially high
inspiration and imagery, the "Psalms outside the Psalter"), and hymns;
they were performed in Latin and arranged in such a way that the entire
psalter could be covered each week. A single office was always part of a
daily and a larger scheme, so that each office was incomplete within it-
self—it may be here that Skelton found it so natural to write *Speke, Parrot*
in discrete yet complementary and vitally linked parts—while "monotony
was avoided," Deanesly tells us, by the application of the fourfold inter-
pretation of Scripture. Moreover, "The psalms of which the offices were
mainly composed were preceded by a solitary verse or antiphon, which
varied with the season, and changed their whole colour and meaning. To
the person who recited them, the psalmist's words might be the words of
Christ in His passion, of the martyr in his torment, or the groans and tears
of his own soul, according to the day and the antiphon. Words like 'The
good shepherd giveth his life for the sheep' might be green and cool like
the shepherd's psalm one day, and take on a new tinge of blood for the
feast of S. Thomas of Canterbury the next" (p. 200). This daily renewal of
changing texts and contexts is also a force in Skelton's poetic imagination;
it allows him to see in *The Bowge of Courte* here a temptation to avarice,
there a temptation to suicide, now a parody of confession, later a sense of
approaching Last Judgment. While certain images can hold two or more
meanings simultaneously—as the scurrying of Hervy Hafter, for exam-
ple—all the meanings function by an easy reference to congruent situa-
tions. The peculiarities of Skelton's poetics, then, are often the direct
results of his Catholic training—and the Catholic training of his audi-
ences. Like the continually renewing cycles of liturgical seasons in which

all the people of his day shared, Skelton's poems transform themselves before us, continually being reborn with related but different references. What may first be puzzling to us, then, was both instinctive and habitual for Catholic Tudor readers.

As shepherd of the flock at Diss, Skelton must have taken up other responsibilities too. Deanesly writes that the church

> was not run on a system of voluntary finance: the parish priest could excommunicate for non-payment of tithe, and the secular courts would enforce the obligation. The parish priest also tilled or let out the glebe land of his church. He was bound to keep the chancel of his church in repair [consider "Ware the Hauke"], and see that the church-wardens repaired the nave: he was also bound to see that no fairs or morris dancings were held in the churchyard and that it was not otherwise profaned.
>
> It was his duty to relieve the poor, and strangers, as far as he could himself: though his stipend was usually too small to permit of much almsgiving. . . . Other important parts of the priest's social work were the reconciliation of parishioners who had quarrelled, and sometimes the duty of acting as chaplain to a parish gild, which was half burial-club and friendly society, half devotional in character. He might also help with the Corpus Christi and other gild plays: miracle and mystery plays were fairly frequent, and indeed the only drama in fourteenth [and fifteenth] century England [we can think of Drede as a kind of fallen man]. It was his duty to bless the crops, with processions through the field, at Rogation tide (to have trodden down growing corn was a sin to be mentioned in confession), and to offer the first fruits of harvest at Loaf-mass, or Lammas. His manual would contain special blessing for sick children, or animals, or houses and natural objects for which the divine protection was desired, and he would exorcise evil spirits and ghosts. But it was his duty to warn his people not to use spells and incantations, or gather herbs by moonlight, saying the Paternoster backwards, or use sortilege or necromancy (pp. 197–98).

It must also have been Skelton's particular pleasure to see pilgrims pass daily along the streets of Diss on their way to two of England's major shrines—to Our Lady of Walsingham to the northwest and to St. Edmund's at Bury to the south and west; as a priest, after all, one of his obligations was to hear confessions of pilgrims and of his own parishioners going to shrines for penance. We tend to forget how essential such

pilgrimages were considered to be by those who wished to draw on the
Church's treasury of merits in preparation for later relief from purgatorial
pain, where the penitent were "rebaptized in the font of their own tears,"
as Benedict of Canterbury put it.[23] But "Pilgrimages were incessant," J. J.
Jusserand sums. "They were made to fulfill a vow as in cases of illness or
great peril, or in expiation of sins."[24] While the long trek to the shrine of
St. Thomas à Becket at Canterbury was diminishing in popularity (despite
the wealth Colet and Erasmus found there),[25] the journey to Walsingham
was not. On 28 September 1443 Margaret Paston wrote her husband that
his mother had promised the Lady of Walsingham a waxen image weigh-
ing as much as he, while she herself promised a pilgrimage there on his
behalf. "Her name," Erasmus writes of Our Lady of Walsingham, "is very
famous all over England, and you shall scarce find anybody in that island
who thinks his affairs can be prosperous unless he every year makes some
present to that lady, greater or smaller, according as his circumstances are
in the world."[26] Bishop Nikke of Norwich made an official visitation there
on 14 July 1514. And Henry VIII walked from Barsham Manor to the
"Slipper Chapel" at Houghton St. Giles and from there barefoot to Our
Lady's shrine in the Abbey grounds (about two miles, all told) early in his
reign, in hopes he might receive a son and heir; he returned there in 1511
after the birth of the prince; and until 1538 he paid 200 shillings annually
to keep his own priest in residence there as well as 48s 8d per annum to
purchase candles for a perpetual flame. This shrine had as its chief relic the
Virgin's milk (and also one of St. Peter's fingers), but this was considered
superior to Bury St. Edmunds which could boast only the knife and boots
of St. Thomas à Becket and some of the coals which burnt St. Lawrence,
or the more distant Peterborough Cathedral with Becket's shirt and sur-
plice and the bloodstained stone against which he fell in his martyrdom.
Indeed, on the eve of the Reformation, Our Lady of Walsingham "ran at
an average of £260 a year [in gifts] when St. Thomas of Canterbury was
taking in as little as £36."[27] Skelton seems to have thought of pilgrimages
even after he moved to Westminster; at the close of his *Commendacions* to
"Phyllyp Sparowe" he offers to go to the shrine of St. James of Compos-
tella himself (1242) while in "The Tunnyng of Elynour Rummyng," one of
the women has just returned from there. Skelton was equally well situated
geographically in Diss regarding the diocese of Norfolk. Either his bishop
sat some 30 miles away in Norwich—home of Dame Julian, of Jane
Scrope, and of Margery Kempe, Skelton's contemporary—or, more often,
in Hoxne, once the parish of St. Edmund, and a short four miles to Diss

where his residence formed a triangle with Redgrave, Wolsey's parish, which lay eight miles in another direction.

Although it has been commonplace to remark that Skelton feels especially akin to the Old Testament prophets, drawing on them for particular references,[28] it is actually the case that he draws primarily on Church liturgy, most often on the Mass itself whose Canon remains virtually unchanged today. For both priest and parish the Mass was a holy meal which not only memorializes but reenacts the Passion of Christ—an image central to "Ware the Hauke," "Phyllyp Sparowe," and "Elynour Rummyng" —and the Passion was the centerpiece of the liturgy as Easter was the central feast of the Christian calendar. For redemption, revelation, and the fulfillment of the Old Testament depended on the Passion. Nothing could compare with it, although Christmas, Candlemas (the day of "Agaynste A Comely Coystrowne"), and Passion Sunday (the setting for "Collyn Clout") came close. But if we turn to the parts common to every Mass, the Ordinary which formed the core of every Tudor's life, male or female, powerful or poor, literate or not, we shall find the common ties on which Skelton rests much of his poetry.

Each service began with Psalm 42, said responsively by the celebrant and his assistants, and followed with the priest invariably saying, "Judge me, O God, and discern my cause." It continued with the Confiteor or confession of faith, an Introit or processional chant or hymn (which could be rather elaborately troped or farced), the *Kyrie eleison* ("Christ, have mercy") in which the priest and choir joined responsorially, and the major doxology, the *Gloria in excelsis* (by Skelton's time also troped) recited by celebrants and assistants at the altar and sung by the choir at their intermediate position between the altar and the nave. The priest called the congregation together in the Collect or prayer, followed by reading the epistle denoted by the Proper in the Sarum rite. Then came the gradual and *Alleluia*, songs of praise, except in the penitential seasons when they were replaced by a more solemn Tract or a Psalm. Perhaps the most beautiful part of the service followed—the Sequence, again part of the Proper and the result of troping, and which has given us some of the most memorable Church music, such as the *Stabat Mater* and the *Dies Irae*.

An ancient custom held that lights were carried in procession before the gospel was read ("Thy word is a lamp to my feet, and a light to my paths," Psalm 118:105); Skelton makes much of such lanterns of light in "Collyn Clout" to underline Wolsey's neglect of the old ways. Next are the Credo, the Oremus (prayer of the faithful), the Offertory (originally tithes of bread and crops), and prayers for preparing the Host, the oblation of the Chalice, and the invocation of the Holy Spirit, the Preface, and the Sanctus (*Hosanna in excelsis*). Then, at last, comes the critical, invariable part of the service, the Commemorations (of living and dead saints and other members of the Church's body), the elevation (to the sacring-bell) and consecration, the prayer at the moment of Transubstantiation (known as the *Summus sacerdos Melchisedech*), the Paternoster, the *Agnus Dei* (alluding to a legend in which the Virgin appeared before a poor carpenter and gave him a medal with a lamb pictured on one side), the Kiss of Peace, the communion of the celebrant followed by his ablutions, the communion of the faithful, the *Communio* (a sentence from the psalter), and the Post-Communion (a final Collect). With this last prayer bringing together the entire congregation, the celebrants, and his assistants, the priest dismisses the people with *"Ite missa est"* (hence the name *Mass*) and his blessing.

Daily Mass, celebrated by the priest alone with perhaps one or two assistants, usually followed the simplified *Ordo missae privatae*. This Mass still centered on the Canon—"Cleanse me, O Lord, from all pollution of mind and body, that being cleansed I may be able to perform the work of the Lord," Skelton would have said each day to prepare for the miracle of Transubstantiation—but it eliminated the music and some of the responsories. Yet it seems to have been the music that influenced Skelton as much as the celebration of the Passion. "It is everywhere obvious," writes Nan Cooke Carpenter, "that Skelton thinks in musical rhythms"[29]—so much so that she is led to believe that he may have been a chorister or even a lutenist before taking holy orders.[30] (Some choirschool training was usually required for those joining the priesthood.) We have sensed Skelton's deep feelings for the *Dies Irae* in *The Bowge of Courte* and *Speke, Parrot*; we will see his deeply felt sense of the *Magnificat* in "Phyllyp Sparowe," but, even more importantly, the form and the rhythm of Church music clearly lay behind his sense of metrics and helped to inspire the Skeltonics, a metrics based more than on leash rhymes, a metrics grounded primarily in stressed and unstressed syllables. For in the sacred chants, responsories, hymns, and motets found in the Kyriale (for the Ordinary of the Mass), the Graduale (for the Propers), and the Antiphonals (for the offices excepting Matins), we can find all the models (save rime royal) that Skelton needed for all of his major poems. Clearly the most important of these, as well as the oldest, was the plainsong ("Gregorian" chant) that was born, developed, and nourished, Alec Robertson tells us, by "the liturgical spirit."[31] This was an art at which the English particularly excelled. Originally, chants were sung by the congregation as well as by celebrants and assistants—graduals, responsories, Tracts, and Alleluias that could be heavily melismatic (having many notes of music to one syllable of text). They account for the bulk of pre-Reformation sacred music and were so vital and yet so adaptable they "successfully served every liturgical function from the simplest to the most solemn," Richard H. Hoppin observes.[32] While it may have been this very versatility that attracted Skelton, the single-line melody of plainsong (not unlike recited poetry) is articulated by means other than regular accentuation; like the simple recitations from which it was born, it can be nonmensural and *spoken*—that is, like Skeltonics, plainsong is strophic, not metric, and it varies the accents and the number of accented syllables at will for better expression, thus emphasizing its feeling for spoken language. Various interpretations of plainsong rhythms exist—mensuralist, rhythmicist, and nonmensuralist—but from the viewpoint of a student of Skeltonics, plainsong is always nonmetrical and allows for a free placing of accents. This sense of line and song has "the elastic ease" praised by John Norton-Smith "with which Skelton graduates from one form of demotic expression to another."[33] Like Skeltonics, lines of plainsong may be in dimeters or trimeters; in the autumn of 1985, Barbara Haggh announced the discovery of a rhymed office written expressly for the Cathedral of Cambrai in the fifteenth century by two of its canons, the Latin verse by one Egidius Carlier and the plainsong by Guillaume Dufay. By Skelton's time, sight-singing of such works was often designated by the hexachord system, such as the notes "*Fa, re, my, my*" (5), which open "Phyllyp Sparowe," or those referred to more humorously in *The Bowge of Courte* and "Collyn Clout." In this connection it is important to note that the poet's first poem in Skeltonics is also his first sacred poem, and it is one that looks, reads, and chants very much like a processional or a Sequence from the Mass.

> Youre ugly tokyn
> My mynd hath brokyn
> From worldly lust;
> For I have dyscust
> We ar but dust,
> And dy we must. . . .
>   O goodly chyld
> Of Mary mylde,
> Then be oure shylde!
> That we be not exyld

> To the dyne dale
> Of boteles bale,
> Nor to the lake
> Of fendys blake.
>   But graunt us grace
> To se thy face,
> And to purchace
> Thyne hevenly place
> And thy palace,
> Full of solace,
> Above the sky,
> That is so hy,
> Eternally
> To beholde and se
> The Trynyte!
> Amen (1–6; 41–60).

Indeed, merely reading these lines with the solemnity they require virtually *forces* us into plainsong. Indeed, only plainsong alone can accommodate the otherwise strange shift in line-length which we find in a passage in "Collyn Clout" where (while discussing sermons) language is the topic.

> But men say
> Your auctoryte,
> And your noble se,
> And your dygnyte,
> Shulde be imprynted better
> Then all the freres letter;
> For yf ye wolde take payne
> To preche a word or twayne,
> Though it were never so playne,
> With clauses two or thre,
> So as they myght be
> Compendyously conveyed,
> These wordes shuld be more weyed,
> And better perceyved,
> And thankefullyer receyved,
> And better shulde remayne
> Among the people playne (758–74).

Any poet writing these lines is clearly aware of line-length and clausal length (with its consistent brevity), and the variable pattern can be accounted for only by something like plainsong; to speak or intone these variable lines we *need* the actual or inferred underlay of music.[34]

Furthermore, extensions of plainsong first connected to the *Alleluia*, known as Sequences, became in time entire independently shaped melodies, which nevertheless could maintain the short line similar to those we call Skeltonics, as in a fifteenth-century manuscript at the Bodleian Library (Selden B26) or as in this instance honoring the Blessed Virgin:

> No messenger mean
> to the barren is sent,
> but an angel of might
> most refulgent in light
> from the lover of men.
> She wonders, believes,
> and in joy she conceives,
> the blest mother of God,
> whom exulting she bore,
> most beloved of all.
> The most excellent maid
> in seclusion abides,
> serving God in her heart,
> sweetly singing apart,
> born a blessing to man.

Hundreds of such Sequences appeared all over Europe from the tenth century on, perhaps sung at times to an accompaniment of organs and bells. A later monophonic song, which may have originated in the processional of a Mass or a liturgical drama, the *conductus*, came to be used with secular texts that dealt seriously with historical or moral themes.[35] We can begin now to see why Skelton finds it so natural and so instructive to draw on Sequences (and hymns) in his poems.

But Skelton also may have taken from Church music other features of his poems which we have thought so original. Centonization, for instance, the construction of new chants from pre-existing melodic figures, when translated into language, leads to the kind of rhythmic response that Jane Scrope provides for her private Requiem Mass of Birds as a conceptualized countermelody to the overheard Office for the Dead—which leads, in fact, to antiphony in the poem. Variety of melodic figures to accommodate different texts helps to account for the sudden shift in poetic line and stanzaic form from rime royal to the song "My propire Besse" in *Speke, Parrot*. Hoppin points out, moreover, that mood in such a monophonic form of music is often defined by the place of the chant in the liturgy, just as Drede and Parrot both make use of placement and crescendo to lend tonal variety to the fixed form of rime royal. Even more fundamentally, the use of troping to extend the text by adding new words leads to the *copia* of which Skelton is sometimes accused, but which, well before humanist rhetoric, had a long-established place in liturgical and related secular chant and song in England. Troping was used with introits, with the Alleluia, and especially with the Gloria, but could be used with any musical part of the Mass, even (on occasion) the Credo. It could be employed to explain or illustrate the text or to apply the text to the occasion on the Church calendar; this is not dissimilar from Skelton's practice of building an entire poem on the images in the text for a particular service or feast day. As the priest of a flourishing parish, Skelton doubtless had access to one or more Graduales or antiphoners, which would illustrate at every Sabbath and every festival these principles of rhythm and song; and over the years they must have influenced his sense of rhythm and poetry. Troping could also enlarge phrases taken from other works as an idea on which to build a new text, as Jane Scrope extracts the *Placebo* in her own office of the dead in "Phyllyp Sparowe." But just as Skelton's poems persistently base themselves on external references, such as Psalm 13 or Psalm 82, so troping always relied on a base text. Troping too would be incomplete without such a basis.

In time, such creative additions led to polyphony (still based on a preexistent source, the *cantus firmus*) and to motets, which could combine various sacred and secular elements (much as Skelton mixes *O lux beata Trinitas* with the ship of fools or the *Salve festa dies* with the Boccaccian parrot) only to conclude with a singular radiant statement. (Some motets strayed far from their liturgical beginnings, however, such as the well-known work based on the plainsong *Rex regum* in which the highest part sang "It must be proclaimed openly at meeting-places, the abominable madness of these ages, the demented frenzy of dogs, launched on the world by eternal Satan" and the next highest part, "O King whom I represent in the first letter of these lines" in a Latin text yielding the acrostic "Robertus"; originally a French work, this song was copied into English manuscript.) Examples of all these musical forms were common and can be found in such manuscripts as the Winchester Troper or the St. Albans Graduale, or, from the fifteenth century, the Old Hall Manuscript used by the Chapel Royal of Henry VII when Skelton was at court, or the

Eton Choirbook, a collection of highly melismatic antiphons and Magnificats, some by John Dunstable and William Cornysh (who later set some of Skelton's poems to music). We also have manuscripts containing both liturgical music and carols, often concerned with the Virgin or the Passion. Such carols, occasionally involving refrains that remind us of the reference to Deucalion's flood in *Speke, Parrot*, were originally intended both for private devotion and for use in the pulpit. Some of them are in brief lines remarkably similar to the Skeltonic: "Loue me brouthte, / & loue me wrouthte, / Man, to þi fere. / Loue me fedde, / & loue me ledde, / & loue me lettet here." Although it is likely that Skelton's understanding of the multiple meanings inherent in a single text and the use of secular forms for biblical themes came from the kind of sermons he preached, surely the liturgical music that surrounded those sermons would have reinforced such principles of composition for him constantly.

As a poet, Skelton shared with the musician a sense of linguistic performance. "The writers composed most often for the performing voice—speaking, intoning, chanting, or singing," J. A. Burrow writes of the period just before Skelton, "and the expressive effects which they contrived tended in consequence to be boldly and emphatically shaped for the voice to convey to the ear"; he further notes that even the solitary reader spoke aloud.[36] Another influential force in Tudor culture, which also shares this sense of performance, was church drama. Cycle plays would have shown Skelton again and again how discrete segments could be correlated to make larger units of meaning, as the need for Gideon fuses the four somewhat distinct parts of *Speke, Parrot*. More importantly, the religious drama reinforced the Tudor sense of seamless time, which in terms of *Heilsgeschichte* or sacred history defined every present event—such as the death of old John Clarke, the exposure of the anonymous curate hawking in church, or the misdeeds of Wolsey—as merely the reappearance of a figural truth. "The mediaeval stage was a mirror," Anne Righter sums, "but it was a glass held up towards the Absolute, reflecting the 'age and body of the time' only incidentally. In a theatre dealing with Creation and Apocalypse, with Incarnation, and the story of Mary and Joseph, the ordinary concerns of those mercers, weavers and riotous apprentices who followed the pageant wagons on the feast of Corpus Christi could have no more substantiality than the shadow shapes in Plato's cave. Continually, the fourteenth-century playgoer was urged to associate illusion with his own life and Reality itself with the dramas enacted before him."[37] The filtering of historical action, such as Wolsey's negotiations at Calais, through the prisms of liturgical ceremony and language such as the *Salve festa dies* and the Sequence for the Mass of St. Nicholas allows for the same sense of recurrence as that on which Tudor liturgical drama was based: biblical events, like Christ, live, die, and are born again. The several places to which Parrot refers in his envoys, like the multiple settings of a pageant wagon, or like the idea of shared places (allowing an altar to be both manger and sepulchre or Mak's cradle to become the manger on a single wagon in the Wakefield *Secondum Pastorum*) show us how events and places that may seem somewhat distinct were quite the reverse in the time of Henry VII and Henry VIII. Moreover, if we follow Rosemary Woolf in determining the theory behind the art of such plays as implied by a widespread Lollard attack on them called *A Tretise of Miraclis Pleyinge*, we shall see how closely the poetics of such drama comes to what seems to be Skelton's poetics as well: mystery plays, this treatise suggests, are devoted to the honor of God, convert men to virtuous living by statement and example as well as warn them of the pride and wiliness of the devil, encourage compassion and devotion through sorrow or pity, and attract by entertaining.[38] "The peculiar paradox" of all this, Frederick B. Artz writes, "is that in seeming to draw drama away from realism into allegory the writers of morality plays succeeded in linking drama closer to actual life and to contemporary types."[39]

Drama, then, contributed greatly to Tudor piety just as services, sermons, offices, and festivals did; here too "the entire population turned out," as Eleanor Prosser has it, "to participate in a community drama of worship and celebration."[40] We have no record of Skelton's participation in or supervision of such drama but, as we have seen, his duties as rector at Diss prescribed some involvement. Nor would he have found this awkward. For the Tudors, drama came directly from the Holy Mass which Skelton celebrated daily. Woolf has noted that "when a choir sings the *Magnificat* they impersonate the Virgin, when the *Nunc dimittis* Symeon" (p. 5); the *planctus*, or lament of the Virgin at the foot of the cross, apparently the first detachable text for a liturgical play (from the time of the Anglo-Saxon *Visitatio*), is one drama Skelton employs to fine effect in "Phyllyp Sparowe."[41] O. B. Hardison, Jr., in a pioneering study, traces the intimate connection between early drama and the Mass back to the *Gemma animae*, written about 1100 by Honorius of Autun.

It is known that those who recited tragedies in theaters presented the actions of opponents by gestures before the people. In the same way our tragic author [i.e., the celebrant] represents by his gestures in the theater of the Church before the Christian people the struggle of Christ and teaches to them the victory of His redemption. Thus when the celebrant [*presbyter*] says the *Orate* [*fratres*] he expresses Christ placed for us in agony, when he comnmanded His apostles to pray. By the silence of the *Secreta* he expresses Christ as a lamb without voice being led to the sacrifice. By the extension of his hands he represents the extension of Christ on the Cross. By the chant of the Preface he expresses the cry of Christ hanging on the Cross. For He sang [*cantavit*] ten Psalms, that is, from *Deus meus respice* to *In manus tuas commendo spiritum meum*, and then died. Through the secret prayers of the Canon he suggests the silence of Holy Saturday. By the *Pax* and its communication [i.e., the "Kiss of Peace"] he represents the peace given after the Resurrection and the sharing of joy. When the sacrifice has been completed, peace and Communion are given by the celebrant to the people. This is because after our accuser has been destroyed by our champion [*agonotheta*] in the struggle, peace is announced by the judge to the people, and they are invited to a feast. Then, by the *Ite, missa est,* they are ordered to return to their homes with rejoicing. They shout *Deo gratias* and return home rejoicing.[42]

This is especially important for us because it emphasizes the powerful centrality of the Passion in the Mass—"I wanted to be actually there with Mary Magdalen and the others who loved him," Julian of nearby Norwich wrote at the end of the fourteenth century, "and with my own eyes to see and know more of the physical suffering of our Saviour, and the compassion of our Lady and of those who there and then were loving him truly and watching his pains. I would be one of them and suffer with him."[43] Indeed, the central presentation of the Tudor liturgical drama "is designed as a sequential experience which begins as it ends," Peter W. Travis reminds us, "by meditating upon the meaning of the image of the Body of God."[44] And from the blood-smeared rood cross of "Ware the Hauke" to the demonically inverted Creed in "Collyn Clout" we shall soon see how the Passion is central to the Christian experience for Skelton too.

But the Mass actually meant to embrace a wider stretch of sacred history. Hardison continues by summarizing the work of the Bishop of Metz (?780–850).

The chapter headings of Amalarius' *Ecologae de officio missae* provide a convenient outline of the rememorative allegory of the Mass. The service is divided into two major parts. The prayers and ceremonies which precede the Gospel represent Christ's life "from His birth to the time when He hastened to Jerusalem to suffer." The Introit is the chorus of Old Testament prophets foretelling the coming of the Messiah, and the Kyrie is the voice of the more recent prophets, especially Zacharias and John. The Gloria (omitted from the beginning of Lent to the Mass of the Easter vigil) announces the Nativity. It echoes the song of the angels (Luke 2:14), and it is chanted antiphonally to suggest a dialogue between heaven and earth. The collect represents Christ in the Temple at twelve years of age. The reading—whether from the Old or the New Testament—is the preaching and prophecy of John. The responsory depicts the good will (*benevolentia*) of the apostles, who, when summoned, came freely. The Alleluia (omitted from the beginning of Lent to the Mass of the Easter vigil) expresses the happiness which the apostles felt when they heard Christ's promises and saw miracles performed in His name. The first "act" of the drama concludes with the Gospel, which makes manifest the words and deeds of Christ during His ministry. The second "act" extends from Palm Sunday to Pentecost. The prayers from the *Secreta* to the *Nobis quoque peccatoribus* represent the prayers of Jesus in the garden of the Mount of Olives, and what follows commemorates His death and entombment. The commingling of the Host and consecrated wine marks the return of Christ's soul to His body. The next action (the Kiss of Peace) is the greeting of the disciples and their joy on learning of the Resurrection. The Fraction is not a "slaughtering of Christ," as it was sometimes considered during the baroque period, but, in the *Ecologae*, the breaking of bread by Christ at Emmaus (p. 45).

Here too single events bear more than one interpretation without denying any. "By the same token," Hardison writes, "the roles of the participants are fluid.

> At times the celebrant is the High Priest of the Temple sacrificing the holocaust on the Day of Atonement, at other times he is Christ, and at one point he is Nicodemus assisting Joseph of Arimathea at the entombment. The congregation can be the Hebrews listening to the prophecies of the Messiah, the crowd witnessing the Crucifixion, the Gentiles to whom the Word was given after it had been rejected by the Hebrews, and the elect mystically incorporated into the body of Christ. Numerous conflicts among levels of interpretation, inconsistencies of chronology, and abrupt shifts of meaning are apparent. On the other hand, in the midst of these anomalies one element

stands out sharply. From beginning to end, but especially during the Canon and Communion, the Mass is a rememorative drama depicting the life, ministry, crucifixion, and resurrection of Christ (p. 44).

On certain festivals, this situation actually grew stronger. Hardison continues,

> On certain feast days this role-playing is intensified by explicitly mimetic actions: on Palm Sunday, for example, there is a formal procession with palms—identifying the congregation with the crowds who welcomed Jesus into Jerusalem—and hymns of praise echoing the Gospel accounts of his entry. During the Gloria the congregation becomes the shepherds and humble folk of Bethlehem who, in the second part of the antiphon, answer the angels, either directly or vicariously through the cantors. During the reading of the Gospel the people stand to bear living witness, as soldiers of Christ, to the events of His life. They bow their heads in sorrow during the terrible events leading to the Crucifixion. They stand bowed before the Cross with the holy women as Christ dies and blood and water pour from His side into the chalice. Following the Communion, the congregation assumes still another role. Allegorically, it becomes the disciples and apostles receiving the blessing of Christ before the Ascension. At the same time, it is, in literal truth, the Gentile nations who have received Christ and who, through him, are gathered into the mystical body. In the period between the Communion and the *Deo gratias*, the congregation enters an eschatological world. It lives in a timeless present, sharing the fellowship of the apostles whose images decorate the nave and of the angels who bring the sacrifice to the throne of God (pp. 46–47).[45]

In Skelton's time the procession of Corpus Christi brought priests and parishioners together, singing responsorially through the church, across the churchyards and down the street and back to the west front and the Galilee door; together they crossed the Red Sea with the living Christ and made for their ship, the church (*navis*).

In such an environment we can see how the altar could by turn be the hill of Calvary or the table at Emmaus while niches along the nave or at the transepts could hold Christmas angels or the Marys at Eastertide. Mary H. Marshall further notes,

> The characteristic movement of the liturgical plays necessitated by the symbolic representation of place, which was already familiar in

church processions, is a foreshortened conventionalized symbol of journeying. So the Magi approach, each from his separate corner as from his region, pointing out the star, or the two disciples journey down the aisle to Emmaus. The characteristic medieval dramatic technique of the simultaneous scene and multiple setting and the movement they entailed are iconically symbolic, as any dramatic convention may be.

The properties give a formalized suggestion of what they are to represent. The star may be a corona of candles let down from the roof and moving before the Magi. The lightning at the Resurrection in a play from Coutances is represented by two angels bearing candelabra of ten lighted candles, at the sight of which the soldiers at the tomb fall terrified as if dead. . . . When the iconic symbolism of things and properties has deep familiarity in sacred uses, emotions may be touched by their very appearance—the altar, or the cross itself, as elevated at the final moment of rejoicing in a *Visitatio* from Fritzlar.[46]

We forget what it must have been like to see the Bible unfold before us, in our own lives, just down the street; at least as late as 1452 such plays were still "at the church gate" in Harling, Norfolk, and still in the churchyard at Bungay in 1566. We forget how it must affect the imagination, too, to see neighbors becoming Joseph and Mary, and to comprehend our own jobs as potentially sacred every day, but that is how the Tudor wine merchants must have felt in staging annually the marriage at Cana, or the fishmongers in presenting the story of Jonah, or the pasterers with Noah's ark, or the bakers with the Last Supper. Such acts not only kept realizing Scripture anew, but did so by importing the liturgy. The Nativity play in Chester drew on the Embers Days' Feast of the Annunciation, while the vintners' and mercers' Magi plays drew on Advent services and the *Officium Stellae* of Epiphany, and the goldsmiths' Herod play drew on traditions of Holy Innocents' Day.[47] The Digby *Slaughter of the Innocents* borrowed a piece of business—the Virgins of the Temple forming a procession bearing candles—from the service for Candlemas, while the Pharoah in the York-Towneley *Exodus* spoke lines openly parodying the *sursum corda* from the Preface of the Mass.

Such broader conceptions of the seasons of the Church year help to remind us that the Crucifixion was answered by the Resurrection and that the Passion brought redemption into the world. Thus the function of such drama "is quite clear," as Sandro Sticca has it; "It constitutes a powerful dramatic statement on the Christian faith at its richest and most complex."[48] The multivalent density by which such works arouse pity and piety and grief and horror and guilt and awe, perhaps all at once, is the sort of Tudor environment in which Skelton can write a poem like *The Bowge of Courte* in which an innocent is a fool, a victim, and a sinner, and a poem in which a parrot speaks prophecy at one moment and makes ardent advances toward ladies of estate the next. The well-known story of Mak and his sheep-stealing as a parody of the Nativity is neither solemn nor sacrilegious; it merely demonstrates by means of farce and celebration the joy of the Christ Child's birth. Even the Passion plays, with Christ's last words and the Virgin's lament, often included rioters dicing and thieves after Christ's garments—and one play has Pilate outbluff the thieves and get the garment for himself so as to provide illustration for a homily on gambling! Such juxtapositions, writes A. C. Cawley, are like "the marginal babewyns of the Gorleston Psalter, the mitred fox preaching to a congregation of hens on a misericord at Boston, and the monkey's funeral (with a cock reading the service) in the nave windows of York Minster."[49] How natural, then, for Skelton to import the babblers Javel and Havell from the Towneley plays into his most caustic attack on Wolsey, "Why Come Ye Nat to Courte?" or, perhaps, recall the monkey's funeral in a window at York Minster when writing of the death of Phyllyp Sparowe.

By the same token, mystery plays could also grow increasingly dark. Taylor has argued convincingly that "the line of sequential action of the Corpus Christi plays has a plot of opposing forces which reenact the struggle of Christ and Antichrist"—or of Melchisedech and Moloch. "The complication presents, first, the division of mankind into basically two strains—the seed of Cain, prolonged in the wicked rulers of men (Pharaoh, Herod, Caesar, Pilate, Caiaphas, and their minions), and the friends and instruments of God, represented by Abel, Noah, Abraham, the prophets, the Magi, Mary, and climactically Christ. . . . In Christ's defeat of evil through love, God asserts and finally vindicates his rule" (pp. 154–55). But the blustering folly of Herod or Pilate (or the shrewishness of Eve or Noah's wife) makes wicked or misguided characters into buffoons—precisely the technique by which Skelton derides Adam Uddersale, old John Clarke, and, of course, Wolsey. Even various miracle plays (on St. Paul from the East Midlands, on St. Catherine in London, on St. Lawrence and St. Susanna and St. James in Lincoln) and morality plays (beginning with the twelfth-century Advent play *Antichristus*) reassert this fundamental opposition as the foundation of liturgical and sacred drama. Thus the boasting of the King of Life in the play of that name is suggestive in reading Skelton, while the play of *Wisdom*, written about the time of *The Bowge of Courte*, "outside of time and human imperfection," as David Bevington notes, "instructs Anima, the soul of every man, in ortho-dox theological explanations of man's fall from grace and hence the sus-ceptibility of man's Mind, Understanding, and Will to the wiles of Fiend, World, and Flesh. This epistemology, interspersed with Latin chant, ap-plies timelessly to each auditor and to the collective soul of mankind in its infancy. . . . The idealized ending of *Wisdom* offers only the conservative solution of self-reform by each erring individual priest, submitting himself once again to 'yowur modyr, holy chyrch so mild.'"[50] A lost play from Cividale—which had its counterpart at York—was an explicit dramatiza-tion of the Creed.

It is pertinent to note, then, that a number of mystery plays came from the north and east of England—the extant cycle from York, the lost cycle from Beverley, a probable cycle at Norwich (the N-Town cycle, once as-signed to Coventry), and the best-known *Abraham and Isaac* from Brome Manor, Suffolk. A recent register by John Wasson and David Galloway lists a great number of individual plays in Norfolk and Suffolk, where the favorite subject for miracle plays seems to have been Thomas à Becket.[51] And it is also pertinent to note that some liturgical plays addressed their sacred matter in lines that resemble Skeltonics, as in the shepherds' prayer at Chester,

> Lord, of this light
> send us some sight
> why that it is sent.
> Before this night
> was I never soe afright
> of the firmament,

or in this processional from the play of St. Nicholas in East Anglia,

> Nove geniture
> cedit ius nature.
> Contra carnis iura
> parit virgo pura.
> Novo quodam iure
> premitur natura,
> nato Christo.
> Audit non auditum,
> servat non attritum

virgineum florem.
Mater preter morem,
irratansque ritum,
retinet pudorem,
nato Christo.[52]

The Wakefield Master (as well as others) anticipates Skelton in employing alliteration, internal rhyme, and a wheel of shorter lines—while the "bewildering sophistication of his rhyming, joking, punning and wild humour" remind us very much of the poet.[53] Indeed, the shepherd's complaint of his wife—

As sharp as a thystyll
as rugh as a brere:
She is browyd lyke a brystyll
with a sowre loten chere—

makes her sound like the sister of Elynour Rummyng.

Such visual drama, at the Mass and on pageant wagons, did not provide the only images that surrounded the early Tudors. Church interiors were intensely, vividly colorful. "Almost every inch of space, whether on walls, ceilings, piers, or screens, was covered with paint. Bright blue, red, and gold were the preferred colors. Windows sparkled with stained and painted glass. Rich vestments and jewels adorned both priests and furnishings. Vessels and ornaments of gold and silver glistened. And against this kaleidoscope of color flickered the fires of countless tapers. It was a rich and vivid scene—far removed from the cool, gray dignity that greets today's visitor as he enters these ancient buildings."[54] There is substantial loss in the destruction wrought by the Reformation, but in Skelton's day, a large cathedral might contain ten thousand figures painted on glass or board or carved in stone, while parish churches were also heavily enriched by art and artifact. Such images were meant to help the priest in his job of instruction. John Mirk in the *Liber Festivalis*, the book Wynkyn de Worde printed in 1493, notes that "þerfor roodes and oþyr ymages ben necessary in holy chirch, whateuer þes Lollardes sayn. . . . For, as Ion Bellet tellet, ymages and payntours ben lewde menys bokys, and I say bo[l]dyly þ þer ben mony þousaund of pepul þat couþ not ymagen in her hert how Crist was don on þe rood, but as þai lerne hit be sy3t of ymages and payntours."[55] Such windows feature scenes from Scripture, saints, and allegorical subjects, such as the Dance of Death in which a richly attired bishop is being led away by a skeleton which is still miraculously preserved in the

north aisle of St. Andrew's Church, Norwich. The more comprehensive
defense of such images made by Walter Hilton, Bishop Pecock, and oth-
ers, is stated compactly in the tract *Dives and Pauper*: "They serve for thre
thynges. For they be ordeined to stere mannys mynde to thynke on
Cristes incarnacion and on his passion and on his lyvynge, and on other
seintes lyvynge. Also they ben ordeined to styre mannys affection and his
herte to devocion, for ofte man is more steryt by sight than be herynge or
redynge. Also they be ordeyned to be a token and a boke to the leude
peple, that they may rede in ymagery and painture that clerkes rede in the
boke."[56] The biblical source on Which such theories are grounded is from
St. Paul: "For I think that God hath set forth us apostles, the last, as it
were men appointed to death: we are made a spectacle to the world, and
to angels, and to men" (1 Corinthians 4:9).

The setting for such images was, as we might expect from such a cul-
ture, figural: by the fifteenth century both great cathedral and small parish
church had added transepts, so that the building was cruciform to keep
the idea of Christ's Passion before the communicants. "His head is the
chancel, surrounded with a diadem of little chapels; the doors are his
pierced hands and feet," Morris Bishop writes. "The church itself is a
symbol of aspiration, with its spire pointing toward heaven."[57] Architec-
ture was both functional and representational, like the enameled dove,
symbol of the Holy Ghost, which hung over the altar and contained
wafers for communion.[58] Chantry chapels were set off from aisles by
parclose screens, while a chancel screen, often with a painting of the Last
Judgment, divided the altar and choir from the nave, as we have seen;
atop this screen stood a large crucifix, the rood cross, with lifesize figures
of the Virgin and St. John on either side—an important factor in "Ware
the Hauke." Stone churches—the one at Diss is made of flint and
freestone (for binding)—featured exterior carvings of full-length saints in
niches or on porches, and often the southern entrances or, later, west
fronts, became decorated with elaborate narrative pictures, such as
Doomsday, or allegorical subjects, such as the seven deadly sins. Stories
also unfolded in episodes as in the series of roundels in the south porch at
Malmesbury, which range from the Creation of Adam to David and Goli-
ath, or the 400 roof-bosses in the nave vault of the cathedral at Norwich,
which extend from the Creation to the crowning of Solomon: each of
fourteen bays around the cathedral (such as the twelfth bay from the east,
showing the Passion) has one main subject from the Creation to the Last
Judgment, 150 bosses in the transepts on the life and ministry of Christ (19

of them featuring St. John the Baptist). The Passion and Resurrection leading to the Ascension are represented in still more bosses at Norwich along the east and north walks of the cloister—still England's longest cloister—with Our Lady on nine and St. Thomas à Becket on another five. There is even one boss showing Henry II doing penance at St. Thomas's tomb and one of the martyrdom of St. Edmund at Hoxne. All these bosses at Norwich Cathedral are figural: the Old Adam is paired with the New Adam, Christ; the flood with Christ's baptism; Abraham's sacrifice with Christ's consecration of bread at the Last Supper.

Signs of the four evangelists and emblems of the Passion are frequent decorations carved into Norfolk fonts: the representative one still in the parish church at Framlingham, where Skelton no doubt attended services with Thomas Howard (or conducted services for him), alternates around the basin symbols of the four evangelists with shields of angels, the emblem of the Trinity, three cups with wafers and emblems of the Crucifixion, while the finial displays a newly bursting acorn to signify the sacrament of baptism. In many churches biblical heroes join English ones as, for example, in the enclosed gateway arch at Kirkham Priory (near Sheriff Hutton Castle in Yorkshire); St. George and the dragon on the east side of a carving of the Crucifixion balance David and Goliath on the west. Wooden choirstalls were also often carved elaborately: bench ends in Chester Cathedral show pilgrims and saints; corbels illustrate the Passion and the deadly sins (such as Gluttony, eating a haunch); and misericords display monsters and grotesques. At the splendid Holy Trinity Church at Blythburgh, Suffolk, a large number of bench ends are carved with lively sins: there Avarice sits sturdily on his money chest, Hypocrisy prays with open eyes, Greed has a distended stomach, Drunkenness is put in the stocks, and Sloth sits up uncomfortably in bed. A hawking scene appears on a misericord at Beverley Minster in a carving similar to one in the cathedral at Ripon, Yorkshire (not far from York Minster), and there is also a fox dressed in the cowl and gown of a friar, rosary in his paws, preaching to seven geese, as well as more traditional grotesques. Along the north aisle in Beverley Minster there remain today carvings of the world's largest aggregation of medieval musicians playing various instruments of Skelton's day. Outside the parish churches and the cathedrals, flying buttresses were decorated with demons and gargoyles, some based on living persons, and all as deformed and ugly as Elynour Rummyng and her customers (or as Skelton's later portraints of Wolsey). "The demons and monsters," D. W. Robertson, Jr., writes, "may not be beautiful in themselves, but like the evil angels and the sinners in St. Augustine's hierarchical universe, they contribute through their significances to the ordered beauty of the whole" (p. 136).[59]

As for the exceptional wall paintings, "Extreme richness of surface quality, very great delicacy and an extraordinary power of technical invention characterize the finest work of the time," E. W. Tristram reports. In the fourteenth and fifteenth centuries, "Allegories and Moralities achieved an intensified popularity, and those most frequently represented were the Seven Deadly Sins, the Three Living and the Three Dead, and the Seven Corporal Works of Mercy. Even in small county churches these subjects were normally depicted competently enough."[60] But the newer works grew grim. Christ bleeding on the Cross and vivid martyrdoms of saints seem to indicate that the fifteenth century was a period of discouragement, a period concerned more and more with death and judgment; perhaps this is one reason why St. Christopher appears so regularly, often on church walls opposite the doors. For example, at Byland Abbey, Yorkshire, a large painting of the Lord's Pity, showing the dead Christ on Mary's knees, decorated the wall of the north aisle, creating a visual analogue, as we shall see, to "Phyllyp Sparowe." Indeed, according to the architectural historian W. W. Williamson, Norfolk was "famous for its wooden screens which are probably the finest in England" and for its painted panels.[61] And Norfolk was also especially rich in painted pulpits, decorated by local men, not foreigners, like Robert Hyelyng (or Jokelyng) and Thomas Barsham of Yarmouth. Tristram has catalogued many of the remaining paintings for us in an indispensable listing, including many Norfolk churches. At All Saints in North Walsham, for instance, there was a Tree of the Seven Deadly Sins prominently featuring *Gula* holding a cup (like Elynour), a witch's or devil's Mass over the north door (in which three couples are in the arms of a huge demon), and, east of the doorway, a St. Christopher of large proportions; between the windows on the east wall is a Passion series. The south wall of St. Mary in Elsing had displayed a history of St. John the Baptist (an important reference for "Ware the Hauke"), which showed the dance of Salomé, St. John preaching before Herod, St. John being led from prison, and the beheading. Another Passion series, a large Doom, and the remains of a St. Christopher can be seen at St. Mary in West Somerton near Yarmouth, while a Tree representing the Seven Corporal Works of Mercy still decorates All Saints, Edingthorpe. Indications of many paintings can still be found in the Cathedral Church of the Holy and Undivided Trinity in Norwich; in the four bays of the Ante-reliquary Chapel are the Virgin, St. Peter, St. Paul, and St.

Thomas of Canterbury. Another has been uncovered in Thomas Howard's church of St. Michael the Archangel, Framlingham, where the Holy Trinity is portrayed by God seated on His throne and the Son on the Cross. Such figures are repeated many times over in the parish churches of East Anglia and elsewhere. What is unusual in Norfolk, however, is the large number of paintings of witchcraft and of witch's or devil's Masses —five of seven Tristram located—at Coton, Little Melton, Seething, Stokesby, and Costwight, where they are over the west front so that parishioners keep them to their backs while watching the correct form of Mass at the east end of the church. (The priests, conversely, would look out at such paintings, seeing in them an alternative congregation to their own.) Thomas Waldensis, in his late medieval *Doctrinale Antiquitatum Fidei Catholicae Ecclesiae*, explains why such images were so frequent. "The Jews did not . . . fashion distinct images of things, because, in the prevailing darkness, everything was shadowy, and they saw nothing distinctly," he says. "But we Christians, having knowledge of Christ, cast out old shadows and, because we have been transformed in His image, praise images."[62]

Paintings also decorated manuscripts, and once more the best illuminators belonged to the East Anglian school, which flourished in the second quarter of the fourteenth century. Their work, influenced by French and Italian illuminators, is known for its realism, three-dimensional solidity, and light and dark sculpturing that shows swaying, graceful figures. These East Anglian manuscripts, made for monasteries and gentry in Norfolk and Suffolk, are characterized by marginal art in which a "rich profusion" of "birds, animals, humans and grotesques join a continuous dance among frames and foliage tendrils."[63] All sorts of sacred books were illustrated—Bibles, psalters, missals—but the best-known now are the Books of Hours that were used for private devotions. Here the inhabited initials for Prime, the first Hour of the Virgin, often show the Mother with the Child in her lap—not unlike the suckling child of wall paintings, which probably suggested one of the emblems behind "Phyllyp Sparowe"— while the Hastings Hours (which, like the others, follows the Sarum Missal) has borders of butterflies, dragonflies, snails, and birds as realistically observed as Jane Scrope's descriptions, and also pictures of the Passion and the English saints Edward, Dunstan, and Thomas à Becket. Still another Book of Hours, now at the University of Liverpool, is a mid-fifteenth-century exemplar illustrating the Office of the Dead recited over a coffin as if portraying Jane's poem. Some illustrations, in fact, can be quite charming, such as the portrayal of Mary at the Annunciation in the

Book of Hours of the Master of Mary of Burgundy, where, rather than listening to Gabriel, she is pictured running to tell Elizabeth her news. Others might have a *trompe l'oeil* effect that seems to resonate in Skelton's picture of "the frytthy forest of Galtres" in *The Garlande of Laurell* (22).

Among the finest psalters is the St. Omer Psalter (British Library Yates Thompson MS 14), begun by artists of the East Anglian school for the St. Omer family of Norfolk in 1330 and completed in the fifteenth century, with its colorful margins and historiated initials. The initial B (for *Beatus*) of Psalm 1, for instance (fol. 7), shows the conventional Tree of Jesse, with Christ's ancestors enclosed in medallions against a checkered blue and pink ground. Delicately drawn animals and birds perch on vines, while elsewhere men are wrestling, felling trees, and escaping a unicorn.[64] Similarly, the East Anglian Ormesby Psalter, named for a Benedictine monk at the Cathedral Priory of Norwich (Bodleian Douce 366), has dense borders of animals and people. One page shows a grotesque of a snail with a man's head (at the top), a musician blowing a shawm (at the left), and two people—the man with a hawk on his wrist—holding up a ring (at the bottom) (fol. 131; see frontispiece). The juxtaposition of the sacred and secular along with the grotesque is a telling one for *Speke, Parrot* and "Phyllyp Sparowe." Here the inhabited initial—*D* for *Domine, exaudi orationem meam* (Psalm 131)—shows David kneeling, his hands raised in prayer.[65] The Cuerden Psalter (Pierpont Morgan Library MS 756) shows Christ's life as a series of delicate and lovely illustrations, but most memorable and most powerful are the illustrated manuscripts of the Apocalypse (The Cloisters Apocalypse, which opens with a prefatory cycle on the early life of Christ).

In such a rich culture as we have been describing, poetry flourished too—and much of it also came from the liturgy. Douglas Gray finds this the "most obvious inheritance" for poetry:

> If we look at the Introits, Offertories and Graduals we find that they are often single verses from the Bible, which, when they are abstracted from their prose contexts to stand alone, become virtually lyrics in miniature. Like this:
>
> > Signum magnum apparuit in caelo:
> > Mulier amicta sole
> > et luna sub pedibus ejus
> > et in capite ejus
> > corona stellarum duodecim.[66]

from the book of Revelation (chapter 12), which was used for the Assumption of the Virgin Mary, a vivid and striking image which particularly appealed to the medieval illustrators of the Apocalypse (p. 4).

Carleton Brown, too, found that some of the best religious lyrics—which far outnumber the secular in this period—come from two preaching books, those of the friar John Grimestone (now in the National Library of Scotland) and Bishop Sheppey (Merton College, Oxford, MS 248). Simple and practical religious verse is found in personal primers, as well as in the rich Harleian manuscript where most of the poems center on the Passion. Besides the Passion, however, in the century in which Skelton began writing poetry there was an increasing interest in Marian poetry—in hymns, antiphons, *Ave*-poems. Often they treated the Seven Joys or Seven Sorrows of the Virgin as a Sequence, the latter growing out of the *planctus* tradition in poetry and centering on the Office of the Compassion, since the Seven Sorrows were the arrest, scourging, condemnation, Crucifixion, death, deposition, and burial of her Son. In other, more personal lyrics, Mary could be treated as a second Eve, an extension of the Pauline idea of Christ as the second Adam (there is some reference to this in "Phyllyp Sparowe") or as the New Testament response to the Eve who was seduced by the words of an evil angel because she brought the redeeming Word into the world (there is an infernal parody of this in "Elynour Rummyng").

That Skelton lived in a culture still largely oral, with a parish still populated by the illiterate, suggests the popularity of poetry, with its strong images, as a mnemonic device: the *Lay Folks Mass Book* is written in a rhyme that shares with Skeltonics short lines and varying numbers of stresses, although they are invariably in couplets. Other brief lyrics are meant to serve for private meditations, as this *memoria* of Christ's Passion:

> The minde of thi passiun, suete Jesu,
> The teres it tollid,
> The eine it bolled,
> The neb it wetth,
> In herte sueteth.[67]

Other poems combine images or exempla into memorable narratives, as Chaucer's Pardoner tells us:

> Thanne telle I hem ensamples many oon
> Of olde stories longe tyme agoon.
> For lewed peple loven tales olde;
> Swiche thynges kan they wel reporte
>   and holde (VI, 435–38).

Carols, too, were not only used in ring dances; they were also employed as
instructive devices.

> Pleasure it is
> To hear iwis
>   The birdes sing.
> The deer in the dale,
> The sheep in the vale,
>   The corn springing.
> Gods purveyance
> For sustenance
>   It is for man;
> Then we always
> To him give praise
>   And thank him than
>   And thank him than.[68]

Such poems work with sharp, simple lines that allow the impact of
straightforward imagery, some of it traditional: darkness and light, wash-
ing, feeding, the manger, the Cross, the dove. Other poems work
thematically, as Chaucer's Prioress freely draws on the Mass for Holy
Innocents Day to tell her modern story of an innocent. Still others, as we
have come to expect, work figurally, as Skelton's usually works. While the
flower often stands for Mary, so too she can be referred to in connection
with the dew that fell on the fleece of Gideon (in Judges 6), taken as a
prefiguration of the Word of God descending and causing Mary to have
the seed of Christ within her. In the same way, the lily among thorns in
the Song of Songs and the rose plant of Jericho in Ecclesiasticus are often
connected to Mary, as she is said to be a branch that bears a flower because
the "rods" of Aaron and Jesse bore flowers in the Old Testament and were
meant to figure her bearing Jesus in the New. For the early Tudors, the
book of nature (God's creation) often accords with—and explains—His
sacred book, the Bible. Indeed, the more we grow accustomed to thinking
of poetic language as a language of signs, and the more we become
habituated to such usage, the more natural it becomes to see Parrot as a

divine incarnation of the Holy Spirit—or Wolsey as an incarnation of Moloch. Thus poems also invited thought and meditation. "The old way of reading," Burrow reminds us, "known in the monasteries as *rumination*, was a slow and noisy process—an audible 'chewing over' of the precious words of the text" (p. 53) of the Bible, a process easily conveyed to inspired poetry.

Moreover, a number of medieval and early Tudor poems are written in short lines that seem to anticipate the Skeltonic line. "Sumer is icumen in" is one that is well known;

> I saw a fair maiden
> Sitten and sing:
> She lulled a little child,
> A swete lording.
> That eche Lord is that
> That made alle thing:
> Of alle lordes he is Lord,
> Of alle kinges King.
> Ther was mekil melody
> At that childes berth:
> Alle tho wern in Hevene blis
> They made mekil merth.
> Aungele bright they song that night,
> And seiden to that child:
> "Blissed be thou, and so be she,
> That is bothe mek and mild."
> Prey we now to that child,
> And to his moder dere,
> Graunt hem his blissing,
> That now maken chere[69]

is another. Most medieval clerical poetry tends to be of urban life or of the aristocracy. "The truth is that the Church tended to be hostile to the peasants," Paul Johnson notes. "Medieval clerical writers emphasize the bestiality, violence and avarice of the peasant" (p. 228), as in the case of Elynour Rummyng. Many such verses illustrate the features of the earlier "Ricardian poetry" which J. A. Burrow tells us is narrative, vigorous, realistic, detailed, structurally segmented, and by turns humorous and solemn, jesting and earnest.[70] Skelton shows us the same range and variety. If "I saw a fair maiden" suggests something of Skelton's tender lines to Jane Scrope, then the light, mocking tone of Skelton's early secular verse is captured in this poem about Jankin, a cleric, who seduces the narrator in the course of divine service:

> Kyrie, so kyrie,
> Jankin singeth merye,
> With Aleison.
> As I went on Yol Day
> In oure prosession,
> Knew I joly Jankin
> By his mery ton,
> Kyrieleyson.
> Jankin began the offis
> On the Yol Day,
> And yit me thinketh it dos me good
> So merye gan he say,
> "Kyrieleyson." . . .
> Jankin at the Sanctus
> Craketh a merye note,
> And yit me thinketh it dos me good—
> I payed for his cote,
> Kyrieleyson. . . .
> Jankin at the Agnus
> Bereth the pax-brede:
> He twinkled but said nowt,
> And on my fot he trede,
> Kyrieleyson.
> Benedicamus Domino,
> Christ fro shame me shilde:
> Deo gracias, therto—
> Alas! I go with childe,
> Kyrieleyson,[71]

while another fifteenth-century poem, strikingly similar to Skelton's, has all the heaviness and despair of "Why Come Ye Nat to Courte?":

> Wise men bene but scorned,
> & wedowȝ eke foryerned,
> Grete men arn but glosid,
> & smale men arn borne doun & myslosed,
> lordis wex euer blynd,
> ffrendis ben vnkynde,

dethe is oute of mynde,
Treuth may no man fynde.[72]

But in many instances, as with "Jankin, the clerical seducer," we approach
the thin line between text and parody-text, as in the Mass and the parody
Mass, or the parody Sequences that were written on wine and beer, and
on Martin Luther.

We are, that is, in the sphere of Goliardic poetry to which Skelton
alludes in attacking "*Goliardum Garnishe*" (iii. distichon, 1b). First con-
demned in 1227 for scandalizing the faithful because they sang verses mod-
elled on the Sanctus and the Agnus Dei, the Goliards were wandering
clerics of the twelfth and thirteenth centuries in Germany, France, and
England. Their irreverent and bantering tone and use of sacred music and
texts as the bases for witty and outrageous poems on wine, women, and
song often catch the energy and tone, if not the thesis and substance, of
Skelton's major work. These Latin verses "glorifying a wandering life or
celebrating the joys of drinking, dicing, and drabbing," such as encoun-
tered in "The Tunnyng of Elynour Rummyng," George F. Whicher
writes, "must surely be the work of vagrom scholars, ribald priests, and
renegade monks, the human detritus of the ecclesiastical and monastic
establishments. . . . Goliardic jesters had to be restrained from interposing
irreverent ejaculations during divine services, but nothing could curb their
satiric ingenuity. In defiance of official displeasure they composed paro-
dies of offices, prayers, and hymns, a Gamblers' Mass, a Paternoster of the
Wine, a Gospel according to the Silver Marks."[73] But their irreverence has
point. They attack much that Skelton attacks—hypocrisy, cupidity, misuse
of power and position. They use gluttony to attack gluttony, as in
"Elynour Rummyng," and despair to attack despair, as in *The Bowge of
Courte*. In fact, J. M. Manly has argued that the putative Archpoet Golias,
after whom they take their name, may be etymologically derived from the
use of Goliath in the three lections of the first nocturn of the fourth
Sunday after Whitsunday,[74] and while this position is no longer favored, it
does suggest how close text and parody-text are in the Goliardic period—
and in Skelton's. One extant poem parodies tithing, but note how:

> Fas et Nefas ambulant
> passu fere pari;
> prodigus non redimit
> vitium avari;
> virtus temperantia
> quadam singulari

> debet medium
> ad utrumque vitium
> caute contemplari.[75]

Others deal with the bidding prayer, with confession, with excommunication—and with sinful prelates.

> Quis est verax, quis est bonus,
> vel quis dei portat onus?
> Ut in uno claudam plura,
> mors exercet sua iura.
> Iam mors regnat in prelatis,
> nolunt sacrum dare gratis;
> postquam sedent iam securi
> contradicunt sancto iuri.[76]

A more ambitious poem, "The Drunkard's Mass," begins with the versicle "I will go to the altar of Bacchus" and a response, "To him who rejoices the heart of man," followed by a confession to Bacchus; it continues with a prayer, introit, more versicles and responses, an *Oratio*, an epistle and gospel that parody Acts 4:32ff. and 6:8ff., a Gradual parodying Psalm 55:23, the Preface, *Sursum Corda*, *Sanctus*, and *Agnus Dei*, the *Paternoster* and the *Communio*; the Post-Communion prayers end, "Ite, bursa vacua. Reo gratias."[77] Other songs parody Church hymns—one in praise of wine, "Vinum bonum et suave, bonis bonum," parodies the Sequence in Praise of the Virgin, "Verbum bonum et suave"; "In Taberno quando sumus" parodies "Lauda, Zion, Salvatorem," the Eucharistic hymn of St. Thomas Aquinas; "Quicunque vult esse frater" is based on the Creed-hymn "Quicunque vult salvus esse." It is difficult, reading these now, not to think of Skelton's trental to old John Clarke, his choruses on Diss and France, or his long burlesque of the Mass in "The Tunnyng of Elynour Rummyng."

Contemporary with Skelton is William Dunbar's Goliardic "Dirige to the King at Stirling." It is, notes the modern editor James Kinsley, a parody of the Matins in the Office of the Dead—the same office Skelton uses in "Phyllyp Sparowe"—in which Dunbar uses the three nocturns, three Psalms, and three lessons to "[contrast] the purgatorial austerities of the Franciscans with the celestial delights of the court at Edinburgh."[78] The cascading lines of several other Goliardic poems remind us once again of the Skeltonic.

Conteramus,
confringamus
carnis desideria,
ut cum iustis
et electis
celestia gaudia
gratulari
mereamur
per eterna secula.[79]

And "The Confession of Golias" combines, in a single stanza, the ship of *The Bowge of Courte* and the bird of *Speke, Parrot*:

Feror ego veluti
sine nauta navis,
ut per vias aeris
vaga fertur avis.
Non me tenent vincula,
non me tenet clavis,
quero mei similes
et adiungor pravis.[80]

It is when we consistently come upon poems like these—as well as the liturgy, its music, its drama, and its art—that we realize John Skelton could find all the substance and stylistics he needed, all the matter and manner that we find in his most significant poetry, in the Holy Catholic Church that he served as ordained priest.

A particularly powerful but representative poem from this culture, found in the Vernon Collection, exemplifies much of the best of the poetics Skelton inherited: the use of startling imagery, references to Scripture and appeal to a preacher, and a sense of human life within a divinely ordained sphere in which man is but a stranger and pilgrim and earthly life but a shadow of eternal truth. It is, adds Douglas Gray, "a reflection on mortality which exhibits in a remarkable and distinctive way the sombre pessimism and scepticism . . . based largely on . . . Ecclesiastes" (p. 212). It opens interrogatively:

I wolde witen of sum wys wiht
    Witterly what this world were:
It fareth as a foules fliht,
    Now is hit henne, now is hit here,

> Ne be we never so muche of miht,
>   Now be we on benche, now be we on bere;
> And be we never so war and wiht,
>   Now be we sek, now beo we fere;
> Now is on proud withouten peere,
>   Now is the selve iset not by;
> And whos wol alle thing hertly here,
>   This world fareth as a fantasy.

Change is illustrated from the world of nature: "The sonnes cours, we may wel kenne, / Aryseth est and geth doun west"; in this context, "each man glides forth as a gest" [stranger]. "Kunredes come, and kunredes gon, / As joyneth generacions, / But alle hee passeth everichon, / For al heor preparacions." "At this point," Gray comments,

> there is introduced the idea of the uselessness of discussion and argument. All these "disputations," the poet says, "idelyche all us occupye," for Christ "maketh the creacions," with the implication that we cannot know his "privete." He asks the Psalmist's question, "What is man?" but does not go on "that God is mindful of him." . . . The only thing that distinguishes man is that he is more "sleyye" (wise, cunning). . . . [And] Man's intellect is of no more avail than his strength. . . . Like the Preacher, the poet launches into a *carpe diem* passage (though it is now in a very pietistic context) . . . and the poem ends with yet another sombre reminder of mutability:

> Thus waxeth and wanieth mon, hors and hounde,
>   From nought to nought thus henne we hiye;
> And her we stunteth but a stounde,
>   For this world is but fantasye.

In summary, Gray goes on, "The coexistence of the different moods—the sombre pessimism, the questioning spirit, the doubts of man's value and of the capacity of his reason, together with the absolute insistence on faith and the need for God's mercy, and the hopeful advice to man to make virtue of necessity, which is almost optimistic yet has undertones of despair—results in a remarkable emotional power. This is an extraordinary and a unique religious poem" (pp. 212–15). Yet in its opening of doubt, its submission to fortune, its concern with disputations, its wise and cunning men, its surrender of intellect and will, its notion of the world as a dream—in all these ideas, and in this order, this poem closely parallels *The Bowge of Courte*. But wherever we turn in the rich culture Skelton inherited, we find something reminding us of him or his work. And with such a vibrant, cohesive culture a fresh presence in our minds, we are prepared once more to turn back to his best poetry.

3

THE EAST ANGLIAN POEMS

SLOTH
Bench end (hand-carved, fifteenth century),
Church of the Holy Trinity, Blythburgh, Suffolk

"EVERYWHERE THERE WAS movement and change," Roger Lock-
yer writes of the period when John Skelton was given the rector's living at
Diss in 1502.[1] London was now rapidly growing as a major port; but for
years East Anglia had carried on important trade with the Low Countries
and there the economic growth was at times staggering. It was, H. L. R.
Edwards tells us, "the most crowded and flourishing corner of all En-
gland. Its prosperity came from the great cloth trade, which was now
(after a century's pause) again expanding at a dizzy rate, filling every
cottage kitchen with looms and decking every high street and hillside with
the grand new mansions of successful clothiers" (p. 83). East Anglia also
enjoyed a prosperous fishing trade, from Harwich to Yarmouth, where
herring fleets added new coastal fishing boats and deep-sea vessels every
year, and many men were buying two or three boats of their own. In the
village of Walberswick in east Suffolk, the people left the old chapel down
by the marsh and built an impressive new church dedicated to St. Andrew
high on the ridge where an especially tall tower could guide ships at sea.
Yet over all East Anglia—then known as the "Dowry of Mary" because the
Virgin had appeared at Walsingham—men were remodelling their parish
churches, or enlarging them into lighter and grander places of worship;
and employing Flemish artists and using imports they were fitting them
with finely wrought, expensive, precious objects—furniture, glass, im-
ages, vestments, books. "These people," Colin Richmond has said re-
cently of the East Anglians, "put their money where their hearts were. By
the fifteenth century the religion which was offered them in the parish
church they participated in, they shared, even in some ways they created:
it was popular religion."[2]

Skelton's parish church of St. Mary the Virgin was at a central cross-
roads in the established town of Diss[3] in the diocese of Norwich (al-
though the bishopric had once been at Thetford). Hoxne, where the
bishop often sat in residence (probably at Hoxne Abbey), was four miles
in one direction; Redgrave, until 1506 Wolsey's parish, lay eight miles in
another direction; Kenninghall Place, a home of the Howard family from
1526, lay fifteen miles in still another; while, in a fourth, but somewhat
farther away, was Framlingham Castle, the Howards' chief residence, often
occupied by the second duke and in Skelton's day the most impressive
castle in East Anglia and one of the staunchest military fortifications in the
whole of Tudor England.[4] Skelton's church in Diss stood on high ground
too, at the intersection of Market Hill and St. Nicholas Street, with the
newly built Guild Chapel, consolidating the wealthy Diss woollen and
linen guilds of Corpus Christi and St. Nicholas, to the southwest, the

graveyard to the east, and, beyond that, the splendid new Guild Hall, certainly the most attractive building in the town, just completed in 1490. Busy shops and hostelries spread around the hillside to the west and south and, below them, the mere for which the town had been named and, below that, the common pasture maintained so as to prevent further enclosures from encroaching on rich arable land. Reflecting her surroundings, St. Mary the Virgin Church, built of sturdy flint and freestone and consecrated in 1290, was unusually ample in proportion and lofty in height. The chancel measured sixty-seven by twenty-two feet; the nave was another eighty-one feet long and as wide as the chancel; north and south aisles (only a little more than eleven feet wide) were divided from the nave by an arcade of five arches on eight-sided pillars. There was a chantry chapel at the end of each aisle (remnants of the two guild chapels that had earlier occupied them), impressive north and south porches, and a stout square bell tower at the west end through which a passageway had been cut to allow church processionals to pass around the building without going into the muddy street against which the church building abutted. Heads of figures support dripstones on the north side of the church, but other exterior statuary has been destroyed; trefoil-headed niches are still visible on two buttresses on the west face. The Reformation also destroyed the glass and wall paintings on the interior, but the church still has twenty-two corbels showing crowned angels in various attitudes of prayer, holding scrolls or an open book, while the aisle parapets still have good sculptures of shields, foliage—and grotesques. Few accounts are extant from the time of Skelton's residency, but an inventory made at the time of the Reformation suggests that the church holdings were even then well above the minimum, including a peal of bells:

> In primis oone payer of Chales of syluer and gylt with the patent
> conteyneng
> xx^{ti} vnces at iij^s viij^d the vnce iiij^{li} xiij^s iiij^d
> Ite' oone Whyte Cope for the mynistracyon
> of the Communyon price xv^s
> Ite' iij albys & Six Surplesses price v^s
> Ite' an olde payer of Organs price xij^s
> Ite' oone belle in the stepole conteyneng in weyght
> vj^c at xv^s the hundred iiij^{li} x^s
> Ite' oone lyttyll bell in the Chauncell conteynyng ij^c
> at xv^s the hundred xxx^s
> (Erased: two towels for the Communion table.)

Ite' remaneng in the handes of the right honorable Henry Erle of
    Suffolk two belles contaynyng in wayte xx^{cs}

Such a modestly prosperous church brought Skelton a little more than a
moderately prosperous income: he cleared per annum £33 6s. 8d. (the two
guild priests each earned £5 6s. 8d. per annum from rents on an eight-acre
landholding in Framlingham). In addition, Skelton had nearly twelve
acres of glebe adjoining his house a short distance from the church (now
the site of Mere Manor), where he could grow corn for sale, have his own
kitchen garden, and raise livestock. Here, amidst the bustle of life in Diss
and in addition to his duties as rector, he found time to perfect the
Skeltonic line he had used for "Uppon a deedmans hed" with a trental,
two mock-epitaphs, a canticle and lamentation, a penitential sermon, and
a macaronic poem incorporating the Vespers from the Office for the
Dead. In short, he established with work at Diss the kind of religious
poetry on which much of his reputation would rest, including his first
masterpiece, "Phyllyp Sparowe."

"Uppon a deedmans hed" may be Skelton's first poem at Diss. Surely
the initial description of the skull as a *memento mori*, used to instruct the
beholder in a sense of frail mortality, is just the sort of image pictured
again and again, as we have seen, in wall paintings and carvings of the
Three Living and the Three Dead so prominent, especially in East Anglia,
while the use to which the image is put reminds us of how much such
illustrations prompted the penitent waiting to make their confessions.
Both the pictorial and the instructive are joined in the poem.

> It is generall
> To be mortall:
> I have well espyde
> No man may hym hyde
> From deth holow-eyed,
> With synnews wyderyd,
> With bonys shyderyd,
> With hys worme-etyn maw
> And hys gastly jaw
> Gaspyng asyde,
> Nakyd of hyde,
> Neyther flesh nor fell (7–18).

Such images were also readily apparent in the Dooms painted on the
chancel arch, surrounding the priest as he is seen from the nave (as we

noticed in connection with *The Bowge of Courte*). The poem goes on to assert the priest's role, not as celebrant but as preacher.

> Then by my councell,
> Loke that ye spell
> Well thys gospell:
> For wherso we dwell,
> Deth wyll us quell
> And with us mell (19–24).

The sudden shift in pronoun here surprises us: rather than set himself apart from the problems of mortality as the authority teaching from the gospel, the narrator becomes equally subject to his fleshly fate. Both the universality and the inevitability of death are then brought, like the Doom, to the physical description of life's end in a verbal portrait as harrowing as any imagery surrounding the congregation standing and kneeling in the nave of the church.

> For all oure pamperde paunchys,
> Ther may no fraunchys
> Nor worldly blys
> Redeme us from this:
> Oure days be datyd
> To be chekmatyd,
> With drawttys of deth
> Stoppyng oure breth;
> Oure eyen synkyng,
> Oure bodys stynkyng,
> Our gummys grynnyng,
> Oure soulys brynnyng! (25–36)

But facing the priest, looking *through* the Doom, the congregation would also see, there over the chancel arch, the rood cross: a huge crucifix with Mary and John standing on either side. Such a thought breaks into the narrator's mind too.

> To whom then shall we sew
> For to haue rescew,
> But to swete Jesu
> On us then for to rew? (37–40),

and, thinking of salvation by meditating on the crucifix overhead, thoughts move to the base of it, to the compassionate Mary, Virgin and

Mother, after whom the Diss parish church was named, and to Christ's recognition of the cost of being human.

> O goodly chyld
> Of Mary mylde,
> Then be oure shylde!
> That we be not exyld
> To the dyne dale
> Of boteles bale,
> Nor to the lake
> Of fendys blake (41–48).

Such thoughts, prompted by the Crucifixion and the Resurrection—or the Mass in miniature—introduce thoughts on the state of grace. Then, having united the congregation much like the closing Collect, the poem concludes with a final prayer and blessing.

> But graunt us grace
> To se thy face,
> And to purchace
> Thyne hevenly place
> And thy palace,
> Full of solace,
> Above the sky,
> That is so hy,
> Eternally
> To beholde and se
> The Trynyte!
> Amen (49–60).

Conceptualizing this brief meditative poem so that it functions like the Canon of the Mass (but admitting the gospel to it), Skelton dwells on the Passion, the heart of Church belief and ritual, in a meter resonant of liturgical music, to mark his commitment to Holy Mother Church. Here the short, chanting lines, troping on the idea of death much as the Sequence might trope a similar scriptural text, transform a solemn sense of a dirge into a glorious recessional at the close. "Ite, missa est"; "Go, the poem and its lesson are finished."

The poem's final line, *"Myrres vous y,"* "Behold yourself therein" (61), returns us to the poem's extended title: "Skelton Laureat, upon a deedmans hed, that was sent to hym from an honorable jentyllwoman for a token, devysyd this gostly medytacyon in Englysh: covenable in sentence,

comendable, lamentable, lacrymable, profytable for the soule." Together,
they suggest the poem may have been written while Skelton was still at
court, since such gifts were not unknown there—indeed, it has been sug-
gested that the token was from the Queen Mother herself, denoting either
Skelton's ordination or his departure for Diss. But in either event, the
poem grows out of hints we find in his early work at court. As early as
1494 or 1495, for instance, Skelton began a *Speculum principis* for the boy
he was tutoring to become Archbishop of Canterbury, young Henry. In
this short treatise of advice—what Edwards calls a sermon (p. 75) and
Heiserman a homily (p. 75)—Skelton begins with Psalm 2 ("And now, O
ye kings, understand: receive instruction, you that judge the earth. . . .
Embrace discipline, lest at any time the Lord be angry, and you perish
from the just way," 10, 12) and ends with Psalm 71 ("Give to the king thy
judgment, O God: and to the king's son thy justice: To judge thy people
with justice, and thy poor with judgment," 2). In between, he argues for
probity (1–34) aided by knowledge and virtue (36ff.), by precept and by
examples (41–72) that begin with Jeremiah, Pilate, Mannasses, and Saul,
before turning to more conventional advice from Cato. Skelton's earliest
extant poem, too, the eulogy for Henry Percy, earl of Northumberland,
ends in an extended but moving prayer to God, to Christ, to the Blessed
Virgin, and to the Trinity which, though traditional, makes of North-
umberland's defeat a moment of figural history that is clearly intended
(Fish, p. 4):

> O Quene of mercy, O lady full of grace,
> Maiden moste pure and Goddis moder dere,
> To sorowfull harttes chef comfort and solace,
> Of all women, O floure withouten pere,
> Pray to thy son above the starris clere,
> He to vouchsaf by thy mediacion,
> To pardon thi servant and brynge to savacioun (204–10).

Even in some of the most secular poetry, such as "Lullay, lullay," with its
parody of the sacred lullaby carols of the Virgin and Child, and "Knolege,
Aquayntance, Resort, Favour, with Grace," a love song to an acrostic
Kateryn, where the poet describes his beloved in epithets normally re-
served for the Virgin ("Refresshyng myndys the Aprell shoure of rayne; /
Condute of comforte and well most soverayne," 11–12), Skelton imports
the conventions of sacred poetry to signal meaning. Perhaps his most
ambitious work along these lines is "Agaynst a Comely Coystrowne," a
pretentious "holy water clarke" (21) or one admitted to minor clerical

orders but still a student, whose ambitions in sacred music ("He solfyth to haute, hys trybyll is to hy," 23) ultimately lead him to confuse the *Custodi nos*, the versicle sung after the hymn at Compline (except on double feasts) and just before the *Nunc dimittis* (57) with the *Sospitati dedit egros* ("He has helped the sick to salvation," 59), an antiphon for the feast of St. Nicholas, patron saint of the Guild of Master Parish Clerks such as this poor chorister (58). Such confusion is parodied by the poet when he dates his poem "Candlemas evyn, the Kalendas of May" (70), for Candlemas Day is 2 February—not 1 May—and pointedly the Feast of Purification, a major Marian feast celebrating the Presentation of the Lord (Luke 2:22) when the Old Dispensation is replaced with the New.

However, such hints as these inadequately prepare us for "Ware the Hauke." This poem, which takes as its title a proverbial cry used to encourage a hawk to obtain its prey, tells the story (presumably autobiographical) of the rector of Diss finding a neighboring curate hawking in his church during his absence. Innocent III had specifically forbidden clergy to hawk in an injunction (Canon 15) of the Fourth Lateran Council, although subsequent clergy on occasion ignored him.[6] The hawking parson was a traditional subject for moral and satirical poetry—he appears in both Chaucer and Gower—but despite this, hawking remained especially popular in Norfolk; visitation records of 1492 for the diocese of Norwich indicate that the monks at Wymondham Abbey both hawked and hunted. Authenticity seems confirmed when the poet notes that

> The church dores were sparred,
> Fast-boltyd and barryd;
> Yet wyth a prety gyn
> I fortuned to come in (91–94),

probably referring to that peculiar archway tower of the church of St. Mary the Virgin that had a door through which Skelton could enter, climb tower stairs, pass over the archway, and then descend other stairs that led into the west end of the nave past the locked outer door.

But from the outset this simple story is given a complex presentation. It begins with a prologue that frames the incident as both lesson and warning and then, bringing us close to the event, suggests that the desecration involved disturbs the very basis of the Church.

> This worke devysed is
> For suche as do amys;
> And specyally to controule

> Such as have cure of soule,
> That be so far abusyd
> They cannot be excusyd
> By reason nor by law,
> But that they playe the daw,
> To hawke or els to hunt
> From the auter to the funt,
> Wyth cry unreverent,
> Before the sacrament,
> Wythin the Holy Church bowndis,
> That of our fayth the grownd is. . . .
> Therefore, to make complaynt
> Of such mysadvysed
> Parsons, and dysgysed,
> Thys boke we have devysed (1–14, 20–23).

Skelton goes on to tell how "a lewde curate, A parson benyfyced" (35–36) "wrought amys" (41) by blasphemously stripping the altar and allowing the hawk to pollute it, and eventually, to defecate on it.

> As preest unreverent,
> Streyght to the sacrament
> He made his hawke to fly,
> With hogeous showte and cry,
> The hy auter he strypte naked;
> Thereon he stode and craked;
> He shoke downe all the clothys,
> And sware horryble othes
> Before the face of God,
> By Moyses and Arons rod,
> Or that he thens yede
> His hawke shulde pray and fede
> Upon a pigeons maw!
> The blode ran downe raw
> Upon the auter stone;
> The hawke tyryd on a bonne,
> And in the holy place
> She mutyd there a chase
> Upon my *corporas* face.
> Such *sacrificium laudis*
> He made with suche gambawdis! (45–65)

In the most sanctified part of the church, atop the altar, the blaspheming priest rejoices in his sacrilege.

Skelton's prologue refers to various handbooks for parsons such as the invading priest has sworn to follow. John Mirk's *Instructions for Parish Priests*, for instance, one of the best known, tells the Catholic clergyman that he must always have his altar ready for Mass.

> So þe cloþes þat þey be clene,
> And also halowet alle by-dene,
> Wyth þre towayles and no lasse
> Hule þyn auter at thy masse (1869–72).

Furthermore, if for any reason blood is spilled about the altar where the Host and Chalice are to be elevated for the miracle of Transubstantiation, the priest should soak up the blood lest any clean thing touch it.

> ʒef a drope of blod by any cas
> Falle vp-on þe corporas,
> Sowke hyt vp a-non-ryʒt,
> And be as sory as þou myʒt,
> Þe corporas after þow folde,
> A-monge þe relekus to be holde;
> On oþer þynge ʒet hyt falle,
> On vestement oþer on palle,
> A-way þow moste þe pece cotte,
> And hyt brenne & a-monge þe relekus putte;
> ʒet hyt falle on sum oþer what,
> Tabul or ston, vrþe or mat,
> Lyk hyt vp clene þat ys sched,
> And schaf hyt after þat ys be-bled,
> And do þe schauynge for to brenne,
> Amonge þe relekus put hyt þenne (1921–36).

By not following priestly behavior, then—much less a Christian's—the priest may be dismissed and excommunicated.

There follows as the body of the poem a sermon in eight parts on the prologue as the day's text. It closely (and correctly) follows the *artes praedicandi*, the preaching counterparts to Mirk's treatise, on the penitential sermon, here divided into eight parts labelled Observate, Considerate, Deliberate, Vigilate, Deplorate, Divinate, Reformate, Pensitate, and followed by a new "tabull" of beliefs (234a). Such new laws, though, can hardly be for the erring curate, for he has been called irredeemable; rather, as the imperative mode of the subtitles suggests, they are meant for the poet's congregation and for us as readers. In its exegesis, this poem as sermon will reveal far deeper significations of the hawking curate's actions.

"Observate" continues the narrative: the first hawk has come to rest in its own mess on the altar, while a second hawk, representing sloth rather than gluttony and avarice, comes to rest on the rood beam next to the crucifix of Christ (the rood cross).

> The fauconer then was prest,
> Came runnynge with a dow,
> And cryed, "Stow, stow, stow!"
> But she would not bow.
> He then, to be sure,
> Callyd her with a lure:
> Her mete was very crude,
> She had not wel-endude,
> She was not clene-ensaymed
> She was not well-reclaymed (71–80).

This is what the poet sees when he first gains entrance to his own sanctuary. It is also what we observe. God will effect judgment through the poet (and us). "Considerate" removes us one step from the situation by suggesting that the further harm committed against the implements of the Mass necessitates both exorcism of evil spirits ("Boke, bell and candyll," 112) and excommunication of the sinner. "Deliberate" contrasts the curate's wrathful self-justification—

> Thys fawconer then gan shoute:
> "These be my gospellers,
> These be my pystyllers,
> These be my querysters
> To helpe me to synge,
> My hawkes to mattens rynge!" (119–24)—

and his blasphemous displacement of the sacring bell by the hawks' bells (137) with the priest's attempt to take the matter to consistory court:

> Delt he not lyke a fon?
> Delt he not lyke a daw?
> Or els is thys Goddis law,
> Decrees or decretals,

> Or holy sinodals,
> Or else provincyals
> Thus within the wals
> Of Holy Church to deale (128–35).

The fourth section, "Vigilate," completes the narrative. The court sits—

> whoso that lokys
> In the offycyallys bokys,
> There he may se and reed
> That thys is matter indeed (145–48)—

but "Mayden Meed" (149), or bribery, is employed, and the curate excused.

> And the Pharasay
> Then durst nothyng say,
> But let the matter slyp
> And made truth to tryp (152–55),

turning the occasion for human justice into another travesty, into a modern act of betrayal by modern-day Pharisees.

This prologue together with the first four sections of "Ware the Hauke," then, show signs of Skelton's Goliardic ancestry in the apparent parody of the introit, gospel, sermon, Eucharist, and postcommunion. But the tone belies this. The description here—of the Church, the ceremonial, and the ritual—is too violent and complete, as the consistory court's inability to render justice shows. In fact, the references are to the four divisions of the liturgy in turn: (1) the prologue inverts the prothesis, or preparation; (2) "Observate" inverts the enarxis, or introductory office of praise or prayer; (3) "Considerate" inverts the synaxis or liturgy of the word, the liturgy of the catechumens; (4) "Deliberate" inverts the Eucharist or canon, the liturgy of the faithful; so that (5) "Vigilate" then asks to take over the ritual of prayer to restore what the earlier sections seem to have destroyed. If read another way, sections 1–4 work out the implications of the prologue that functions as the primary text—they become, in effect, interpretive repetitions of the prologue, which cause the curate and his hawks in that prologue to become figural, much as Melchisedech and Moloch become figural in *Speke, Parrot*.

That the figural reading of the curate is what Skelton has chiefly in mind is further suggested in the opening lines of "Considerate," which date the poem.

On Saynt John decollacyon
He hawked on thys facyon:
Tempore vesperarum,
Sed non secundum sarum (100–103).

According to the Sarum missal, the feast day of the Decollation of St.
John the Baptist, 29 August, is also the feast day of St. Sabina; the further
direction *(Tempore vesperarum)* directs us particularly to the service in
memory of St. John. There the gospel according to the Sarum rite recalls
the Passion of St. John (Mark 6:17–29), prefiguring the Passion of Christ
and reenacted in the Diss church by the bloodstained crucifix on the altar
and the threatened crucifix tenoned to the rood beam. In the same way,
the curate is prefigured by Herod as the poet's means of emphasizing his
wrath at the fellow parson's blasphemy. Confronted now by such an act,
Skelton sees no possibility of a subsequent miracle such as that recounted
in *The Golden Legend*, where St. John's thumbprints appear on the altar
cloth.[7] Instead, the bloodstains of the martyr's thumb are horribly paro-
died in the blood of the pigeon slaughtered by the hawk at the altar of
Christ. The act of the curate has thus renewed the possibility of the kind
of treachery that killed St. John the Baptist.

Sections 5–8 introduce an unexpected reversal, but one necessary if all
eight relatively discrete segments of the poem are to constitute, at one
level of significance, a *penitential* sermon. For "Deplorate" describes both
the desecration of the Temple and its restoration:

Loke now in *Exodi*
And *De Archa Domini,*
With *Regum* by and by—
The Bybyll wyll not ly—
How the Temple was kept,
How the Temple was swept,
Where *sanguis taurorum*
Aut sanguis vitulorum
Was offryd within the wallys
After ceremoniallys;
When it was polutyd,
Sentence was executyd
By way of expayacyon
For reconcylyacyon (164–77).

While the holy Ark of God (Exodus 25:10–22) led to slaughter (1 Kings 6:19), the tyranny of Achaz (2 Paralipomenon 28:21–25) allows the cleansing of the temple by Ezechias (2 Paralipomenon 29:1–24), expiating Israel:

> And the priests went into the temple of the Lord to sanctify it, and brought out all the uncleanness that they found within to the entrance of the house of the Lord, and the Levites took it away. . . .
> And they went in to king Ezechias, and said to him: We have sanctified all the house of the Lord, and the altar of holocaust, and the vessels thereof, and the table of proposition with all its vessels,
> And all the furniture of the temple, which king Achaz in his reign had defiled, after his transgression; and behold they are all set forth before the altar of the Lord (16, 18–19).

But the following section of "Ware the Hauke," "Divinate," shows that in Skelton's day there is no Ezechias but only an Achaz. Much like Moloch in *Speke, Parrot*, Achaz remains stoutly unregenerate even though, as a priest of Holy Mother Church, the lessons of Scripture and the life of Christ should have taught him to behave otherwise.

> Then moch more, by the rode,
> Where Crystis precyous blode
> Dayly offryd is,
> To be polutyd this!
> And that he wysshyd withall
> That the dowves donge downe myght fall
> Into my chalys at mas,
> When consecratyd was
> The Blessyd Sacrament—
> O pryeest unreverent!
> He sayd that he wold hunt
> From the aulter to the funt (178–89).

To define such behavior, Skelton once more returns to scriptural history, listing in "Reformate" a long catalogue of Roman emperors who persecuted Christians and more recent pagans, such as the Turks, who destroyed the recent Temple (the Church of St. Sophia in Constantinople, mother church of the Eastern papacy and the place to which St. John's head was taken as a relic). Such pagans are meant to link the Old Testament Achaz with the present-day curate. Skelton seems to be saying that, if teaching by precept will not work (as in "Considerate"), perhaps preaching by example will. And if not, the last section of the sermon (and the poem), "Pensitate," will offer "in a tabull playne" new laws which will replace the Laws of Moses and Christ by spelling them out through enigmatic new Scripture (for truth, we remember, is seen only obliquely when it is the truth of God). Unscrambled and decoded by Henry Bradley,[8] the table reads,

> Thus just as there is the phoenix of the Arabs, a bird so greatly unparalleled,
> So the land of Britain bears Skelton, its poet.
> May this document stand, I pray, to be violated by no horned attacker.
> A man will not ravage these lines but an evil cow.
> In part, give heed to the matter of the table in plain language; insert there the Arethusan muse (239–45).

As God provided an Ezechias to overcome the savage destruction of Achaz, so God has allowed Skelton to see (and to overcome, through this poem) the destruction wrought by the curate; this phoenix will answer to the desecration of the hawks. The dark language is to suggest that this is a matter of God's prophecy, not an idle boast by Skelton who, after all, had not expected to see the curate hawking. That was the doing of God. What derives from such authority, however, is a stern denunciation in which Skelton keeps confronting the curate with his crime, calling him alternately *"Domine* Dawcock" (251, 275, 318) and "Doctor Dawcocke" (265, 284, 305, 329), in order to assert his position in the divine scheme of meaning through a series of *puncti* that give to the final section of the poem the unity and harmony of a motet.[9] The condemnations themselves, macaronic in form, work antiphonally:

> Maister *Sophista,*
> Ye *simplex silogista,*
> Ye develysh *dogmatistia,*
> Your hawke on your fista,
> To hawke when you lista
> *In ecclesia ista,*
> *Domine concupisti,*
> With thy hawke on thy fysty?
> *Nunquid sic dixisti?*
> *Nunquid sic fecisti?*
> *Sed ubi hoc legisti*

> *Aut unde hoc,*
> Doctor Dawcocke?
> Ware the hawke! (253–66).[10]

Such applications of the figural lesson of Ezechias and Achaz, each one ending in an antiphonal chorus of condemnation ("Doctor Dawcocke") and apparent encouragement ("Ware the hauke!") that was first realized in the confrontation of Skelton and the curate in "Observate," ends with a broad sweep across Spain (perhaps because of the major shrine at Compostela) and across England ("From Granade to Galys, From Wynchelsee to Walys," 322–23). Skelton concludes jubilantly:

> *Libertas veneranda piis concessa poetis*
> *Dicendi est quecunque placent, quecunque juvabunt,*
> *Vel quecunque valent justas defendere causas,*
> *Vel quecunque valent stolidos mordere petulcos.*
> *Ergo dabis veniam* (342–46).[11]

Ergo dabis veniam: consequently you will grant indulgence. Those who read this line (or, indeed, much of the poem) as a preposterous boast or as an excessive, monophonic denunciation miss the point. For "Ware the Hauke," like *The Bowge of Courte* and *Speke, Parrot,* is another poem as parable, in which a straightforward event is invested with meaning because it is seen as a *sign* of *figural truth,* in this case, as an example of heresy sent by God, which must be condemned despite the actions of the episcopal court. It is not the event, but the *significance* of the event that matters. And Skelton has told us where to find that: in the Proper of the Mass for St. John the Baptist. For this Mass *celebrates* the beheading of St. John, much as Skelton celebrates the hawking curate by writing a poem about his hawking, as an evil event which nevertheless provides an occasion for the renewal of belief. For if the gospel of the Proper of the Mass is the story of the beheading (and therefore one text that a priest like Skelton is invited to preach on), the other text, from the lesson (Proverbs 10:28–32; 11:3, 6, 8–11), points to the message Skelton chooses:

> The just shall never be moved; but the wicked shall not dwell on the earth.
> The mouth of the just shall bring forth wisdom: the tongue of the perverse shall perish. . . .
> The justice of the righteous shall deliver them: and the unjust shall be caught in their own snares.

Thus the poem ends with Skelton's righteous indignation—and with the curate's silence. Such an outcome realizes the Collect which opens the Proper for the Decollation of St. John the Baptist—

> We beseech thee, O Lord, that in honouring the feast of thy holy martyr John Baptist, we may aid and further our own salvation—

through to its conclusion in the Secret—

> We offer gifts unto thee, O Lord, for the passion of thy holy martyr John Baptist, beseeching thee that they may be profitable to our salvation, by the aid of him who now that his course is finished on earth, hath an everlasting seat in heaven—

and the Postcommunion—

> We beseech thee, O Lord, that the feast of St. John Baptist may confer upon us a twofold benefit, that we may reverence the magnifical sacrament which we have received as betokened in our prayers, and may rejoice in it as more fully set forth within us.

Like the closing of Skelton's sermon, these passages nearly repeat one another in proclaiming the happiness that can come even out of suffering, because through it salvation is made possible. "Ware the Hauke" is, then, a figural sermon that, like the Mass dedicated to the Decollation of St. John, finds joy in the Passion of the saint whose death, figuring Christ's, renewed the lesson of redemption. The poem's title is thus transformed into a message of hope, and well worth repetition.

This much is clear; but what of the antiphonal chorus? Why should the poem have as its title not simply a warning to beware of the hawk but a proverbial expression urging the hawk on to the kill? And why should that call be repeatedly reinforced in the closing portion of the poem? How can this lead to penitence? The answer to all these questions lies in the action in the first section of the poem, "Observate," where the text for its sermon was laid out.

> The fauconer then was prest,
> Came runnynge with a dow,
> And cryed, "Stow, stow, stow!" [Come, come, come]
> But she wold not bow,
> He, then, to be sure,
> Callyd her with a lure:
> Her mete was very crude,

> She had not wel-endude,
> She was not clene-ensaymed
> She was not well-reclaymed (71–80).

The narrative is working out dramatically one of the Church icons familiar to the early Tudors (but largely lost to us) in which the hawk is the soul of man and the curate himself represents Christ. This icon is still seen in the famous thirteenth-century Angel Choir of Lincoln Cathedral, where a series of 28 emblematic angels are carved in the spandrels of the magnificent triforium arches. There an angel holds out the leg of a large bird to an alighting hawk alongside other angels who hold attributes referring to the Passion or to the Last Judgment—St. Michael holding a scales to weigh souls, and angels holding a small naked soul, presenting a soul to Christ, and holding up the crowns of victory. Like Skelton's curate, the hawking angel is one who, according to a fifteenth-century manuscript poem in the British Library, "when his hawk fro him does flee / Shows to the hawk red flesh to see." This calls the hawk back: "And when the hawk looks thereunto / Fast to his master he hastes to go." The angel, writes M. D. Anderson, is "a symbol of Christ who hung bleeding upon the 'tree' to win back the soul of man [that is, the hawk]."[12] There is a similar reference in another poem, a poem of repentance, "Reuerte!," found in Lambeth MS 853, where the poet sees the hawk as the heart or soul that departs from thoughtless and sinful youth:

> ȝouþe beriþ þe hauke upon his hond
>   Whanne ioliite farȝetiþ age:
> This hauke is mannis herte, y vndirstonde,
>   For it is ȝong & of hiȝ romage.
> He puttiþ his hauke fro his fist,
>   He þat schulde to god be free;
> He me tip and wexiþ a weel poor gist
>   Whanne he comeþ to reuertere [repent] (p. 61).[13]

Skelton's curate, who stands before the bloody, messy Cross and altar in the church of St. Mary the Virgin, Diss, is reenacting the Passion of the Lord, then, but also the loss of the soul and the need to recall those souls who have lost touch with the traditions of the Church—with those who fail to see in such acts, as in the Scripture behind them or the Masses based on them, the figures for the need and existence of salvation. This "Dawcocke" (fool), therefore, is also a "Doctor" and a "Domine" (Lord) —quite literally—because he is a holy fool, whose actions appear foolish only to the ignorant. To them he is unrevealed, mistaken. But this curate's own willful ignorance of the significance of his act—his heresy in taking Christ's iconic role but to slaughter rather than to save—is what provokes Skelton's deep outrage. To the episcopal court at Norwich this might look like an idle prank or unfortunate event, but to someone whose mind always seems to work figurally, this is clearly grounds for demanding excommunication. Indeed, it is for those who do not see figurally that "This worke devysed is" (1). In this sermon for those who forget that all events are potentially sacred, Skelton fashions a parable on heresy that is its own lectionary, a new Golden Legend. But for those Tudors who heeded the message of the poem, the holy texts behind it, and the holy truths for which it serves as a sign, this event might renew the feast day, revitalizing God's providence in the beheading of His saint.

Understanding the way in which the skull and the curate work as signs in Skelton's figural poetry will help us with his other East Anglian poems too. The canticle lamenting the two fires that raged during four days in April 1507 in the cathedral city of Norwich and consumed "more than 18 score households and the most parte of their goodys" on 4 and 5 June of that year,[14] the "Canticum dolorosum: Lamentatio urbis Norwicen," while attributing such destruction to the pagan gods Jove and Vulcan, pointedly recalls Jeremiah's grief and helplessness before the destruction of the temple city of Jerusalem. Skelton writes,

> *O lachrimosa lues nimis, O quam flebile fatum!*
> *Ignibus exosis, urbs veneranda ruis;*
> *Fulmina sive Jovis sive ultima fata vocabant,*
> *Vulcani rapidis ignibus ipsa peris.*
> *Ah decus, ah patrie, specie pulcherima dudum,*
> *Urbs Norwicensis labitur in cineres!*
> *Urbs, tibi quid referam? breviter tibi pauca reponam:*
> *Prospera rara manent, utere sorte tua;*
> *Perpetuum mortale nihil, sors omnia versat:*
> *Urbs miseranda, vale! sors miseranda tua est* (1–10),[15]

deliberately echoing the Old Testament prophet:

> He hath bent his bow as an enemy, he hath fixed his right hand as an adversary: and he hath killed all that was fair to behold in the tabernacle of the daughter of Sion, he hath poured out his indignation like fire. . . .
>
> To what shall I compare thee? or to what shall I liken thee, O

daughter of Jerusalem? to what shall I equal thee, that I may comfort thee, O virgin daughter of Sion? for great as the sea is thy destruction: who shall heal thee? (Lamentations 2:4, 13).

The text was familiar to the Tudors, for this book served as the basis, in the Sarum Missal, for the important Mass of the Compassion of Blessed Virgin Mary, a movable feast that could be celebrated during Lent, the time of the first fire at Norwich.

"Epitaphes of Two Knaves of Diss," written about the time of "Ware the Hauke," is a better known poem. It was copied down (in our sole extant source) by the Curate of Trumpington, official Scribe to Cambridge University, on 5 January 1507—suggesting Skelton may have kept some contact with Cambridge since it was not far from Diss. This work joins two mock-epitaphs, one for John Clarke, soul priest, and one for Adam Uddersale, bailiff, both reminiscent of Goliardic predecessors. "Epitaphes," called a "tretise," begins much as "Ware the Hauke" does:

> This tretise devysed it is
> Of two knaves somtyme of Dis:
> Though this knaves be deade,
> Full of myschiefe and queed [bad],
> Yet wheresoever they ly,
> Theyr names shall never dye (1–6).

The final line parodies the immortality of the soul, for these two quarrelsome troublemakers (if we are to believe Skelton) are immortal because of his poetry. Such a poem is meant to be a *"Compendium"* (5a), an epitome or verbal icon, following in the tradition of various *Spottepitaphien* written on popes, bishops, and abbots as well as on lords and kings throughout the Middle Ages.[16] That these two irksome citizens of Diss are paired may also be meant as a parody of the equally quarrelsome disciples John and James (Mark 10:35–41; Luke 9:54–56), for Skelton makes much of St. John the Evangelist in connection with old John Clarke, as we shall see. And as Skelton will write of Adam in *The Garlande of Laurell,*

> "Of one Adame All-a-Knave, late dede and gone—
> *Dormiat in pace*, lyke a dormows—
> He [i.e., Skelton] wrate an epitaph for his gravestone,
> With wordes devoute and sentence agerdows;
> For he was ever ageynst Goddis hows:
> All his delight was to braule and to barke
> Ageynst Holy Chyrche, the preste and the clarke (1247–53).

In addition to information supplied in the poem, we know that Clarke was appointed soul priest of Diss in 1504 (presumably to the Guild Chapel rather than to a chantry in St. Mary the Virgin), that he along with Skelton witnessed Margery Cowper's will that year, and that on 2 February 1506 he made his own will, proved on 14 April 1507, which sees to the state of his soul after death and gives money to the local guild foundation—but it pointedly excludes Skelton's benefice.

> JOHN CLARKE; he ordered his executors to pay to the purchase of *Framlingham*, quarterly, to each of the two *Gilds, 8d*. He left money "to a pylgrym, a priest, to be in prayer and pilgrimage at *Rome* the whole Lent, there to pray and syng for me and myn children, my fader and moder, *Robert* and *Cate, John Kew* and *Maut, Steven Brightled*, and *John Payne*, the which I am in dett to (Blomfield, 1, 27).

But Skelton must have known of this will, too, because it affected his parish, and it may be the trental of the pilgrim's prayers at Lent that prompted Skelton's parody of a trental (thirty Masses, said one after another over thirty days).

John Clarke's trental is itself subtitled "*Dulce melos / Penetrans celos*" ("A sweet song, / Penetrating the heavens"), and begins, "*Carmina cum cannis / Cantemus festa Joannis*" ("With our pipes / Let us sing festive songs"). This opening refers us to the *Festum S. Joannis Evangelistae*, the feast day of St. John the Evangelist (6 May) when a sweet Sequence is indeed sung for St. John and other evangelists too:

> To Christ your voices raise
> in glorifying praise,
>   ye reverential quire;
> Who the evangelists,
> truth's earnest dogmatists,
>   did with his grace inspire:
> Who, as him doth beseem,
> who by the lightning's gleam
>   unto the world gives light;
> By these whom he chose out
> he heresies doth rout,
>   and schism puts to flight.

Indeed, the other John, John Skelton, will expose such "heresies" as those committed by these two contentious parishioners who refused to serve him with proper respect. With witty irony the gospel for this feast day, John 21:19–24, tells of Peter's betrayal of Christ at *His* death, followed by the lesson for the Proper of the Mass (Ecclesiasticus 15:1–6):

> He that feareth God, will do good: and he that possesseth justice, shall lay hold on her. . . .
> And in the midst of the church she shall open his mouth, and shall fill him with the spirit of wisdom and understanding, and shall clothe him with a robe of glory.
> She shall heap upon him a treasure of joy and gladness, and shall cause him to inherit an everlasting name (15:1, 5–6).

Therefore it follows that Skelton, playing off the account of the Last Supper, on the night of Peter's betrayal, pictures this new traitor in his parish as one who mocks the Eucharist by his desire to acquire a red amice (24), the liturgical color for the Passion as well as for those who celebrate the Black Mass. Old John Clarke continually mocks the Mass. He eats the intestines of sheep, goats, and oxen rather than the blessed elements (28–29); he reverses the prayer *Orate, fratres* in the Canon (45); he kneels before a football as if it were the Host (53); he chants *Bibite multum* instead of the proper *bibite ex eo* at the elevation of the Chalice (56); and he kisses the Devil's *culum* rather than the sacred elements (60): all these reiterate John Clarke's heresies as he celebrates his mock-Mass, a soul priest whose own soul is misdirected. Elsewhere he is compared to the Chaldeans (7), "bitter and swift" (Habacuc 1:6ff.), who remind Skelton of how "He did so hector / His very own rector" ("*Rectori proprio / Tam verba retorta loquendo*," 11–12) as well as the Jebusites (8), the foes of Israel doomed to destruction (Genesis 10:16, 15:21; Exodus 3:8, 13:3–5) and defeated by Joshua (Josue 10–12).

Just as Clarke betrayed his function as soul priest, so Uddersale is blamed for misusing his authority as bailiff.

> *Adam degebat:*
> *Dum vixit, falsa gerebat,*
> *Namque extorquebat*
> *Quicquid nativus habebat,*
> *Aut liber natus; rapidus*
> *Lupus inde vocatus* (1–6).[17]

Like Clarke, he subverts the talents and office given him by God—he betrays his trust in the Lord and his obedience to Him. But, unlike

Clarke, he is not beneficed, and so he is compared not to a Jew but to a
Gentile who is contemporary to St. Peter.

> *Ecclesiamque satus*
> *De Belial iste Pilatus*
> *Sub pede calcatus*
> *Violavit, nunc violatus:*
> *Perfidus, iratus,*
> *Numquam fuit ille beatus:*
> *Uddersall stratus*
> *Benedictis est spoliatus,*
> *Improbus, inflatus,*
> *Maledictis jam laceratus* (7–16).[18]

He is likewise compared to a foe of Israel—Agag, King of Amalec (1
Kings 15:32), slain by Saul. His mock-epitaph ends in antiphonal versicles
that could serve for both these modern-day embodiments of John and
James, Peter and Pilate:

> *Adam, Adam, ubi es? (Genesis) Responsus: ubi nulla requies,*
> *ubi nullus ordo, sed sempiternus horror inhabitat* (Job) (32d-e).
>   And the Lord called Adam, and said to him: Where art thou
>   (Genesis 3:9)
>   A land of misery and darkness, where the shadow of death,
>   and no order, but everlasting horror dwelleth (Job 10:22).

Once more, Skelton has taken an actual event, turned it into a figural
representation, and then into a poem as parable—but the wickedness this
time is extremely funny.

These mock-epitaphs, like the skull and even the curate, suggest how
prominently death figured in the minds of East Anglian churchgoers and
in Skelton's imagination. Death is also the subject of Skelton's best known
poem at Diss and arguably his most memorable, "Phyllyp Sparowe"
(1505). The occasion for this poem was the death of a pet sparrow trained
and beloved by Jane Scrope, who was living with her mother, the recently
widowed Lady Eleanor Windham, at the Benedictine Priory of St. Mary at
Carrow.[19] The priory was a favorite of Bishop Nikke's; begun in 1146 from
a grant of King Stephen on uncultivated lands in Norwich field between
Ber Street (or Southgate) and Trowse-bridge, it was still small in early
Tudor times: a census shows thirteen nuns there in 1492 and ten in 1514.
But despite its size it was well known. For a time the celebrated Dame

Julian—called Saint Julian then, although she was never canonized—was indifferently attached to Carrow as an anchoress; the priory was also well known for admitting daughters of good local families for their school-ing,[20] so it is not unlikely that Skelton visited Carrow and that he knew Jane Scrope.

But Robert S. Kinsman has suggested that rolls of the dead, *rotuli mortuorum*—such as the beadrolls Jane mentions (12)—may also have helped to shape this poem. Such *rotuli* not only recorded deaths but invited prayers of intercession from others for the souls of the departed. Names of the dead were inscribed on them by written formula and the rolls then taken from one religious community like Carrow to another; occasionally, according to Kinsman, these rolls were concerned with the death of a single person. For the lowly, the form on such a *rouleau in-dividuel*, he writes,

> was quite simple and purely informative, stating merely that such an one has died and asking prayers for his soul. It was quite otherwise with the roll announcing the death of an important religious. Here, in the fully developed forms, a regular *planctus* was devised in which allusions from the Fathers and the Bible were heaped, proclaiming the nothingness of things below and damning Adam's Fall. To this there succeeded a list of the virtues of the dead person, followed by the reflection that even he was mortal, leading to a request for pray-ers ("Titulus," pp. 477–78).

In addition to such tributes, the Divine Office of the Dead employed in Skelton's poem—originally designed to be used only at individual deaths but by the poet's time a necessary prelude to all Solemn Requiem Masses and, in priories like Carrow, a daily tribute to the souls of the dead—was an important and moving petition. (John Fisher tells us that Skelton's putative benefactor, the King's mother, would also say her dirges and commendations daily.[21]) Thus the form itself is not puzzling; what is puzzling is why Skelton would provide such an elaborate petition for a pet sparrow. The poem offers answers.

Part 1 of "Phyllyp Sparowe," the *Placebo*, is based on a single liturgical service, the Vespers of the Office of the Dead, one of the three hours of the original Office (Matins and Lauds as well as Vespers) and, writes F. W. Brownlow, one that is "rich with metaphorical implications and full of elegiac feeling."[22] The actual order for Vespers opens with a brief antiphon after which the service is named, "Placebo Domino in regione vivorum"

("I shall please the Lord in the land of the living"), continues with Psalm 114—

> I love the Lord because he has heard my voice in supplication,
> Because he has inclined his ear to me the day I called.
> The cords of death encompassed me; the snares of the nether world seized upon me; I fell into distress and sorrow,
> And I called upon the name of the Lord, "O Lord, save my life!"—
> Gracious is the Lord and just; yes, our God is merciful.
> The Lord keeps the little ones; I was brought low, and he saved me.
> Return, O my soul, to your tranquillity, for the Lord has been good to you.
> For he has freed my soul from death, my eyes from tears, my feet from stumbling.
> I shall walk before the Lord in the land of the living,
> Eternal rest[23]—

and *concludes* with an *augmented* antiphon "Placebo Domino in regione vivorum" to which there is the reply, "Hei mihi, Domine, quia incolatus meus prolongatus est" ("I shall please the Lord in the land of the living. Woe is me, O Lord, that my sojourn is prolonged").

But Jane's *Placebo* begins antiphonally and remains that way.

> *Pla ce bo,*
> 　　Who is there, who?
> *Di le xi,*
> 　　Dame Margery,
> *Fa, re, my, my.*
> 　　Wherfore and why, why?
> 　　For the sowle of Philip Sparowe,
> That was late slayn at Carowe,
> Among the Nones Blake.
> For that swete soules sake,
> And for all sparowes soules
> Set in our bede rolles,
> *Pater noster qui*
> With an *Ave Mari,*
> And with the corner of a Crede,
> The more shal be your mede (1–16).

These opening lines indicate the thrust of the entire *Placebo* of the poem: clearly what Jane has done—the entire first half of the poem is in her voice and in her thoughts—is to turn the actual *Placebo* that is being sung (hence the syllabication of the words and the names of neumes) into a continuous, unending antiphon to which she constantly sings the responds with the plainsong of her own stream-of-consciousness. The traditional *Placebo* also directs that stream-of-consciousness, because her entire thought pattern will be a projection, into her own suffering over the recent loss of her sparrow, of the antiphonal exchange following the opening Psalm of the Office of the Dead. *She* is sorrowing at *her* prolonged sojourn, separated as she is from Phyllyp; she asks how she, left in the land of the living without her sparrow, can possibly be expected to please the Lord? The dialectic proposed by the text in her primer, then, becomes the basic dilemma that her private meditation must work out even as the more public service is sung around her.

That Jane is prompted to such thoughts is parodic in a special, figural sense meant to underscore how seriously, how *personally*, she applies the text of the Divine Office. We know this because all of her thoughts in Part I will be prompted by the text of that Office (in which Psalm 114 is followed by Psalms 119, 120, 129, and 137, interspersed with versicles, the Paternoster, the Ave Maria, and closing antiphons). But we can see this parodic arrangement from the outset. Her opening meditation takes the posture of supplication (Psalm 114:1) as she calls upon the Lord (114:2, 4); she relies on His justice and mercy (114:5) in which He has promised to care for the least of creatures (114:6) like Phyllyp, and like herself. By realizing Psalm 114, then, rather than merely chanting it, she is told by the text of the Offices that her soul will regain tranquility (114:7). Brought low (114:6) in prayer (114:1) she has caught the attention of the Lord Himself (114:2) and He has promised her eternal rest (114:10). Why must she continue to sojourn alone, without Phyllyp; why, she asks, is she not permitted to join the one she has lost, that one eventually becoming Phyllyp and the Lord, indistinguishably? On the one hand, "Phyllyp Sparowe" will examine and celebrate the liturgy; on the other, the poem will celebrate Jane by means of the liturgy. Realizing the "swete soule" of Phyllyp (10) and setting the bird's name on her own private *rouleau individuel*, along with the Paternoster, Ave Maria, and Credo, she attests to her own unself-conscious orthodoxy. For her private lament, through the stages suggested by the text of the Office of Vespers for the Dead, will realize the lesson implied in that text and also beyond it, that Phyllyp

Sparowe is the biblical icon for Christ and for the soul. For this she also has scriptural authority. Elsewhere the Psalmist writes,

> How lovely are thy tabernacles, O Lord of hosts! my soul longeth and fainteth for the courts of the Lord.
> My heart and my flesh have rejoiced in the living God.
> For the sparrow hath found herself a house, and the turtle a nest for herself where she may lay her young ones:
> Thy altars, O Lord of hosts, my kind and my God (83:2–4).

> Hear, O Lord, my prayer: and let my cry come to thee.
> Turn not away thy face from me: in the day when I am in trouble, incline thy ear to me.
> In what day soever I shall call upon thee, hear me speedily. . . .
> I have watched, and am become as a sparrow all alone on the housetop (101:2–3, 8),

while the evangelist has comforted her by quoting Christ's assurance that "Not one [sparrow] shall fall on the ground without your Father" (Matthew 10:29). Jane Scrope thus anticipates Hamlet in knowing that there is special Providence in the fall of a sparrow (5.2.220), an idea also dramatized in the Wakefield *Secunda Pastorum* and perhaps other mystery plays.[24] Such an understanding further allows Jane to realize the Church's teaching of *misericordia*, which St. Thomas Aquinas, quoting Augustine, defines as *"heartfelt sympathy for another's distress, impelling us to succour him if we can. For mercy takes its name misericordia from denoting a man's compassionate heart (miserum cor) for another's unhappiness"* (*Summa Theologica*, 2, ii, Q.30a1.). Of "all the virtues which relate to our neighbour," this is the greatest (Q.30.a.4). From the beginning of the poem, then, Jane may find the opening antiphon of the *Placebo* bewildering but her beliefs are instinctive and her faith finally sure and unshaken.

Jane's personal service recalls the fact of the sparrow's death, when he was killed by Gib the cat ("My sparowe dead and colde," 40); her subsequent grief; Phyllyp's soul endangered by Hell (68–94); her memories of what they did; and how she best remembers him (Phyllyp "wold syt upon my lap . . . And many tymes and ofte / Betwene my brestes softe / It would lye and rest— / It was propre and prest," 121, 124–27). Such memories give way alternately to joy (157ff.), innocence (171ff.), a sense of loss (186ff.), vengeance (273ff.), admiration (324ff.), and prayer ("*Kyry, eleyson*," 379–81). Thus her entire meditation (1–844), through her personal involvement, encloses her grief, her compassion, and her faith, other scraps of liturgy and other excerpts from Scripture—all of which are appropriately conceived and aptly applied—as well as a Requiem Mass for Phyllyp (386– 602), an epitaph (heavily troped, as she ransacks her mind and her reading for adequate comparisons, 603–825), and an elegy (826–44). Each of these interruptions, however, also realizes the text of the Vespers service, both because that text suggests the ostensible digression and because the mood dramatized by the digression (to mourn, to record, to celebrate or eulo- gize) is precisely the mood that the Office is then initiating by way of Psalms and versicles. In fact, fragments of those Psalms and antiphons, apparently overheard by Jane, are registered in the poem to remind us, lest we forget, that the subtext is always this Divine Office, which motivates Jane's meditation. Thus we have the beginnings of Psalm 114 at lines 1,3; antiphon 1 at 64; Psalm 119 at 66; antiphon 3 at 95; Psalm 120 at 97; antiphon 4 at 143; Psalm 129 at 145; antiphon 5 at 183; Psalm 137 at 185; and the closing antiphon at 239. Following Psalm 137 in the *Placebo* are versicles sung (or chanted) antiphonally and a chanting of the Magnificat, after which

> At the end is said:
> Eternal rest.
> Ant. All that the Father gives to Me shall come to Me, and him
> who comes to Me I will not cast out—

at which point Jane awards Phyllyp with a fitting Requiem Mass of Birds. Subsequently in the *Placebo* the Paternoster is said aloud in unison (or silently) while kneeling, followed by another antiphonal exchange—"V. O Lord, hear my prayer. R. And let my cry come to You"—that prompts Jane's thought of an epitaph (where she properly rejects all secular sources in a trope implying the superiority of her, and Skelton's, religious verse). Then, after a Collect, there come final versicles.

> V. Eternal rest grant unto them, O Lord.
> R. And let perpetual light shine upon them.
> V. May they rest in peace.
> R. Amen.

These versicles, which close the Office, motivate Jane's elegy that closes her section of the poem. Thus nothing in Part 1 is extraneous; everything is subordinated to the devotional mind and mood that the Office itself establishes.

The Mass of Birds, which has seemed to some readers intrusive, is meant to suggest Jane's heightened sense of death, of the occasion of

Requiem, and of the beauty of the Mass itself. It is her own creative troping on the plainsong of the Office, at a point roughly analogous to where the Sequence of the Proper of any Mass might be troped (there was almost never any troping in reciting the Offices). This is, then, a dramatic device. But it is not an unusual one. For one thing, bird Masses abounded in medieval poetry—as later too in Caxton's Mass for, and burial tomb and epitaph of, "Coppe Chanteklers Doughter, / Whom Reynart the Fox hath byten" or the dream vision in *The Fantasy of the Passion of the Fox* printed by Wynkyn de Worde in 1530.²⁵ In addition, birds were often associated with the religious houses. We may think of the revered St. Francis of Assisi, but there was a popular legend in Skelton's day describing an island tenanted by monks, on which birds joined the pious in singing praises to the Lord, while St. Guthlac was said to have lived with swallows in his cell. Yet despite the convention, Jane's Mass is peculiarly her own: she chooses more than seventy birds, all of them (with three exceptions) landbirds and shorebirds native to her East Anglia and mostly predators (like Gib the cat), who were transformed—*without* exception— in the medieval bestiaries where they possess truly moral signification.

Jane's special service begins with the summoning of communicants.

> Some to synge, and some to say,
> Some to wepe, and some to pray,
> Every byrde in his laye (392–94).

All will mourn together, that is, but some will perform special functions. Robyn Redbreast, for instance, is priest, "The Requiem masse to synge, / Softly warbelynge" (401–2), with numerous assistants, described with ornithological accuracy, while the raven chants "His playne songe to solfe" (415; cf. 5), the parrot (popyngay) "Shall rede the Gospell" (423), and the song-thrush (mavys) "with her whystell / Shall rede there the Pystel" (424–25) followed by the versicles of the choir.

> But with a large and a longe
> To kepe just playne-songe,
> Our chaunters shalbe the cuckoue,
> The culver, the stockedowve,
> With Puwyt the lapwyng,
> The versycles shall syng (426–31).

The peacock, "Because his voyce is lowde" (439), sings the gradual; the puffin and teal take the Offertory; and even the luckless, untalented ostrich will be allowed to ring bells. But the most important place is reserved for the phoenix as priest.

> This corse for to sence
> With greate reverence
> As Patryarke or Pope
> In a blacke cope.
> Whyles he senseth [the herse],
> He shall synge the verse,
> *Libe ra me*,
> In *de, la, soll, re*,
> Softly bemole
> For my sparowes soule (526–35).

The choice is deliberate—"Of whose incyneracyon / There ryseth a new creacyon / Of the same facyon / Without aleracyon" (540–43)—for she sees the phoenix as a figure of both Phyllyp and, ultimately, heself. "This matter trew and playne, / Playne matter indede, / Whoso lyst to rede" (547–49).

But with the censing of the body, we move from the Requiem Mass to the Absolution over the Tomb, the *Absolutio super Tumulum*, where the phoenix, as celebrant, is served by birds appropriately feathered in "theyr amysse of gray" (560)—the eagle as subdeacon, the hobby (small falcon) and musket (sparrowhawk) as acolytes, and the kestrel, who carries the holy water (550–70). All this, too, is a theological and liturgical, as well as a meditative and emotional, outgrowth of the Vesper service. "In the medieval English rite," E. O. James records,

Placebo was sung overnight, and early the next morning the *Dirige* preceded the *Commendatio animarum* and the Mass of Requiem. While the choir were singing the *Commendatio* over the corpse, the priest, vested in alb and stole, retired to the churchyard, where he made the sign of the cross over the piece of ground assigned for the grave, and sprinkled it with holy water, having marked out the length and breadth by digging the shape of a cross upon the ground with the words of Psalm cxvii. 19, 20, "Open ye to me the gates of justice; I will go into them, and give praise to the Lord. This is the gate of the Lord; the just shall enter into it." Then he returned to the church to sing the mass.

This strong sense of justice had prompted Jane's thoughts of vengeance on Gib (237ff.) but she has now put that behind her. James continues, "After Mass the priest exchanged his chasuble for a cope, and preceded by the subdeacon carrying the processional cross, and accompanied by the acolytes and deacon, he placed himself at the foot of the coffin opposite the subdeacon, . . . He [the priest] then censed the body, sprinkled it with holy water, and exhorted all present to join with him in saying a *Pater noster* for the soul of the deceased. In later times prayers and antiphons were added supplicating that the departed, who, while he lived, was signed with the seal of the Holy Trinity, might deserve to escape the avenging judgment." Following the *Kyrie eleison*, the Paternoster, and further censing came a prayer substantially from the Gregorian Sacramentary: "O God, Whose property is ever to have mercy and to spare; we humbly entreat Thee for the soul of Thy servant N., which Thou hast this day called out of this world, beseeching Thee not to deliver it into the hands of the enemy, not to be unmindful of it at the last, but command Thy holy angels to receive it, and to bear it into paradise; that as it has believed and hoped in Thee, it may not suffer the pains of hell, but may possess eternal joys through Jesus Christ our Lord."[26] In the liturgical ceremony of this poem, Jane has succeeded in putting Phyllyp to eternal peace with God; in the dramatic story of the poem, she has passed through grief and vengeance to peace herself.

> God sende my sparoes sole good rest!
> *Requiem eternam dona eis, Domine.*
> *Fa, fa, fa, my, re,*
> *A por ta in fe ri,*
> *Fa, fa, fa, my, my.*
> *Credo vydere bona Domini,*
> I pray God, Phillip to heven may fly!
> *Domine, exaudi oracionem meam,*
> To heven he shall, from heven he cam;
> *Do mi nus vo bis cum,*
> Of al good praiers God send him sum!
> *Oremus!*
> *Deus, cui proprium est miserere et parcere,*
> On Phillips soule have pyte! (574–87).

The mood is exactly right. "The Eucharist cannot avoid being a thanksgiving," A. S. Duncan-Jones tells us. "'*Requiem aeternam*'—rest eternal—sounds at the beginning, and is the burden of the whole,"[27] and Jane concludes with epitaph and elegy. Rather than being a digression at all, then, the Requiem, epitaph, and elegy are the liturgical and ceremonial completion of what was only begun with the *Placebo*, although the narrative setting of the poem requires that Part 1 return us to Dame Margery's actual *Placebo*, now woefully incomplete, in the Priory chapel. Jane, however, moves from her own *Placebo* to her own *Ordo Commendationis* at the close: *Tibi, Domine, commendamus*, "We commend *ourselves* to thee, O Lord." Through this richer, truly polyphonic texture of liturgical services and ceremonies, Jane's personal service for Phyllyp moves from sheer density to a simple radiance not unlike a motet, and one which resolves the dilemma of the opening antiphon in the *Placebo*: *Placebo Domino in regione vivorum*: "I will *please the Lord* in the land of the *living*." Her cycle of thought and feeling, in fact, will be exactly paralleled by the poet himself in Part 2 of the poem, the *Commendacions*, when he moves from his day of wrath (in a trope on envy) to his own day of light (in praise of Jane).

But as we might expect from so rich and careful a poem and from a poet who prefers the complex multivalency of various referential texts and traditions, there are considerably more than the Vespers, the Requiem, and the *Ordo Commendationis* and *Absolutio* behind this poem; and we stand no chance of getting Part 2 right until we consider them. The *Commendacions* proceeds by matching the poet's compassion for Jane with Jane's for Phyllyp. For he understands—as too few of his readers have understood—that Jane's sorrow over the loss of her bird resembles the Virgin's weeping for the loss of Christ. Part 1 of the poem is, in fact, a reenactment of the *planctus*, as Fish remarked some time ago (p. 104), followed by Rosemary Woolf.[28] The reference Skelton provides could not be plainer, as a comparison of Jane's thoughts—

> I syghed and I sobbed,
> For that I was robbed
> Of my sparowes lyfe.
> O mayden, wydow, and wyfe,
> Of what estate ye be,
> Of hye or lowe degre,
> Great sorowe than ye might se,
> And lerne to wepe at me! (50–57)—

with a representative Marian lament—

> So my soon is bobbied
> & of his lif robbid
> forsooth than I sobbid,
> Veryfying the wordis she seid to me,
> Who cannot wepe may lerne at thee[29]—

confirms. In the tradition of the *planctus* lyric, which emphasized the Virgin's faith and steady composure, particularly in the fifteenth century, "we find a direct address and appeal to the meditator," Woolf writes, "the speaker fixed in a static visual image, and the enumeration of many scenes of dramatic action which successively pass in front of that of the speaker" (p. 239). Jane's "dolorous mater" (398) makes her the Mater Dolorosa. But Skelton combines the *planctus* tradition with that of the *Stabat iuxta,* as Woolf defines it. "In contrast to the more emotional *Stabat mater dolorosa,* the *Stabat iuxta* is chiefly concerned to establish and correctly circumscribe a doctrinal statement of the Virgin's sufferings. It emphasizes the much-repeated point that what Christ suffered *foris* the Virgin suffered *intus,* and neatly stresses the intellectual parallels between the Nativity and the Crucifixion, that at the Crucifixion the Virgin endured *cum usura* the pains of childbirth, which against the laws of nature she had been spared when Christ was born" (pp. 243–44). Jane too figures the Nativity juxtaposed to her lament when she recalls of Phyllyp

> How pretely it wolde syt,
> Many tymes and ofte,
> Upon my fynger aloft!
> I played with him tyttell-tattyll,
> And fed him with my spattyl,
> With his byll betwene my lippes,
> It was my pretty Phyppes!
> Many a prety kusse
> Had I of his swete musse;
> And now the cause is thus,
> That he is slayne me fro,
> To my great payne and wo (354–65; cf. 124–27).

At least twice the picture her mind calls up is that of the Christ Child being fed or suckled by the Virgin. This is another Church icon given vivid descriptions in the pseudo-Bonaventura's *Meditationes Vitae Christi* (translated into English by Nicholas Love in 1410), the *Dialogus Beatae Mariae et Anselmi de Passione Domini* and the *Liber de Passione Christe,* and illustrated too in the wooden roof boss at Salle, Norfolk, and in a window of St. Peter Mancroft, Norwich. The *Placebo* itself, we recall, *includes* the *Magnificat* (Luke 1:46–55). "The best Nativity lyrics very often express dramatically the relation between the mother and her child," Douglas Gray notes (p. 110). Here is one:

> On her lap she him layde,
> And with her pappe he playde,
> And ever sang the mayde,
>   "Come basse thy mother, dere."
> With lyppes collyng.
> His mouth ofte she dyd kysse
> And sayd, "Sweete hert myne,
>   I pray you make good chere."[30]

Many were lullabies, like the one Skelton had parodied in his court days.

> Whan it gan wepe, that child so swete,
> Sho stilled him with mylk of tete;
> Sho clipte hym oft and keste also
> Gret was the joye betwene hem to.
> The yonge child whan it gan wepe,
> With song she lulled him aslepe;
> That was so swete a melody
> Hyt passet alle mynstralcy;
> The nyghtyngale sang also,
> Hure wois is hors and noght therto.[31]

In drawing on various developments in the Marian tradition and the relatively new Church meditation on the Seven Sorrows of the Virgin (by Skelton's day in every primer and every Book of Hours), Skelton transforms Jane Scrope's personal loss into another figural lesson, an occasion when her lament can aid us, as the institution of the Mater Dolorosa coupled with that of the nursing Mother was meant to aid the sorrowing supplicant by mediating among the grief of death, the meaning of sacrifice and loss, and the glory of salvation. An early poem, extant in at least five manuscripts, "Offe alle women þat ever were borne," begins,

> In a chirche as I gan knele,
> This enders daye to here a masse,
> I sawe a sighte me liked wele,
> I shal you tell what it was.

> I saw a pite in a place,
> Owre lady and her sone in feare;
> Ofte she wepte and sayd, "Alas.
> Now lith here dede my dere son dere!"

and goes on, in subsequent stanzas, to address "all women" and then "al mankynde."[32] Jane mediates, too, by transforming her modest little sparrow ("Are not two sparrows sold for a farthing?" Matthew asks, 10:29), who is named Phyllyp—that is *filip*, a trifle—into a lesson of the glorious fact of Redemption itself.

"Phyllyp Sparowe," consequently, is a poem of intercession—in Part 1, Jane intercedes on behalf of Phyllyp; in Part 2, Skelton intercedes on behalf of Jane. It is as if the poet, named John, joins the girl, figuring Mary, in attempting to comprehend the meaning of death and redemption signified in the Passion—rather as if they were embodying the elements imaged on the rood cross found in Skelton's church at Diss, the Priory chapel at Carrow, and in nearly every church across England—as well as the front chapels and altar in the parish church at Skelton, Yorkshire, four miles from Sheriff Hutton Castle where Skelton's career began.[33] This is a poem of intercessions as mediation, then, a poem which tries to translate that figural act into daily activity. It is a mediating poem in another way: it attempts to mediate between the *Placebo* and the *Magnificat*. "Are not five sparrows sold for two farthings, and not one of them is forgotten before God?" Luke writes of the small birds (12:6); and of man, "He hath put down the mighty from their seat, and hath exalted the humble" (1:52).

Part 2 of "Phyllyp Sparowe" follows exactly a service complementary to the *Placebo*: the Commendation of All Souls, found in the same primers and Books of Hours. Brownlow, who has also made this connection, notes that this service is one

> consisting of Psalm 119, Psalm 138, concluding versicles and responses, and the formula of commendation: *Tibi, Domine, commendamus animam famuli tui N. et animas famulorum famularumque tuarum* ("To thee, O Lord, we commend the soul of thy servant N. and the souls of thy servants both men and women"). This latter formula, which ends the devotion, naturally provides the last liturgical reference in the poem (1241). Psalm 119 contains twenty-two eight-verse parts called octenaries which the makers of the books of hours treated as eleven pairs. Skelton takes the opening verse of each pair of octenaries in succession and uses it to open a section of his

"Commendacions." He changes *Dominus* (Lord) to *Domina* (Lady), and he equips each of the verses with extra material in the manner of a liturgical antiphon. For instance, to the opening verses of the third pair (*Legem pone mihi, Domina, viam justificationum tuarum*: "Teach me, O Lady, the way of thy statutes") he adds the first verse of Psalm 142 (*Quemadmodum desiderat cervus ad fontes aquarum*: "Like as the hart desireth the waterbrooks"). Each of the eleven sections of Skelton's "Commendacions" also has for response an English refrain and the couplet, *Hac claritate gemina / O gloriosa femina*.

Not all the "antiphonal" matter is scriptural. The fifth and seventh sections have verses from a hymn of St. Thomas Aquinas, properly sung at Matins on the feast of Corpus Christi. The sixth has a quotation from a Latin lullaby of the Virgin (*Quid petis filio, mater dulcissima? ba-ba!* "What do you ask of your son, sweetest mother? ba-ba" [set as a carol with Latin burden and English verse by Richard Pygott, Master of the Children in Wolsey's chapel until 1524]), and the eleventh and last has some Skeltonic Latin verses. . . . The phrase *O gloriosa femina* forms the first words of the hymn at the Lauds of the Virgin, and Skelton's *Haec virgo est dulcissima* has a parallel in the phrase *virgo dulcis* from the Marian hymn, *Salve regina*. Even Skelton's change of *Dominus* to *Domina* has a devotional model. In St. Bonaventura's *Psalter of the Virgin* . . . we find the same thing; the saint takes the opening words of each of the biblical psalms and makes them the beginning of a psalm of his own composition addressed to the Virgin, and in doing so changes *Dominus* to *Domina*: *Domina probasti me et cognovisti me* (Psalm 139): "O Lady, thou hast searched me out, and known me." The *Psalter of the Virgin* also provides parallels to the imagery of precious stones, stars, and flowers with which Skelton praises Jane. These, however, are the common materials of writing in praise of the Virgin ("*Boke of Phyllyp Sparowe* and Liturgy," pp. 8–10).

Indeed, the eight main sections in Part 2, introduced by versicles from Psalms, have appeared to many as erotic stanzas cataloguing Jane's physical charms, but that of course is not the point, any more than it was the point of Parrot's song to Galathea. Rather, these stanzas are Skelton's attempt to benefit from Jane's lesson and to succeed her enactment of the *planctus*, representing the Seven Sorrows of the Virgin, with his own poems celebrating the Seven Joys of the Virgin—that is, returning, as Jane has with the *Magnificat*, to the relationship between Mother and Child when it was marked by pleasure and happiness. (Just as the Seven Sorrows, the Seven Joys were in the primers and Books of Hours.)

In his discussion of the *planctus* tradition, Gray cites a typical lyric which introduces this kind of erotic cataloguing by the Compassionate Virgin as she observes Her Son upon the Cross—carefully she details His head, breast, hands, and feet (p. 138). But "religious lyrics (and especially those which are addressed to the Virgin) make extensive use of the language of the *fine amour* of the secular poets," he writes. "We find rather worldly-sounding descriptions of the Virgin's beauty" (p. 56). Sometimes poets parody secular love songs with songs to the Holy Mother, such as a "love rune" by Friar Thomas of Hales; according to the chronicler William of Malmesbury, St. Aldhelm, bishop of Sherborne, stood on a bridge singing secular songs until he had won the attention of passers-by, whereupon he began to introduce more traditional religious ideas into those songs.[34] Perhaps poems of adoration to Christ were models—poems such as this well-known one by Richard Rolle:

> Lufe es hatter þan þe cole; lufe my nane be swyke.
> Þe flawme of lufe wha myght it thole, if it war ay ilyke?
> Luf vs comfortes, and mase in qwart, and lyftes tyl heuenryke;
> Luf rauysches Cryste intyl owr hert; I wate na lust it lyke.[35]

By the fifteenth century there were also a large number of English carols to the Virgin, which, while written in popular song styles, with refrains or as rounds, were not secular. Woolf notes that instead "They are liturgical, not in the sense that they were intended solely or primarily for liturgical use, but because in style and content they resemble the Latin hymns and sequences that formed part of the church's liturgy. In their reiteration of clear doctrine and in their enumeration of types, they resemble vernacular lyric genre, but recall unmistakably the typological sequences of writers such as Adam of St. Victor."[36] For imagery some employed the erotic images of the Canticle of Canticles; others saw Judith or Esther as types of Mary in much the way that Skelton sees Jane. Even more to the point were the St. Valentine's Day poems to the Virgin such as Lydgate's "Saynt Valentyne, of custume yeere by yeere," which begins with the tradition of selecting a mistress and then continues,

> Tesbe þe mayde borne in Babyloun
>   Þat loved so weel þe yonge Pyramus,
> And Cl[e]opatre of wilful mocyoun
>   List for to dye with hir Antonyus.

Sette al on syde oone is so vertuous
Whiche þat I do my soverein lady calle,
Wham I love best for she excelleþ alle.[37]

So common was this sort of love poetry, in fact, that Skelton introduces it in the *Commendacions* with a trope to Envy (902–99) which is meant to point the difference of his ostensibly similar but actually more figural poem; it is also a parallel to Jane's search through pagan sources for a suitable epitaph (603–812; almost twice the length), as well as an introduction to his own part of the longer poem. Owst has recorded similar imagery in sermons on the Virgin, often to celebrate the Feast of the Assumption (pp. 18–20); indeed, Skelton's descriptions of Jane imitate the Proper for the Mass of the Assumption, celebrated on 14 August (following its own special vigil) and drawn from the Canticle of Canticles:

How beautiful art thou, my love, how beautiful art thou! thy eyes are doves' eyes, besides what is hid within. Thy hair is as flocks of goats, which come up from mount Galaad. . . .

How beautiful are thy breasts, my sister, *my* spouse! thy breasts are more beautiful than wine, and the sweet smell of thy ointments above all aromatical spices.

Thy lips, my spouse, are as a dropping honeycomb, honey and milk are under thy tongue; and the smell of thy garments, as the smell of frankincense. . . .

Let my beloved come into his garden, and eat the fruit of his apple trees. I am come into my garden, O my sister, *my* spouse, I have gathered my myrrh, with my aromatical spices: I have eaten the honeycomb with my honey, I have drunk my wine with my milk: eat, O friends, and drink, and be inebriated, my dearly beloved (4:1, 10–11; 5:1).

The opening of the Sequence in the proper echoes the epistle:

From our first mother Eva's sickly branch
Mary the blooming rose proceedeth forth;
Bright as amidst the stars the morning star,
And fair in beauty as the moon she came;
Sweet beyond balsam, ointments, frankincense;
As violet glowing, dewy as the rose.

The Holy Mother and Compassionate Virgin is now celebrated as Queen of Heaven. Skelton's portion of "Phyllyp Sparowe" draws on this, for in the girl who can comprehend the significance in the fall of a sparrow, he can find a figure of the Virgin Queen herself. Little wonder that he concludes Part 2 with this exclamation concerning Jane: "She is worthy to be enrolde / With letters of golde!" (1258–59).

But "Phyllyp Sparowe" also has a third intercessor—the sparrow and, behind him, St. Philip himself. He was frequently the subject of Norfolk church paintings, some of which may still be seen at North Elsham, South Lynn, and Salle, and he was a particular favorite with early Tudors because he was the disciple who was thought to intercede with Christ most often on behalf of others. In fact, this commonplace belief somewhat strains its Scriptural source (John 12:20–23), yet so popular did it become that it served as the basis for the further development of St. Philip as the disciple known for inspiring conversions. *The Golden Legend* emphasizes this point:

> Philip means a mouth of light or a mouth of hands. Or, it comes from *philos*, love, and *yper*, above; and means a lover of higher things. He is called a mouth of light because of his illuminating preaching, a mouth of hands because of his diligent labours, a lover of higher things because of his divine contemplation. . . .
>
> Isidore tells us, in his book, *Life and Death of the Saints*: "Philip the Galilean preached Christ, brought the faith to the barbarian peoples who sat in darkness on the coasts of the ocean, and brought them light and led them into the harbour of faith, and in the end was crucified, stoned, and put to death, at Hierapolis, in the province of Phrygia, where he is buried between his two daughters." Thus says Isidore (pp. 260–61).

The early Tudors celebrated the feast of St. Philip on 1 May. The lesson given in the Proper to his Mass is from Wisdom and it too is apposite to "Phyllyp Sparowe": "Then shall the just stand with great constancy against those that have afflicted them, and taken away their labours. . . . Behold how they are numbered among the children of God, and their lot is among the saints" (5:1, 5).

Still the liturgy from the Sarum Missal that best reflects the entire poem is, as we might expect, the movable feast of the Compassion of the Blessed Virgin. The Proper for the Mass has a lesson from Lamentations while a brief gospel lesson tells of the Holy Mother at the foot of the cross (John 19:25–27). But now the troped text becomes the centerpiece. In what is probably the Sarum rite's most moving Sequence (and surely one of its longest), we are returned to Jane's meditation from which we began. The Sequence opens,

> Alas! now recall to mind,
> O people redeemed with the blood
> of the gentle Lamb,
> the tears of Mary,
> the mournful mother of Christ.
> Who having suffered blood-stained wounds
> on the empurpled cross,
> washed out the stain
> of the fallen human race,

and proceeds to allude to the Magnificat,

> Is that the favour thou broughtest unto me,
> O Gabriel, when thou saidst to me,
> Hail, Mary, full of grace?
> 'Tis the contrary
> of that thou first didst promise,
> when now instead of grace to me
> there cometh grief and suffering.

Then, after a narrative of the Seven Sorrows, the Sequence proceeds, like the Virgin carols and St. Valentine's Day poems, to Old Testament pre-figurations—to Anna, mother of Samuel; Rachel; and Naomi; and concludes, "Thus, O virgin, full of sorrows, / make us so to sympathize / with thy tears and sighs, / that after this unhappy life / we may have thee as our conductress / into joys eternal." Skelton's most haunting poem works on us as Origen has said Scripture works on us—*figurally*, with historical, allegorical, and moral meanings—and with a double *anagogia*, one mystical, the other eschatological. In a poem which throughout its many parts keeps returning to death and salvation, it recalls the double *anagogia* of Christ's death, as derived from Origen: the first resurrection, by which the soul rises from the death of sin (as Phyllyp rises from death by Gib) and the second resurrection—Phyllyp's, Jane's, *ours*—by which the body finds occasion to be freed from all corruption, to renew its spiritual dedication and health. Jane herself could not have wished a more splendid—nor a more devotional, a more profound—tribute.

We can share Skelton's astonishment, then, at the reception given his best work at the time. As he remarks in *The Garlande of Laurell* (published in 1523),

> What ayle them to deprave
> Phillippe Sparows grave?
> His *Dirige*, her Commendacioun
> Can be no derogacyoun,
> But myrth and consolacyoun
> Made by protestacyoun,
> No man to myscontent
> With Phillippis entremente (1267–74).

Earlier the poem had been misunderstood too—perhaps, as Skelton implies, by envious poets who deliberately misconstrued the *Commendacions*, much as some modern critics have—but in a third section to the poem, the *Addicyon* (1267–1382), he managed to fashion his outspoken reply so as to complement the earlier parts of "Phyllyp Sparowe." He makes the new Part 3 (?1508–1516) follow Part 1 (the intercession of Jane for Phyllyp) and Part 2 (the intercession of Jane to God) by interceding on behalf of Jane to the poem's readers. Thus this final act of intercession becomes, as the other two had become, also an act of commendation; and all three become acts of pleasing (*Placebo*). Yet *The Garlande of Laurell* tells us that even with a third statement of what Skelton was attempting to do in "Phyllyp Sparowe" some missed the point. Consequently, in his later poems, Skelton uses Church liturgy, sacrament, and ritual more openly. But he does not depart from using these sources. And it is to these later major works, written during the final decades of his life in Westminster, that we now turn.

4

THE WESTMINSTER POEMS

GLUTTONY
Bench end (hand-carved, fifteenth century),
Church of the Holy Trinity, Blythburgh, Suffolk

W I L L I A M M A N E, prior of Westminster Abbey, noted in the household accounts book for Saturday, 5 July 1511, "this day at dyner w*ith* you*r* maistrchip the Soffrecan and Skeltun the poet w*ith* others."[1] This is the first record of Skelton's association with Westminster—where he seems to have moved and eventually died in 1529—and the first indication of his friendship with the orthodox and influential abbot of Westminster, John Islip. Descended from the family of Simon Islip, archbishop of Canterbury, Abbot Islip had entered the monastery about 1480, had been elected prior in 1498, and abbot in 1500. Almost at once he had persuaded the King's Council to move the body of Henry VI from Windsor to Westminster Abbey, and in the next few years he began planning with Henry VII the splendid chapel named for him which replaced the old Lady Chapel. Doubtless it was Islip who appointed three extra priests (Skelton may have been one of them) who at the direction of Henry VIII's will were to join the abbey to serve the altars of the new Lady Chapel. By 1511, when he was dining with Skelton, Abbot Islip was at work raising the roof of the abbey and supplying new statuary for its niches. In 1512 he requested from Skelton an epitaph for the tomb of Henry VII, a moving and dignified poem that Skelton completed on the eve of St. Andrew (the last day of the year in the Church calendar); in 1516, after he had joined the King's Council, he asked Skelton for a second epitaph for the tomb of Lady Margaret Beaufort, the King's mother. (An observer in 1631 found both epitaphs still hanging there on parchment.[2]) But by then Skelton had apparently settled on abbey lands within the sanctuary of Westminster; a lease from 1518 notes that when the convent of Westminster made arrangements with Alice Newebery regarding a tenement located on the south side of the Great Belfry, together with attached houses, solars, and cellars, John Skelton was then in residence—"*In quoquidem tenemento Johannes Skelton laureatus modo inhabitat.*"[3]

What sparse records we have suggest that the priest and the abbot, who were about the same age, remained good friends—as well they might, since they both shared common interests in serving Church and state. Skelton's first poem, we remember, had been a eulogy for the earl of Northumberland and it is pronouncedly royalist:

> The grounde of his quarell was for his soveryn lord,
> The well concernyng of all the hole lande,
> Demaundinge soche dutes as nedis most acord
> To the right of his prince, which shold not be withstand;
> For whos cause ye slew hym with your awne hande (64–68).

Except for his time in Diss, in fact, Skelton combined the two interests in his poems. His "Lawde and Prayse Made for Our Sovereigne Lord the Kyng" (1509), one of the first works to emphasize "The Rose both white and Rede" (1) which, for Skelton, *"Grace* the sede did sow" (5), and his revised *Speculum Principis* (1511) both imply that he wished to return to court now that the boy he had tutored had ascended the throne. Yet he must have remained in Diss through at least part of 1513, because he tells us that his next two significant works, the two Diss choruses, were performed there. The first, "Chorus de Dys contra Gallos," which celebrated the King's victories in France at the Battle of the Spurs (16 August) and at Thérouanne (22 August), was sung solemnly on the eve of the Decollation of St. John, 28 August (*"cantavit solemniter hoc Elogium in profesto divi Johannis ad decolationem"*). The poem, however, figures Henry not as St. John but as the legendary St. George, soldier, martyr, and patron saint of England, who, according to *The Golden Legend,* defeated the dragon and saved the country on the condition that men believe in Christ and be baptized. (Henry's troops advanced, crying the names of God and St. George.) The clear implication is that Henry is equally fighting as much for the Christian cause as against the French.

> *Salve festa dies, toto memorabilis evo,*
> *Qua Rex Henricus Gallica bella premit.*
> *Henricus rutilans Octavus noster in armis*
> *Tirwinne gentis menia stravit humi.*
> *Sceptriger Anglorum, bello validissimus Hector,*
> *Francorum gentis colla superba terit.*
> *Dux armis nuper celebris modo dux inermis*
> *De Longvile modo dic quo tua pompa ruit?*
> *De Cleremount clarus dudum dic, Galle superbe,*
> *Unde superbus eris? carcere nonne gemis?*
> *Discite Francorum gens cetera capta, Britannum*
> *Noscite te magnanimum, subdite vosque sibi.*
> *Gloria Cappadocis, dive milesque Marie,*
> *Illius hic sub ope Gallica regna reget.*
> *Hoc insigne bonum, divino numine gestum,*
> *Anglica genus referat semper ovansque canat.*[4]

The companion poem, the "Chorus de Dys contra Scottos," celebrates Surrey's defeat of the Scots at Flodden Field (9 September 1513). A headnote says the song was sung in procession on 22 September, significantly the feast day of a second legendary saint, the martyred St. Maurice, patron saint of soldiers, to whom eight English parish churches were dedicated.

> *Salve, festa dies, toto resonabilis evo,*
> *Qua Scottos Jacobus, obrutus ense, cadit.*
> *Barbara Scottorum gens, perfida, plena malorum,*
> *Vincitur ad Norram, vertitur inque fugam.* . . .
> *Jam quid agit Jachobus, damnorum germine cretus?*
> *Perfidus ut Nemroth, lapsus ad ima ruit.*
> *Dic modo, Scottorum dudum male sane malorum,*
> *Rector, nunc regeris; mortuus, ecce, jaces!*
> *Sic Leo te rapidus, Leo Candidus, inclitus ursit,*
> *Quo Leo tu Rubeus ultima fata luis.*
> *Anglia, duc choreas, resonent tua tympana, psalles;*
> *Da laudes Domino; da pia vota Deo* (1–4, 13–20).[5]

Just as Surrey is meant to figure St. Maurice here, whose exploits are also the material for legend, so King James of Scotland is a modern-day Nimrod, rebel descendant of Ham (Genesis 10:8–10). This second chorus, moreover, effectively tropes the epistle for the Proper of the Mass for St. Maurice and, if sung as a traditional interior processional just before the Canon of the Mass, could suitably replace the Sequence that usually troped the day's lesson at that point. The epistle, taken from Hebrews, pictures St. Maurice (and by extension, Surrey) as one

> Who by faith conquered kingdoms, wrought justice, obtained promises, stopped the mouths of lions,
> Quenched the violence of fire, escaped the edge of the sword, recovered strength from weakness, became valiant in battle, put to flight the armies of foreigners (11:33–34).

And as this text supplies the military imagery used in both choruses, so the Sequence for the feast day of St. George (23 April) supplies the musical imagery that both choruses share.

> In them, as though in instruments of music,
> faith doth with her own finger touch the strings
> discoursing high of virtues excellent;
> As on each single string she lays her hand
> she blends it in the fourfold melody,
> which she, that mother of all grace, evokes,
> Composing their harmonious symphony,

> without which all is dissonant,
> yes, trifling, poor, and vain. . . .
> Aided by faith the just in holy lives,
> seeking to climb the heights of starry heaven,
> sing forth new songs, and tune their harps in gladness.

Even more fundamentally, the choruses are linked parody-hymns (as the earlier poems on Clarke and Uddersale were linked mock-epitaphs). The first lines of each chorus refer us to the *Salve festa dies*, a hymn by Fortunatus, bishop of Poitiers, which by Skelton's day was the Church's favorite. Originally an Easter hymn, the *Salve Festa Dies* was still used on Easter because—figuring Thérouanne and Flodden in Skelton's allusion—it tells of Christ's harrowing hell and conquering death to ascend to His triumph at the Resurrection. By Skelton's time it had more than fifty variants and was used in both the Sarum and York rites for Ascension, Whitsunday, Corpus Christi, and Visitation as well as Easter—that is to say, for all the glorious ceremonials. Skelton follows this popular tradition by writing in elegiac distichs and by modelling his first line after the original—"Salve, festa dies, toto venerabilis aevo"—but pointedly changing "venerabilis" to "memorabilis" and "resonabilis." He may also have known that the hymn was used for English saints (such as St. Dunstan and St. Hugh of Lincoln) and for such legendary saints as St. Patrick and St. George himself. (St. George's own version,

> Salve festa dies, toto venerabilis aevo
> Qua pugil Anglorum migrat ab orbe polo,

can be found in an English manuscript of the early fifteenth century celebrating the English victory at Agincourt.[6]) When Skelton turned his attention to writing occasional poetry on political events, then, he drew as usual on scriptural and liturgical texts and on Church forms and ceremonial to figure modern-day occurrences as further evidence of sacred history.

This remained his strategy for much of his major work in Westminster. His flytings against Sir Christopher Garnesche written "by the kynges most noble commaundement" (?1514) reduce the Christian images in his model, William Dunbar's "Flyting of Dunbar and Kennedie" (1500–1505), to an occasional reference to the crucifix in Garnesche's native town (i.16) or to the mediocre refrain of ii, "Ye cappyd Cayface copious, your paltoke on your pate, / Thow ye prate lyke prowde Pylate, beware of chek-mate!" (6–7 *et sub.*), but his drama *Magnyfycence* (1516) is an orthodox morality play, set at court, which deals with the definitions of magnanimity and providence in a traditional story of temptation, fall, suffering, and repentance. Events enlarge upon a theme from Wisdom, alluded to by Measure (119)—"Yea and without these, they might have been slain with one blast, persecuted by their own deeds, and scattered by the breath of thy power: but thou hast ordered all things in measure, and number, and weight" (11:21)[7]—and it is when the nobleman Magnyfycence comes to realize that "In welth to beware yf I had had grace, / Never had I bene brought in this case" (1975–76) that he is able to dismiss Fansy (as Largesse) and the masqueraders Counterfet Countenaunce (as Good Demeanance), Crafty Conveyaunce (as Sure Surveyaunce), Cloked Colusyon (as Sober Sadnesse) and Courtly Abusyon (as Lusty Pleasure) and with the aid of Adversyte, Poverte, and even Dyspare, find Good Hope, Redresse, Sad Cyrcymspeccyon, and Perseveraunce. In his final address to the audience, Magnyfycence remarks on the need for Holy Mother Church,

> Of the terestre rechery we fall in the flode,
> Beten with stormys of many a frowarde blast,
> Ensordyd with the wawys savage and wode;
> Without our shyppe be sure, it is lykely to brast;
> Yet of magnyfycence oft made is the mast;
> Thus none estate lyvynge of hymselfe can be sure,
> For the welthe of this worlde cannot indure (2553–59),

a passage that returns us to ideas and motifs in *The Bowge of Courte*. He also returns us to the mock epitaph in the diatribe against William Bedell, former Treasurer of the Household for Lady Margaret Beaufort, whom Skelton pictures as "*Belial incarnatum*":

> *Ismal, ecce, Bedel, non mel sed fel sibi des, El!*
> *Perfidus Accitephel, luridus atque lorell;*
> *Nunc olet iste Jebal; est Nabal, ecce, ribaldus!*
> *Omnibus exosus atque perosus erat;*
> *In plateaque, cadens animam spiravit oleto:*
> *Presbiteros odiens sic sine mente ruit* (1–6).[8]

This poem is also based on Scripture as an internal reference to Psalm 73 (14a), called "*A prayer of the church under grievous persecutions*" in the Vulgate, makes plain:

> Lift up thy hands against their pride unto the end; *see* what things the enemy hath done wickedly in the sanctuary.

And they that hate thee have made their boasts, in the midst of
thy solemnity. . . .
They have set fire to thy sanctuary: they have defiled the dwelling
place of thy name on the earth.
They said in their heart, the *whole* kindred of them together: Let
us abolish all the festival days of God from the land. . . .
Arise, O God, judge thy own cause: remember thy reproaches
with which the foolish man hath reproached thee all the day.
Forget not the voices of thy enemies: the pride of them that hate
thee ascendeth continually (3–4, 7–8, 22–23).

But the difficulty between Skelton and Bedell is unknown, and the cause
of the poem obscure.

This is not at all the case with "Against Venemous Tongues" (1516). In
this poem the attack is openly against Thomas Wolsey, archbishop of York,
who was elevated to Cardinal of the Church (and chief prelate in all
England) in 1515 and made Lord Chancellor (upon William Warham's
return to Canterbury) in 1516.

Al maters wel-pondred and wel to be regarded,
How shuld a fals lying tung then be rewarded?
Such tunges shuld be torne out by the harde rootes,
Hoyning like hogges that groynis and wrotez! (1–4).

The reference to "hogges," alluding to Wolsey as a butcher's son, makes
that clear. What appears especially galling to the poet is the Cardinal's new
ostentatious display of his badge of office—

For before on your brest and behind on your back,
In Romaine letters I never founde lack (16–17)

—yet "never founde lack" is a turning point in the poem, for while there is
a surplus of letters ("T" and "C" for "Thomas Cardinalis") on his livery,
this sign belies the true "lack," which Skelton finds

In your crosse-rowe nor Christ-crosse-you-spede,
Your *Pater noster*, your *Ave*, nor your Crede (18–19)

and this is the text the Cardinal forgets both to speak and to practice. At
the same time Wolsey has added so splendidly to his own livery, and to the
livery of his men who form a continually expanding retinue, that he has
seen fit to "Controlle the cognisaunce of noble men" (22). In connection
with the visit of the King's sister, Queen Margaret of Scotland, Wolsey

had actively sent out spies to count the retinues of others and to diminish them. A. F. Pollard tells us that one Thomas Allen reported hearing "my Lord Cardinal command them to bring in every man's name which was with them in their livery at the said time,"[9] and in May of 1516 the Marquis of Dorset, the Earl of Surrey (young Thomas Howard, son of the victor at Flodden), and Lord Abergavenny were put out of the Council chamber and with other nobility were indicted in King's Bench and called before Star Chamber (where Wolsey sat) over the matter of keeping retainers. What is more, Skelton says, such intemperate and distasteful treatment has been maliciously rumored to have had his, Skelton's, support.

> Whosoever that tale unto you tolde,
> He saith untruly, to say that I would
> Controlle the cognisaunce of noble men,
> Either by language or with my pen (20–23).

Instead,

> My schole is more solem and somwhat more haute
> Than to be founde in any such faute.
> My scoles are not for unthriftes untaught,
> For frantick faitours half mad and half straught;
> But my learning is of another degree,
> To taunt theim like liddrons [rascals], lewd as thei bee (24–29).

Clearly Skelton is implying that his "school" is one that "instructs" men in precisely those things the Cardinal ignores—the Paternoster, *Ave*, and Credo. Therefore, he is impervious to their Satan-like tongues,

> For though some be lidder and list for to rayle,
> Yet to lie upon me they cannot prevayle;
> Then let them vale a bonet of their proud sayle,
> And of their taunting toies rest with il hayle (30–33),

although it is true that we are told both in Proverbs (25:15) and Ecclesiasticus (28:21) that

> Malicious tunges, though they have no bones
> Are sharper then swordes, sturdier then stones
> Sharper then raysors that shave and cut throtes,
> More stinging then scorpions that stang Pharaotis.
> More venemous and much more virulent
> Then any poysoned tode or any serpent (49–54).

Next to Skelton's knowledge of Scripture and the authority it gives him, the political maneuverings of Wolsey are inconsequential and even laughable:

> "What tidings at Totnam, what newis in Wales?
> What shippis are sailing to Scalis Malis?" [Cadiz]
> And all is not worth a couple of nut shalis! (64–66).

In language that means to separate Truth from falsehood, Skelton's own words must therefore be trusted, and his own inquiry and accusations are the ones with force.

> For his false lying, of that I spake never,
> I could make him shortly repent him forever;
> Although he made it never so tough,
> He might be sure to have shame ynough (75–78).

Although ostensibly a poem of denunciation, the poet here must find a way to salvage language when it has been all but destroyed by debasement. His means for achieving this is to make an analogy between proper and improper use of language and the good and bad men who are responsible for its corruption; further, he makes good men (such as himself) those who remain responsible to the beliefs of the Church and the lessons of Scripture and the evil ones those who flout their office at the expense of their faith. Thus the poem is really a colloquy between the priest of the Church, who calls on the Church's authority for his credentials, and the prelate of that Church, who has apparently forgotten what he learned from Her.

This deeper structure is indicated plainly enough at the outset in the colloquy of Psalms (119, 51) that are excerpted to form an epigraph, and augmented by two more (11, 13) quoted in the rubrics to the poem. These passages from Scripture also juxtapose sharply two voices employed by Skelton in his poem. One is initially the voice of concern and, finally, of petition.

> Salvum me fac. *The prophet calls for God's help against the wicked.*
> Save me, O Lord, for there is now no saint: truths are decayed from among the children of men.
> They have spoken vain things every one to his neighbour: *with* deceitful lips, *and* with a double heart have they spoken.
> May the Lord destroy all deceitful lips, and the tongue that speaketh proud things.

Who have said: We will magnify our tongue; our lips are our own; who is Lord over us?

By reason of the misery of the needy, and the groans of the poor, now will I arise, saith the Lord.

I will set him in safety; I will deal confidently in his regard.

The words of the Lord are pure words: *as* silver tried by the fire, purged from the earth, refined seven times.

Thou, O Lord, wilt preserve us.: and keep us from this generation for ever.

The wicked walk round about: according to thy highness, thou hast multiplied the children of men (11:1–9).

Ad Dominum. *A prayer in tribulation.* A gradual canticle.

In my trouble I cried to the Lord: and he heard me.

O Lord, deliver my soul from wicked lips, and a deceitful tongue.

What shall be given to thee, or what shall be added to thee, to a deceitful tongue?

The sharp arrows of the mighty, with coals that lay waste.

Woe is me, that my sojourning is prolonged! I have dwelt with the inhabitants of Cedar: my soul hath been long a sojourner.

With them that hated peace I was peaceable: when I spoke to them they fought against me without cause (119:1–7).

The other voice is that of accusation and judgment.

Dixit insipiens. *The general corruption of man before our redemption by Christ.*

The fool hath said in his heart: There is no God.

They are corrupt, and are become abominable in their ways: there is none that doth good, no not one.

The Lord hath looked down from heaven upon the children of men, to see if there be any that understand and seek God.

They are all gone aside, they are become unprofitable together: there is none that doth good, no not one.

Their throat is an open sepulchre: with their tongues they acted deceitfully; the poison of asps *is* under their lips.

Their mouth is full of cursing and bitterness; their feet are swift to shed blood.

Destruction and unhappiness in their ways: and the way of peace they have not known: there is no fear of God before their eyes.

Shall not all they know that work iniquity, who devour my people as they eat bread?

They have not called upon the Lord: there have they trembled for fear, where there was no fear.

For the Lord is in the just generation: you have confounded the counsel of the poor man, but the Lord is his hope.

Who shall give out of Sion the salvation of Israel? when the Lord shall have turned away the captivity of his people, Jacob shall rejoice and Israel shall be glad (13:1–7).

But this second voice is made even more emphatic by citing Psalm 51 that in the course of the poem figures Skelton as David and Wolsey as Doeg, Saul's chief herdsman (1 Kings 21, 22).

Quid gloriaris. *David condemneth the wickedness of Doeg, and fore-telleth his destruction.*

Why dost thou glory in malice, thou that art mighty in iniquity?

All the day long thy tongue hath devised injustice: as a sharp razor, thou hast wrought deceit.

Thou hast loved malice more than goodness: and iniquity rather than to speak righteousness.

Thou hast loved all the words of ruin, O deceitful tongue.

Therefore will God destroy thee for ever: he will pluck thee out, and remove thee from thy dwelling place: and thy root out of the land of the living.

The just shall see and fear, and shall laugh at him, and say: Behold the man that made not God his helper:

But trusted in the abundance of his riches: and prevailed in his vanity.

But I, as a fruitful olive tree in the house of God, have hoped in the mercy of God for ever, yea for ever and ever.

I will praise thee for ever, because thou hast done it: and I will wait on thy name, for it is good in the sight of thy saints (51:3–11).

Yet this is more than Skelton using Scripture for his own purpose—and more than calling attention to his own vocation and his own stalwart faith. It is a matter of *using the Scriptures to condemn a prelate*. If Wolsey is to look up the references spelled out in the epitaph and the rubrics, he will find only a repetition of the poem itself: and this means that to deny the poem is to deny the Scriptures. Either way, through ignorance (by refusing to acknowledge the biblical passages) or by knowledge of the Scriptures, Wolsey is declared guilty of bad faith.

Nor can it be coincidental that when we search the Sarum Missal for the use of these Psalms, we find that the two Psalms of the epigraph, 51 and 119, as well as Psalm 13, are recited in their entirety only once in the church year—and then *on the same occasion*, the Office of Compline for Maundy Thursday, a major feast day near the May date when Skelton composed and circulated his poem, and a day and feast that recall the betrayal of Christ (the Church) by Judas (the fallen). It is a particularly moving service of penitence, in which priests wash the altars and one another's feet to the responsory "Lying men compassed me about" and following a strikingly apposite set of versicles:

2 Responsory.

Lying men compassed me about; they scourged me without a cause. But thou, O Lord, my defender, avenge me.

V. For trouble is hard at hand, and there is none to help. But thou, O Lord, etc. . . .

6 Responsory.

Judas, the wickedest trafficker, sought the Lord with a kiss; he as an innocent lamb refuseth not the kiss of Judas. For a sum of money he betrayed Christ to the Jews.

V. Drunken with the poison of covetousness, while he seeks for gain, he finds a noose. For a sum of money etc.

7 Responsory.

Could ye not watch with me one hour, ye who encouraged [each other] to die for me? See ye not even Judas how he sleepeth not, but hasteneth to betray me to the Jews?

V. Sleep on now, and take your rest; behold, he is at hand that will betray me. See ye not etc. . . .

9 Responsory.

O Judas, who hast cast away the counsel of peace and hast covenanted with the Jews for thirty pieces of silver, thou hast sold the blood of the just one, and bestowedst the kiss of peace, which thou hadst not in thy breast.

V. Thy mouth was full of malice, and thy tongue did set forth deceit. And thou bestowedst etc.

This liturgical drama ends with further memorable antiphonals.

R. We wait for thy loving-kindness, O God,
V. In the midst of thy temple.
R. Thou hast charged,
V. That we should diligently keep thy commandments.

Thus this service both warns and instructs Wolsey, after condemning him and his allies for playing Judas to Church robes and ceremonials. But it is not exactly Skelton who is condemning the prelate. It is the Church liturgy itself, which the prelate has spent a lifetime celebrating.

We may be astonished at the abruptness and force of Skelton's outburst. But it was probably not sudden from his perspective, nor from the Tudor perspective either. Aristocratic families like the Howards—a distinguished and powerful family in East Anglia, whose family homes at Kenninghall Place and Thetford Priory were not far from Diss—headed a powerful, conservative faction on the King's Council, upholding an orthodox and traditional England and opposing Wolsey. Moreover, Thomas Howard's son Thomas II, who had helped his father at Flodden, was one of those whom Wolsey accused in court. Skelton's special faction—and all Skelton stood for as this conservative faction represented it—was thus being undermined by the effrontery of the man who called himself chief prelate of the Catholic Church in England.

Yet from the beginning there had been doubts about Wolsey. When Skelton's patron, the King's mother, had seen her grandson succeed to her son's throne, she quickly formed for him a new King's Council that continued the appointments of Warham, of Richard Fox, bishop of Winchester, and of Thomas Howard I—but she had only suspicions of Wolsey.[10] Within two years she was proven right: on 26 May 1511, Pollard reports, Wolsey as the King's secretary "produced for the chancellor a signed bill which had gone through none of [the] official [channels]" (p. 15); already he was short-circuiting procedures and taking charge. His servant George Cavendish tells us how this happened. Young King Henry did not like the bother of administrative details, says Cavendish, and he gladly left them to Wolsey, who excelled at them.[11] By May 1516 Wolsey was persuading the King to send the earl of Northumberland to Fleet prison and Sir William Bulmer to the Tower for preferring to serve the Duke of Buckingham.[12] By 1518 he would also sit in his own court in Westminster Hall as head of the English judiciary—although he was not a lawyer, had never practiced law, and, unlike many Tudor ecclesiastics, had never even taken a degree in canon or civil law.[13] "The cardinal," the Venetian ambassador Giustiniani remarked in 1518, "for authority, may in point of fact be styled *ipse rex*." Even Thomas More complained that Wolsey made decisions for the King's Council and only later reported them to the Council.[14] It was no good, with a distracted king, concentrating the chief positions of Church and state—chief prelate and cardinal and lord chancellor —in the same hands.

Not that Wolsey did not manage the jobs he assigned himself. Yet with all his industry, energy, and devotion to work—he would not leave the court even in times of plague—he was blind to the reactions of others. Surely his great pride and pomp exacerbated the situation. But it seems to have been contagious; Cavendish writes fondly and at length about Wolsey's household servants "whereof the number were about the sum of five hundred persons, according to his checker roll" (p. 22). Wolsey used such numbers to maintain power: he worked by means of a glorious intimidation, employing spectacle to establish authority and rule. Pollard tells us that his excessiveness is seen in the autumn of 1515 when he was elevated to the cardinalate.

> The protonotary of the papal court, who brought [his red hat from Rome], was stopped on his arrival in England in order that he might be more sumptuously arrayed in Wolsey's apparel for the occasion; a bishop and an earl were dispatched to Blackheath to meet it; the mayor and aldermen of London on horseback and the city gilds on foot were turned out to do reverence as it was borne through the city on Thursday, 15 November, to Westminster abbey; and there it reposed upon the high altar until the following Sunday. On that day a ceremony, "as I have not seen the like" says Cavendish, "unlesse it hath bin at the coronation of a mighty prince," heralded the reign of Shakespeare's "cardinal-king." The archbishops of Canterbury, Armagh, and Dublin, eight bishops, and eight abbots [including John Islip] assisted in the service. Warham said mass, the bishop of Lincoln read the epistle, and the bishop of Exeter the gospel; and eighteen temporal lords, led by the dukes of Norfolk [Howard] and Suffolk [Charles Brandon], conducted the cardinal back to his palace at York place (p. 56).

Wolsey's expanding authority finally forced Warham out, too; he returned to Canterbury (where, to Wolsey's irritation, Warham would outlive him), and upon Warham's resignation of the Great Seal, Wolsey took up the Lord Chancellorship in less than two months, installing himself in another magnificent service on Christmas Eve 1515 in the chapel at Eltham—the very palace where Skelton had tutored prince Henry—after the singing of

Vespers and in the presence of the King. Wolsey also promoted luxuriousness by encouraging clergy to wear silk and velvet publicly for the first time (while burgesses were restricted to homespun), and he devised a new regulation whereby the ordinary gentleman was limited to three dishes at each meal, lords of parliament, lord mayors, and knights of the garter to six—but the cardinal was allowed nine, and so were any of those who had the good fortune to dine with him.[15] So, by the time Skelton wrote "Against Venemous Tongues" in the late spring of 1516, Wolsey was thoroughly established, and the lines against him were drawn.

Cavendish tells us that each morning from that time forward, Wolsey celebrated two Masses in his private closet with his personal chaplain before going forth from York Place to Westminster Hall in a grand procession, riding, says Harvey, a

> mule, the great symbol of humility that Christ himself had used, covered too as all the servants in crimson livery, gold flashings, copper gilt, black velvet, and everywhere the golden glinting of the great man's badge: his cardinal's hats and his initials T. C.
>
> It was a daily demonstration of splendor wherever the cardinal might go. In all there were 160 personal attendants, 60 priests in residence, 16 doctors and chaplains, 4 councillors of law, 2 secretaries and 3 clerks. To these were added his retinue as chancellor, numerous clerks and running footmen, armorers, and minstrels, sergeants-at-arms and heralds. For them alone, the stables kept more than one hundred horses. For himself he kept six gray and white ambling mules.
>
> But of all this vast assembly, the part that attracted the greatest attention, well-deserved attention, was his choir of twelve singing priests, twelve singing boys, and sixteen singing laymen.

"It was," she sums, "a choir unequaled by any in England" (p. 99). Then, at the Field of the Cloth of Gold in 1520 Wolsey managed, for Henry and for himself, 5,172 men and women and 2,865 horse—"Never before had the English court moved abroad in such strength and in such style," Williams tells us (p. 38)—and he showed the world his newly designed arms, displaying a sable shield and cross engrailed and azure leopards' faces to claim descent from the Ufford earls of Suffolk and the de la Poles, a lion to represent his connection with the papacy, dragons supporting pillars to symbolize his legatine authority, and (again by decree and not descent) the choughs believed by the College of Arms to have been borne by Thomas à Becket, whom Wolsey took as his patron saint. In France Wolsey appointed not John Skelton, laureate and *orator regius*, but Alexander Barclay, the Benedictine monk, to serve as poet in residence, giving him a leave of absence to compose mottoes for the walls of banqueting houses and apartments.[16]

So only a moment's reflection will tell us why Skelton was so personally offended by Wolsey: they must have been life-long rivals. They were about the same age; they had both come from undistinguished backgrounds (whatever Skelton's was); they had gone to the university and begun life as scholars (Wolsey to Magdalen, Oxford; Skelton presumably to Peterhouse, Cambridge); they were both rectors at about the same time in similar towns in East Anglia (Wolsey was made vicar of Redgrave, Suffolk, by the abbot of Bury St. Edmund in 1506). Then, when Skelton was dismissed from royal service, Wolsey entered it, as royal chaplain to Henry VII in 1507, and, later, as almoner. By the time Skelton returned to court, Wolsey was heading it, invincible. (In time each of the English universities that gave Skelton a laureateship would offer Wolsey the chancellorship, and Oxford would pass a resolution "that whoever preaches at Oxford or at London henceforth shall mention Wolsey's name in the bidding prayer."[17]) Worse even than this galling success, Wolsey managed in his titular administration of Holy Mother Church to corrupt Her. It was not simply that the lavish ceremony he engineered replaced the Church liturgy as the center of Wolsey's rituals; it was his ambition to the papacy, and finally his papal appointment (in 1518) as *legatus a latere* that threatened the foundation of the Church. This last appointment enormously extended his ecclesiastical powers: acting in place of the Pope in England, he could remit sins, take jurisdiction of wills from English bishops, demand tribute from all levels of the clergy, and (in time) legitimize bastards, chastise the clergy, grant degrees in theology, arts, and religious orders, appoint benefices at will, absolve those excommunicated or under other sentences, and reform the monasteries.[18] Wolsey violated the trust of these privileges and the sanctity of his papal appointment from the start. Rather than recognize the wishes of Rome, Roger Lockyer writes, to which Skelton would doubtless have agreed, Wolsey

came instead to epitomize all the abuses of the Church. He always had one other bishopric as well as his Archbishopric of York, thereby introducing episcopal pluralism to England, and he had non-resident Italians appointed to the sees of Salisbury, Worcester, and Llandaff, to whom he paid a fixed salary so that he could pocket the surplus. He had himself elected Abbot of St Albans, one of the

richest monasteries in England, although he was not and never had
been a monk. He interfered in every diocese, appointing his own
protégés, regardless of the rights of patrons, and set up legatine
courts to which he summoned men from all over England. He
charged large sums for probate and was notoriously greedy for
riches. He was non-resident on a princely scale, never even visiting
three of his sees and first entering the diocese of York sixteen years
after he had been made Archbishop.[19]

He made a game out of appointments for himself, trading up the sees
by turning in Bath and Wells when Durham fell vacant, and exchang-
ing that for the see at Winchester. But most disastrous of all for the
Church, Lockyer continues, "He dissolved twenty-nine monasteries on
the grounds that they were hopelessly decayed, and used their confiscated
property to endow the colleges which he was building at Ipswich and
Oxford" (p. 38), and to endow extensive alterations to York Place and to
Hampton Court. "Assuredly no other extended his jurisdiction so much
as Wolsey," Pollard comments, "and not one of his successors has wielded
more than a fraction of his authority" (p. 59). Yet, as head of the Catholic
Church in England, "he left nothing in writing that could be called the-
ology" (p. 26). In sum, he was "a born fighter encumbered by clerical
garments and spiritual professions to which he had no vocation" (p. 305).

It is, in fact, the dissolution of the nunneries of Lillechurch, Kent, and
Bromehall, Berkshire, effected at Wolsey's directions in October 1521, that
partly prompts Skelton's third attack on the chief prelate, following
"Against Venemous Tongues" (1516) and *Speke, Parrot* (late 1520–1521). He
calls this poem "Collyn Clout" (1521–1522). Here he comments that

> the selfe-same game
> Begon, and now with shame,
> Amongest the sely nonnes:
> My lady nowe she ronnes,
> Dame Sybly our abbesse,
> Dame Dorothe and Lady Besse,
> Dame Sare our pryoresse,
> Out of theyr cloyster and quere
> With an hevy chere,
> Must cast up theyr blacke vayles
> And set up theyr fulke sayles
> To catche wynde with theyr ventayles (387–98).

The thought of the hapless dispossessed now prey to any misfortune and sin was not enough. Skelton reminds us that in addition there was destruction of the church and of the consecrated ground on which it stood and in which troubled souls still lie, now unprotected from the anguish of purgatory:

> Ye do them wronge and no ryght
> To put them thus to flyght:
> No matyns at mydnyght,
> Boke and chalys gone quyte;
> Plucke away the leedes
> Over theyr heedes,
> And sell away theyr belles
> And all that they have elles. . . .
> How ye breke the dedes wylles,
> Turne monasteries into water mylles,
> Of an abbey ye make a graunge—
> Your workes, they say, are straunge—
> So that theyr founders soules
> Have lost theyr bedde roules,
> The money for theyr masses
> Spent among wanton lasses;
> Theyr dyriges are forgotten,
> Theyr founders lye there rotten;
> But where theyr soules dwell,
> Therwith I wyll nat mell.
> What coude the Turke do more
> With all his false lore—
> Turke, Sarazyn or Jewe?
> I reporte me to you (404–11; 417–32).

Such practices mock the liturgy; the *Gloria* ("*In secula seculorum*") is inverted in this exhortation to liberty that caused some in Skelton's day to link Wolsey's actions—his quick rise to power and influence—to witchcraft.

> Relygyous men are fayne
> For to tourne agayne
> *In secula seculorum,*
> And to forsake theyr *corum*
> And *vacabundare per forum,*

And take a fyne *meritorum*
Contra regulam morum,
Aut blacke *monacorum,*
Aut canonicorum,
Aut Bernardinorum,
Aut Cruciferorum,
And to synge from place to place
Lyke apostataas (374–86).[20]

No one—not the Benedictines, Augustinians, Cistercians, or Trinitarians
—is safe before a prelate whose greed sweeps up everything without dis-
tinction. As for Wolsey himself, he appears very much as Cavendish has
pictured him—although Skelton precedes the familiar icon with a sharply
disjunctive portrait of the learned and saintly Thomas Scrope, the wander-
ing bishop of Norwich in the later fifteenth century, who is cited by
Holinshed as one of the learned men in the reign of Henry VII:

Over this, the foresayd lay
Reporte howe the Pope may
An holy anker call
Out of the stony wall,
And hym a bysshop make,
Yf he on hym dare take
To kepe so harde a rule,
To ryde upon a mule
With golde all betrapped,
In purple and paule belapped,
Some hatted and some capped,
Rychly bewrapped,
God wotte, to theyr great paynes,
In rotchettes of fyne raynes,
Whyte as mares mylke;
Theyr tabertes of fyne sylke;
Theyr styrops of myxt golde begared,
There may no cost be spared;
Theyr moyles golde dothe eate,
Theyr neyghbours dye for meate (301–20).

Yet these examples, of the chaos of the world and of the singular force of
the chief prelate, juxtaposed, limn all of "Collyn Clout." Although this
poem seems peculiarly puzzling among Skelton's major works—because

the perspective and ideas are clear but they appear strangely jumbled—this is not at all the case. Like the juxtaposed passages from the Old and New Testaments which form the epigraph—

> *Quis consurget mihi adversus malignantes,*
> *aut quis stabit mecum adversus operantes iniquitatem?*
> *Nemo, Domine!* (a-c)

("Who will rise up with me against evil-doers? Or who will stand up with me against the workers of iniquity?" [Psalm 93:16]; "No one, O Lord!" [John 8:11])—this poem is persistently a poem of contrasting forces. Collyn is opposed to Wolsey because he is simple, blunt, and honest. His observations, moreover, are addressed to us.

> My name is Collyn Cloute.
> I purpose to shake oute
> All my connynge bagge,
> Lyke a clerkely hagge, . . .
> Yf ye take well therwith,
> It hath in it some pyth (49–52, 57–58).

> And let Collyn Clout have none
> Maner of cause to mone!
> Lay salve to your owne sore,
> For elles, as I sayd before,
> After *gloria, laus,*
> May come a soure sauce!
> Sory therfore am I,
> But trouth can never lye (478–85).

But as the poem spirals outward into a lengthy series of critical observations, it reviews both the spiritual and the temporal realms (61–62). For Wolsey is both chief prelate and Lord Chancellor: this poem, like the opening colloquy, keeps splintering and doubling. In the course of the investigation, Wolsey becomes both the origin of evil and simply the worst example of it, both type and prototype. Collyn, too, becomes more than simply Collyn; he also becomes the spokesman for a whole community of honest, suffering laymen.

> . . . I, Collyn Cloute,
> As I go aboute,
> And wandrynge as I walke,
> I here the people talke (285–88).

What follows from passages such as this one—passages Collyn always identifies—are his reports buttressed by, or simply mirroring, a broader consensus of those who remain faithful to scriptural precept and liturgical practice. Like the others, Collyn is a character who is victimized by the world around him; unlike the others, Collyn will also speak for them. In addition, he will be both narrator and judge.

In all his characteristics—his simplicity, his clearsightedness, his bluntness, his pain, his anxiety, and his stubborn faith—Collyn represents the ordinary early Tudor whose belief in the Church and Her teachings is being undermined by the chief prelate. Collyn is no Parrot, no figure of the Holy Ghost and divine prophecy; his roots are with the commoner. But as Skelton deliberately tells us in the epigraph, Collyn does figure the anonymous Psalmist of Psalm 93 with a cry of tribulation and a prayer for deliverance that, in his case, is further bolstered by the common Tudor knowledge of the Bible and of Church liturgy (as we shall see) and further authenticated by Christ's own testimony on behalf of the Psalms (Luke 24:44). Like the author of Psalm 93, Collyn is at the same time peculiarly personal and impersonal in his complaints; his charges are both general (cf. 93:5) and specific (cf. 93:6), individual (93:16–19) and collective (93:4–7, 20–21). Thus the double quality of Collyn's poem follows that of the Psalmist's cry and prayer. Indeed, a close examination of Psalm 93 will show us at once that, just as Parrot had found form and sense in the world outside his cage by seeking prefigurations in the events of Genesis and Exodus, Collyn is able to see a pattern and make judgments about the apparent chaos of the Church by writing his own lament that closely parallels the form, mood, and intention of Psalm 93.

Psalm 93 can be analyzed (like many Psalms) in relatively independent parts. Verses 1–3 are an opening cry for help.

> The Lord is the God to whom revenge belongeth: the God of revenge hath acted freely.
>
> Lift up thyself, thou that judgest the earth: render a reward to the proud.
>
> How long shall sinners, O Lord: how long shall sinners glory?

Like Collyn, the Psalmist (1) is able to identify what is wicked and even its source; (2) is seeking restitution, although (3) is unable to provide it himself, for vengeance belongs to God; and (4) is despairing because the removal of wickedness and the restoration of what is good is long in coming. Psalm 93 continues (4–7) by describing the Psalmist's situation, although he sees his misfortunes as typical of the corruption of his age.

Shall they utter, and speak iniquity: shall all speak who work injustice?

Thy people, O Lord, they have brought low: and they have afflicted thy inheritance.

They have slain the widow and the stranger: and they have murdered the fatherless.

And they have said: The Lord shall not see: neither shall the God of Jacob understand.

Then, in the style of the wisdom writers, the Psalmist appeals to the people he represents to understand the ways of the Lord while shoring up his own beliefs (8–15); it is here Collyn will allude to other Scripture and liturgical practices in the course of the poem.

Understand, ye senseless among the people: and, you fools, be wise at last.

He that planted the ear, shall he not hear? or he that formed the eye, doth he not consider?

He that chastiseth nations, shall he not rebuke: he that teacheth man knowledge?

The Lord knoweth the thoughts of men, that they are vain.

Blessed is the man whom thou shalt instruct, O Lord: and shalt teach him out of thy law.

The Psalmist's prayer for deliverance concludes as Collyn's will—in the rhetorical questions that function as the poem's epigraph (93:16). The next section of the Psalm (17–23) regains some assurance, although it is tentative and conditional—"Unless the Lord had been my helper, my soul had almost dwelt in hell" (17)—because the source of wickedness is in the position of power: "Doth the seat of iniquity stick to thee, who framest labour in commandment? / They will hunt after the soul of the just, and will condemn innocent blood" (93:20–21). It is precisely these varying tones and moods that Collyn will enlist to make sense of his own age to those he addresses. At times he will pray for relief too (433–40) but his preoccupation will always be with the current state of corruption. Yet the precise ordering of Psalm 93—a cry for help, a description of current wrongs, an appeal, and the fear that such an appeal will be fruitless—will provide the model for each of the sections of "Collyn Clout" for which Collyn himself is responsible.

It is important to note, however, in connection with Collyn's use of the Psalm as his organizing model, that he stresses the cry of lament (as

Skelton does, with his choice of epigraph) at the expense of what solace the Psalmist finds. In some small ways, Psalm 93 is more hopeful, finally, than Collyn's denunciation. The reason for this is the intervening centuries between the days of the Psalmist and those of Collyn, centuries in which the evil ways of men have continued to go unconquered. It is to make this single reservation that Skelton provides the second part of the colloquy that serves as epigraph. The passage in John 8 is, pointedly, from the narrative portion of St. John's gospel, addressed to the common man; it is the story of the woman taken in adultery.

> And early in the morning he came again into the temple, and all the people came to him, and sitting down he taught them.
>
> And the scribes and Pharisees bring unto him a woman taken in adultery; and they set her in the midst,
>
> And said to him: Master, this woman was even now taken in adultery.
>
> Now Moses in the law commanded us to stone such a one. But what sayest thou?
>
> And this they said tempting him, that they might accuse him. But Jesus bowing himself down, wrote with his finger on the ground.
>
> When therefore they continued asking him, he lifted himself up, and said to them: He that is without sin among you, let him first cast a stone at her.
>
> And again stooping down, he wrote on the ground.
>
> But they hearing *this*, went out one by one, beginning at the eldest. And Jesus alone remained, and the woman standing in the midst.
>
> Then Jesus lifting up himself, said to her: Woman, where are they that accused thee? Hath no man condemned thee?
>
> Who said: No man, Lord. And Jesus said: Neither will I condemn thee. Go, and now sin no more (2–11).

Christ's teaching has also intervened since the Psalmist's writing, and Collyn knows that too. Unlike the Psalmist who can share God's sense of justice and righteous indignation, Collyn knows from Christ's teaching that all men are in a fallen state. Therefore, complaint *but not vengeance* is his lot. Indeed, the moving inner drama of "Collyn Clout" is his sense of possible complicity, and his struggle to maintain the force of the Psalmist's lament alongside that Christian understanding of man's need, from time to time, for charity and divine support. It is this conflict within Collyn that makes his poem so rich and so powerful. His strength is that he is a kind of Everyman, whose instincts and common knowledge, when accusing the prelate, can best define the extent of Wolsey's wrongdoing. This strength is what causes Skelton to give the poem over to him after a brief prologue. Indeed, the transparency of the truths he announces arouses a third voice in the poem, obviously meant to be Wolsey's, to confirm Collyn's charges and to remove Collyn's doubts (1151–1227). But Collyn has also confirmed the poet, and he too enters the poem (1228–66) to reassert Collyn's judgment and to suggest that in silencing him, Wolsey has not (nor could he have) silenced complaint or silenced truth.

Collyn Clout, in short, is a singer who figures the Psalmist; like St. John he is one who has great faith in the power and truth of the Word. Moreover, he is a necessary spokesman for Skelton, who tells us that as a poet he could either become a seer and make his subject appear foolish (13–25) or speak directly and announce his subject's foolishness (26–32). Either he will convince no one (33–37) or else frighten them with the wretchedness and instability of a world gone mad under the chaos of misrule (38–46). Collyn, however, as a member of the broader populace, has a different but unimpeachable authority. He will be able to witness to conditions and events as others witness to them; and he will also dramatize the effect of those conditions and events. If he lacks Parrot's ability at prophecy he shares Parrot's figural sense of Scripture. He believes.

Collyn's observations fall into discrete episodes in each of which he lists a number of wrongs, assesses their similarities, and then discovers, in each instance, that Wolsey is at the root of them. He begins with a common complaint: very much like the Psalmist, he finds shepherds no longer care for their flocks.

> Laye men say in dede
> Howe they take no hede
> Theyr sely shepe to fede,
> But plucke away and pull
> Theyr fleces of wull (75–79).

This leads Collyn to expand on ignorant bishops (92–114), their effect on clergy (115–31), their sloth and greed (132–61), and their decline since the days when St. Thomas of Canterbury, the antitype of Thomas Cardinal Wolsey, was archbishop of England (162–77), and he finally concludes that the self-indulgence and lechery of Wolsey (in reference to Wolsey's liaison in 1515 with Mistress Lark, 193) best exemplify what is wrong with Holy Mother Church (178–95).

The concrete thought of Wolsey jolts Collyn, and so he begins again:

"What have laye men to do / The gray goos for to sho?" (196–97). The second section of Collyn's investigation opens with his proverbial recognition that his task of challenging such a situation is impossible—he is keenly cognizant now, that is, of John 8:2–11—and this leads him to thoughts of food, and that leads to the greed of the clergy and their violations of the Church customs regulating the diet during Lent (205–19). This in turn calls to his mind the service of ordination, the *Sicientes* (222), when priests take vows which they break in a whole litany of parodied services (222–29). Furthermore,

> . . . whan they have ones caught
> *Dominus vobiscum* by the hede,
> Then renne they in every stede,
> God wote, with dronken nolles;
> Yet take they cure of soules
> And wotteth never what thei rede,
> Pater noster nor Crede;
> Construe nat worth a whystell
> Neyther gospell nor pystell;
> Theyr matyns madly sayde,
> Nothynge devoutly prayde;
> Theyr lernynge is so small
> Theyr prymes and houres fall
> And lepe out of theyr lyppes
> Lyke sawdust or drye chyppes (229–43).

Although they begin with the Chalice at Mass (230), they wind up at the alehouse (249–61). Thus Collyn concludes by returning to Wolsey's well-rumored gluttony.

After another pause Collyn begins section three, reinforced by the conversations of others (285–89), this time to examine simony (again with an emphasis on bishoprics, "Myters are bought and solde," 290, a reference to Wolsey), and continues with the memory of Wolsey on his mule. Such wealth is accumulated "With sommons and citacyons / And excommuny-cacyons" (324–25) that only Wolsey was empowered to give. Such misuse of power overtaxes and so impoverishes the common man (360–73). But not only the laity are impoverished. Collyn's next subject is the dissolution of religious houses (374–432). Before continuing, he pauses, like the Psalmist, in a brief song of petition:

O mercyfull Jesu,
You supporte and rescue,
My style for to dyrecte,
It may take some effecte!
For I abhorre to wryte
Howe the lay fee despyte
You prelates, that of ryght
Shulde be lanternes of lyght (433–40),

with Collyn returning to the traditional metaphor for the function of bishops. Their betrayal of their office leads him in section four to thoughts of the Crucifixion (449–55) when "He dranke eysell and gall / To redeme us with all" (454–55) but present-day spiritual leaders are content with "swete ypocras" (456). Collyn continues his accusations, noting the misuse of language (486ff.) and scriptural misinterpretations (517–18) which result in heresies (521ff.). Such ambition invites the prelate to wish "To rule kynge and kayser" (604). Collyn concludes with a long section on the actions of heretics encouraged by such an upstart prelate (605–70).

"Yet over all that, / Of bysshoppes they chat" (671–72): the next section contrasts Collyn's positive recommendations to the "lanternes of lyght" (440) by calling on them directly to carry out proper reform:

Ye bysshopes of estates
Shulde open the brode gates
For your spirytuall charge,
And com forthe at large,
Lyke lanternes of lyght,
In the peoples syght,
In pulpyttes autentyke,
For the wele publyke
Of preesthode in this case (690–98).

Collyn provides good examples (737–57) and discusses good preaching (758–80), but just as St. Thomas of Canterbury reminded him of Thomas Wolsey, the antitype, so once again he is reminded, following the form of the colloquy, of bad preaching (796–829), bad friars (830–87), and bad priests subject to bad bishops (887–924), who live, like Wolsey, in excessive palaces (935–69).

Nowe trewly, to my thynkyng,
That is a speculacyon

> And a mete meditacyon
> For prelates of estate,
> Theyr courage to abate
> From worldly wantones,
> Theyr chambres thus to dresse
> With suche perfytenesse
> And all suche holynesse;
> Howbeit they let downe fall
> Theyr churches cathedrall! (970–80).

Once more Collyn has returned to Wolsey—and to Hampton Court this time, and so he makes a fresh start. But "all temporall people" who keep "talkynge and tellynge" (983, 985) will not let Collyn achieve the distance he had earlier. Instead, they remind him that

> It is a besy thynge
> For one man to rule a kynge,
> Alone, and make rekenynge
> To governe over all,
> And rule a realme royall
> By one mannes wytte (989–94).

Now, showing signs of extreme tribulation, Collyn becomes relentless (995–1079). For given the state of the world, he cannot write differently from the way he has (1080–95). He concludes with a disclaimer for good churchmen (1118–29) and a confirmation of his own honesty (1130–50).

At line 1151, Collyn is suddenly interrupted by a stern and tyrannical voice which identifies itself ("us prelates") as Wolsey.

> "Shall they taunt us prelates,
> That be theyr prymates?
> Nat so hardy on theyr pates!
> Harke, howe the losell prates
> With a wyde wesaunt!" (1151–55).

This new voice threatens punishment, a court hearing, and then reviews the charges Collyn has levelled against him, allowing Skelton to repeat once more a number of Wolsey's own crimes.

> "Ye prechers shall be yawde:
> Some shall be sawde,
> As noble Isaias,

The holy prophet, was;
And some of you shall dye,
Lyke holy Jeremy;
Some hanged, some slayne,
Some beaten to the brayne;
And we wyll rule and rayne,
And our matters mayntayne" (1205–14).

Collyn has won his case; he has forced Wolsey to open confession. But perhaps he is also defeated; perhaps he has been taken off to Fleet Prison (1166) or the Tower of London (1168) for we do not hear from him again. Instead, the poet who provided the prologue provides an epilogue, led to conclude that "this is the gyse nowe-a-dayes!" (1228).

Collyn's thoughts, then, in his colloquy with himself, his colloquy with others, and his colloquy with us, are limited to what he witnesses around him. He is no great prophet like Parrot. Conversely, he is not nearly so timid as Drede. Like the Psalmist, who also denounced, pleaded, praised, and oversaw his times from the plain man's perspective, Collyn is deeply aware of the presence and force of the Lord and as a good Tudor Christian he is also deeply aware of God's Word. He can pair passages of Scripture to strengthen his case, from Parrot's examples from 4 Kings 16:10–11 and Exodus 32:1–6 (152) to his own from Matthew 25:31–36 (106–61), Isaias 5:1 (1207), and Hebrews 11:37 (1211ff.). Moreover, Collyn has not lost touch with his Church. A true Englishman, his favorite saint is Thomas à Becket, whom Henry VIII, with the Holy Roman Emperor Charles V at his side, venerated during a special journey to Canterbury in 1520; and in citing three lines from the antiphon *Studens livor Thomas Supplicio* sung at Lauds in the Office to St. Thomas—

Theyr lessons forgoten they have
That Saynt Thomas of Canterbury gave:
Thomas *manum mittit ad forcia,*
Spernit dampna, spernit opprobria;
Nulla Thomam frangit injuria (169–73)—

he may have in mind that Thomas Wolsey has usurped St. Thomas's name and crest and declared himself, in effect, the new St. Thomas of England. The point is doubly ironic; for through his constancy and his fearlessness, Collyn has resembled St. Thomas more than Wolsey has. If we are to assume that Wolsey's interruption in Collyn's colloquies silenced him for

all time, then Wolsey has guaranteed this second association. Collyn's
sense of type and antitype calls to mind the Sequence for the feast of St.
Thomas the Martyr (29 December):

> Let every living soul rejoice,
> And with free voice to Christ sing praise.
> Let Canterbury at this feast
> Devoutly homage pay.
> The furious soldier band
> Shouts forth the tyrant king's command,
> Lawless will and fierce decree
> Forced their way full haughtily.
> Armed men with passion wild
> Places dear to Christ defiled:
> But Christ's footsteps following,
> Thomas with unswerving tread
> Stood unshaken, undismayed,
> In obedience to his King
> Meets the sword with steady eye,
> Counting it all gain to die.
> Thomas, rejoice, thy victory adds a lay
> To swell the praise of Christ's own natal day.

The Mass for St. Thomas—which opens with another Psalmist's plea,
"Hear my voice, O God, in my prayer: preserve my life from fear of the
enemy" (63:2)—like the Offices for his feast day fall within the octave of
Christmas, and so renew the Church's celebration of the Nativity, as
Collyn reiterates in citing the *Letabundus* ("Greatly rejoicing"), one of the
Sequences used at Christmas (248), although here corrupted (249). But
Collyn's attempt to cheer himself up does not work. In time the need to
rejoice recalls the triumphal processional of Christ into Jerusalem, and
Collyn thinks of the *Gloria, laus et honor* (449), the well-known proces-
sional hymn for the Proper of Palm Sunday—and this in turn recalls the
mockery Wolsey, on his mule, makes of Christ's entering Jerusalem (as
told in the day's gospel, Matthew 21:1–9, and prefigured in the day's
lesson, Exodus 15:27–16:10). The Tudor service for Palm Sunday is cen-
tered on just this processional featuring the hymn of praise which Collyn
cites. It begins with hope, when the main celebrant, in a red silk cope,
stands before a gathering of palms and flowers and exorcises and blesses
them. "I exorcise thee, O creature of flowers and leaves, in the name of
God the Father almighty, and in the name of Jesus Christ his Son our

Lord, and in the power of the Holy Ghost. Henceforth all power of the adversary, all the host of the devil, all the strength of the enemy, all assaults of demons, be uprooted and transplanted from this creature of flowers and leaves, that thou pursue not by subtlety the footsteps of those who hasten to the grace of God. Through him who shall come to judge the quick and dead, and the world by fire. Amen." The celebrant then recites the Collect, which recalls the biblical story of Christ's entry on an ass, and, following "*A lantern of light, with an unveiled cross*" picturing precisely Collyn's dilemma, he leads the clergy in a processional around the church, stopping at various stations to continue the dramatic story of Christ's trial and Passion. Initially there is the joyous entry (at the first station) and the appearance of Lazarus (at the second). At this point "*seven boys, from a very elevated position*" sing the *Gloria, laus et honor* to which Collyn twice refers (449, 482). At the third station, the celebrant and his assistants recall the story of the bad priest, Caiaphas, and the mood suddenly grows somber. The choir sings a sobering responsory which we have heard before, in "Against Venemous Tongues":

> Lying men compassed me about; they scourged me without a cause. But do thou, O Lord, my defender, avenge me.
> V. Deliver me from mine enemies, O Lord: defend me from them that rise up against me

(Psalm 58:2). They continue with a solemn Tract in alternation:

> My God, my God, look upon me: why hast thou forsaken me.
> V. And art so far from my health, and from the words of my complaint?
> V. O my God, I cry in the day-time, but thou hearest not: and in the night season also I take no rest.
> R. And thou continuest holy, O thou worship of Israel. Our fathers hoped in thee: they trusted in thee; and thou didst deliver them.
> V. They called upon thee, and were holpen: they put their trust in thee, and were not confounded,

also drawn from Psalms (21:2–6), at which point the deacon prostrates himself, facing East, absorbed in a private Paternoster. Again Collyn is confounded. A burst of hope erupts in grief. He returns, then, to the lantern of light carried on this processional (440, 694) which figures Christ as Saviour. The senior clerk remarks in the course of the service, "Hail, light of the world, king of kings, glory of heaven, with whom abideth dominion, praise and honour, now and for ever"; his source is the

Scripture with which "Collyn Clout" begins—John 8:12. There, immediately following the story of the woman taken in adultery, Christ's proclamation—"I am the light of the world: he that followeth me, walketh not in darkness, but shall have the light of life"—fulfills Old Testament Scripture (Isaias 49:6; 60:1–3).

Thus Collyn's reference to St. Thomas unleashes a whole series of significant ideas that, supported by other references in his poem, allow us to define more precisely his thoughts and attitude. Clearly, for Collyn, St. Thomas, archbishop of Canterbury, was martyred because he would not allow the union of Church and state—he would keep pure the doctrine of Holy Mother Church and her spiritual (rather than her temporal) purpose, falling out with Henry II over the jurisdiction of Church courts. But Thomas Wolsey, an archbishop of York, and St. Thomas' antitype, performs just such an unholy alliance to effect his tyranny and to support his unholy ambition for the papacy. The reference to Palm Sunday, furthermore, reminds us of the betrayal of Christ and of the Church in Christ by those Pharisees of the spirit who only think themselves religiously sanctified and politically loyal.

As the sense of Passion Week with its treachery spreads across the imagery of the poem and through Collyn's thoughts and observations, so he seizes on the salvation represented by the lanterns of light promised by Isaias, proclaimed by Christ, and practiced in one of the Church's seven sacraments. It is the sacrament of *Sicientes* to which Collyn refers (222), that is, the sacrament of ordination when, on a special day outside the four proper days of ordination (the Saturdays in Ember Weeks), bishops admit men to holy orders. Collyn's immediate point is that men like Wolsey crowd all the year's possible occasions into one, thus ignoring the four regularly scheduled times in the Church year. But when we couple this reference with the two references to "lanternes of lyght," we see that such a service can also extend to the consecrations of bishops—like Wolsey. At this sacred service, (1) the candidate is presented as a supplicant, (2) a bidding prayer is said in his behalf, (3) the Book of Gospels is laid on his head and neck while he is prostrate and prayers are said over him, (4) a subsequent prayer refers to him as the servant of all the people, a shepherd and teacher and steward of episcopal grace, (5) the Book of Gospels is removed and he is presented with the Pastoral Staff by which he is to feed his flock, (6) he rises to his feet, ascends to the apse to sit on the bishop's throne, and (7) he partakes in the celebration of the Eucharist. From Collyn's anguished thoughts it is clear that Wolsey has mocked the duties, significance, and spirit circumscribed by his pastoral vows; in short, that he has demeaned himself as the shepherd who lets his flock starve (75–81, attributed as a charge against Wolsey by "Laye men," 75). It is true that Collyn mentions this at the very outset of his report, but Skelton refers to it when he re-enters the poem at the close (1228–38).

But Skelton, if not Collyn, may have a further reference in mind. E. O. James reminds us that "The Christian priesthood . . . is historically a descendant of the divine kingship in its essential elements along three lines of development. In the first place it derives its origin and significance from the royal priesthood of its invisible and divine Author, Who was regarded by His followers as the Spiritual King of the New Israel. Secondly, it was at a very early period associated with the Jewish hierarchy, which had inherited the position formerly occupied by the king in the days of the monarchy. Thirdly, through the papacy and Byzantium, it derived its authority very largely from that of the emperor. This royal descent is brought out clearly in the ordination ritual" (pp. 88–89). "Lanternes of lyght," as a symbol of both Christ, the King of Kings, and the function of bishops, is meant to convey this relationship; Skelton is accusing Wolsey of being both tyrannical cardinal and tyrannical king. It is further underscored by Wolsey's own remarks in the poem when they take on the role of a tyrant who acts first in the temporal realm—

> "Take him, Wardeyn of the Flete,
> Set hym fast by the fete!
> I say, Lieutenaunt of the Toure,
> Make this lurdeyne for to loure;
> Lodge hym in Lytell Ease,
> Fede hym with beanes and pease!
> The Kynges Benche or Marshalsy,
> Have hym thyder by and by!" (1166–73),

referring specifically to those courts Wolsey took over, as well as invoking the tyrannical voice of a latter-day prophet in the spiritual realm: " 'Shall they taunt us prelates, / That be theyr prymates? / Nat so hardy on theyr pates!' " (1151–53). Wolsey's treason is complete. The divided sense of colloquy with which the poem began—like all colloquies in the Mass—is at last resolved into a singular Collect in which we can all participate. The prelate who for Parrot had been Moloch, the Antichrist, is even for the simple plainspoken Collyn, an anti-priest, anti-prelate, and anti-king who stands convicted by his own admissions. As an attack on Wolsey, "Collyn Clout" is even more precise and more detailed than *Speke, Parrot*—and surely more outspoken.

On Whitsunday 1522 Wolsey celebrated the *missa solemnis*, High Mass, before the Holy Roman Emperor Charles V, archduke of Burgundy, in St. Paul's Cathedral, London, with twenty mitred prelates and Charles's courtiers in attendance. When it came time for the ablutions, the country's two leading noblemen, the dukes of Norfolk and Suffolk, served him the water, assisted by two earls and two barons. DeSalino noted in disgust that this splendid service was conducted by "the Pope who is the Cardinal."[21] For Wolsey's ostentation knew no bounds. He probably had not seen *Speke, Parrot* or "Collyn Clout," but it would not have mattered: he was now impervious to criticism. York Place, his palace in London (which in time Henry VIII would take from him and transform into Whitehall) was now the great chamber where he held court in majestic style. "One traverses eight rooms before reaching his audience chamber, and they are all hung with tapestry, which is changed once a week," a visitor reported. Williams adds that the floors were probably covered with damascene carpets that he had "wheedled out of the signory of Venice," concluding that "York Place put Lambeth Palace, renovated by Cardinal Morton, into the shade and it was the finest house owned by a subject since Humphrey, Duke of Gloucester's 'Bella Court' at Greenwich" (p. 55). Now that he had such a fine town residence, Wolsey turned his attention more and more to rebuilding and vastly extending Hampton Court, some twenty miles west of London on the Thames in Surrey. He complained he suffered from the bad air and the polluted water of the city and approved the designs of elaborate piping systems to Hampton Court from the springs at Coombe Hill three miles away. The court itself—another palace—was built around one courtyard where the windows ran sixty-five feet on either side of the gallery, but then everything was on an elaborate scale: the kitchen, for instance, was forty-eight feet long and, on completion, Hampton Court had 280 guest chambers, each with two rooms.[22] The walls of the public rooms were painted in oil with scenes of the Nativity, the Passion, and other events in the life of Christ, while on one occasion, the better to furnish the Clock Tower alone, he purchased twenty-one sets of tapestries, 132 pieces, which displayed, among other subjects, the stories of Hester, Samuel, Tobias, Moses, David, Jacob, Susanna, Judith, Solomon, Christ, and the Virgin Mary—as well as a set that portrayed the allegory of man's pilgrimage of life while others were allegorical scenes of Love, Chastity, Eternity, Death, Time—and Fame.[23] The loyal Cavendish saw all this as a sign of the Cardinal's deep piety. His lord, he tells us, wore hair shirts at all times, for self-mortification, always having three of them packed to take on his travels, and he always wore "a little chain of gold made like a bottle chain with a cross of gold hanging thereat, wherein was a piece of the holy cross (which he wore continually about his neck next his skin)" (p. 106). To his contemporary, Skelton, as to the members of the King's Council, such luxuriousness must have been annoying indeed.

We are not surprised then that Skelton's next poem, "Why Come Ye Nat to Courte?" (late 1522) is even more direct in its bitter attack on Wolsey than "Collyn Clout." It is far simpler and more forceful. The structural principle is also plainer, because Skelton announces it in his incipit and repeats it twice in his opening lines, lines this time addressed to a specified audience. "All noble men, of this take hede, / And beleve it as your Crede" (1–2).[24] In light of Skelton's priestly vows to instruct others in the beliefs of the Church and his precise use of the Creed elsewhere, this directive is not to be taken lightly. His prologue begins with the general state of the world that produces such a replacement of the Nicene Creed as he is about to propose.

> To hasty of sentence,
> To ferce for none offence,
> To scarce of your expence,
> To large in neglygence,
> To slacke in recompence,
> To haute in excellence,
> To lyght of intellegence,
> And to lyght of credence;
> Where these kepe resydence,
> Reson is banysshed thence,
> And also Dame Prudence,
> With sober Sapyence (3–14).

Such fundamental and summary charges concerning selfish, negligent, and ignorant leadership cause him to repeat the damning charge that the Church Creed from the Council of Nicea, in use since the sixth century (as a replacement for the Apostles Creed) and part of the Church's teaching since the eleventh, has been overturned by the practices of this new apostle to the devil: "All noble men [of this take hede, / And beleve it as your Crede]" (15–16). Such general usurpation of principle and duty leads to an antiphonal response in a long versicle that points to specific actions that the poem's context calls not merely political but heretical, such as the execution of Edward Stafford, third Duke of Buckingham, on charges of treason.

> Than without collusyon,
> Marke well this conclusyon:
> Through suche abusyon,
> And by suche illusyon,
> Unto great confusyon
> A noble man may fall,
> And his honour appall;
> And yf ye thynke this shall
> Not rubbe you on the gall,
> Than the devyll take all!
>   [All noble men, of this take hede,
>   And beleve it as your Crede] (17–28).

The closing couplet—"*Hec vates ille, / De quo loquuntur mille*" ("These things [saith] that bard [Skelton] / Of whom a thousand speak"), 29–30, repeated again at the poem's close—has led some scholars to believe that the first thirty lines were circulated separately, perhaps at Buckingham's death, in May 1521; the poem proper, then, begins with a new, slightly longer, colloquy that refines the earlier one. It begins by characterizing the general situation, one marked by both anger and dread. The opening versicle,

> For Age is a page
> For the courte full unmete,
> For Age cannat rage,
> Nor basse her swete swete;

is followed by the response,

> But whan Age seeth that Rage
> Dothe aswage and refrayne,
> Than wyll Age have a corage
> To come to court agayne (31–38).

This same sort of statement-and-reply continues for two more antiphonal exchanges between voices, the one clearly immediate and wrathful and the other more distant and conciliatory.

> But
> Helas, sage Overage
> So madly decayes,
> That Age for dottage
> Is reconed now-adayes: (39–43)

Thus Age—*a graunt domage*—
Is nothynge set by,
And Rage in arerage
Dothe rynne lamentably (44–47)

and

So
That Rage must make pyllage
To catche that catche may,
And with suche forage
Hunte the boskage (48–52),
That hartes wyll ronne away—
Bothe hartes and hyndes,
With all good myndes—
Farewell, than, have a good day! (53–56),

finally being resolved in a Collect that comes as close as such times of heresy will allow to a petition to Christ:

Than, have good daye, adewe!
For defaute of rescew,
Some men may happely rew,
And some theyr hedes mew;
The tyme dothe fast ensew
That bales begynne to brew.
I drede, by swete Jesu,
This tale wyll be to trew—
"In faythe, Dycken, thou krew!" (57–65).

This authentic account of Dicken (that is, the devil) and the crew (the crow or chough on St. Thomas's and Wolsey's crests) will take the form of historical biography—that is, it will literally be a New Creed by supplanting the life of Christ as given in the Nicene Creed with the life of Wolsey as portrayed in the chaos of England under the rule of Dicken. If we recall that tradition assigned a particular part of the Creed to each apostle, moreover—as still pictorially conveyed in the fifteenth-century window at Beverley Minster—then this poem suggests that Wolsey would usurp the Creed by proclaiming himself greater than all the apostles. The poem proceeds by a strategic argument in three parts: (1) it begins with a general statement full of interpretive details to give a concrete and comprehensive view of the present condition of men under the dispensation of the New

Creed; (2) it supplies, through a series of questions and answers, an itinerary of events, often in foreign countries, which are a direct consequence; and, finally, (3) it locates the cause of all these evil acts and crimes in the biography of Dicken, who alone is responsible for them.

Such a tri-partite organization, when Skelton's readers have been aware of it, has puzzled them, but to a nation trained from childhood in the Creed and saying it at least weekly in the Ordinary of the Mass, such organization would have been clear at once in a poem by a priest about a prelate, each of whom would have intoned the Creed at least once daily after taking orders. So would the division of the poem, because it follows the three stages of the catechism that Skelton at Diss (and Wolsey at Redgrave) were obligated to employ in teaching parishioners the Creed. After the Council of Lambeth in 1281 all priests were required to provide such instruction four times a year on feast days, "without any fantastic weaving of subtle adornment." Besides the Creed, on which this poem declares it will concentrate, such instruction included the Paternoster, the Ten Commandments, the seven sacraments, and the seven sins (here treated in lines 573–76), and it might also include the seven acts of mercy, the *Ave*, and the Virgin's Seven Joys and Seven Sorrows. But the Creed remained primary at each of the three stages: at initial instruction before baptism, for example, when Christ laid his hands on the children (Mark 10:16), transformed in this poem to the knowledge of a world under the New Dispensation; a second stage of examination, by question and answer, at the time of baptism, as Christ taught the apostles (John 20:22), in this poem a series of questions about particular events; the third, an adult stage of post-baptismal instruction in "the last and deepest mysteries" involving redemption and sanctification traced to Christ's teaching after the Resurrection (Acts 1:3), now in the poem the deepest mysteries about Wolsey. It is in this manner, Henry Holland says as late as 1606, in *The historie of Adam*, that "in elder ages the babes of Christ were carefully taught the first grounds of Religion: and so being well grounded they were admitted by confirmation and laying on of hands to the Lords Supper" (sig. A3). It is also important to remember that for the Tudors the catechism was conceived not only as the teachings of the Church undergone before full membership but also as subsequent tests of orthodoxy, because this test is what Skelton means to show Wolsey failing dramatically and excessively in the course of the poem.

In Part 1, Skelton addresses Dicken directly (67ff.), with the authority invested in him by the Church and with the Church as first and last recourse by which the chief prelate and author of the New Creed will stand condemned. He finds that under this New Dispensation "There hath ben moche excesse, / With banketynge braynlesse, / With ryotynge rechelesse" (69–71); in the case of the losses at the Calais conference in particular, "Chefe counselour was carlesse, / Gronynge, grouchyng, gracelesse" (78–79). As a result, in Christian terms, the people under their chief pastor suffer. "Our shepe are shrewdly shorne, / And Trouthe is all totorne" (91–92) because rather than guide his life by that of the Saviour, Who, the Old Creed tells us, was miraculously born, served man, and suffered for him, the prelate is instead guided by the single principle of selfish pride. "For Wyll dothe rule all thynge— / Wyll, wyll, wyll, wyll, wyll— / He ruleth alway styll" (104–6), and this leads to a despotism where he who "hathe the strokes alone; / Be it blacke or whight, / All that he dothe is ryght" (113–15). Clear evidence is found in the way he has dealt with the members of the King's Council—William Warham, archbishop of Canterbury; Richard Fox, bishop of Winchester; Thomas Grey, third marquis of Dorset; and Buckingham (119–22). He has usurped his privileges of *legate a latere* by becoming Pope himself, and making his office one inspired by the Devil (thus inverting Christ's mission too):

> From the Pope of Rome,
> To weve all in one lome [loom],
> A webbe of Lylse Wulse [linsey-woolsey],
> *Opus male dulce*—
> The devyll kysse hes cule! (128–32).

Such infernal havoc reaches throughout the north ("From Baumberow to Bothombar," 138) and in the south ("From Croydon into Kent," 144), affecting the Cinque Ports ("From Wynchelsey to Rye," 146) and the defense of Carlisle ("From Wentbridge to Hull / Our armye waxeth dull," 148–49). As antitype to this, there is "Yet the good Erle of Surray, / Of chevalry he is the floure" (152, 158)—"Our Lorde be his soccoure!" (159). For the prelate has traded in his bishopric at Tournai (in 1518) for French crowns and Italian scuti (169), like Judas selling the Church of Christ for pieces of silver. Skelton underlines this inversion of the Old Creed with a vengeance: "With scutis and crownes of golde / I drede we are bought and solde; / It is a wonders warke!" (170–72). Yet it must be acknowledged of one who has "his eyen so dased, / That he ne se can / To know God nor man" (180–82). Thus even at home he undermines justice by arbitrarily extending his power and the power of the Star Chamber where he sits—

"That in the Chambre of Sterres / All maters there he marres" (187–88), now parodying the Resurrection in his arrogant dismissal of God. For he is himself the source of all triumph:

> With braggynge and with bost;
> Borne up on every syde
> With pompe and with pryde,
> With "Trompe up, Alleluya!" (201–4).

Such sinful actions cause him to figure evil as practiced in the Old Testament, by resembling Asmodeus (Tobit 3:8) and by associating with the likes of Delilah (Judges 16), "That wanton damosell" (208–11). The conclusion to all this is obvious.

> *Adew*, Philosophia,
> *Adew*, Theologia!
> Welcome, Dame Simonia,
> With Dame Castrimergia [Gluttony],
> To drynke and for to eate
> Swete ypocras and swete meate! (212–17),

Part 1 ends with this horrible corruption of the Last Supper denoted in the Old Creed.

Part 2 of the poem, rather than examine the catechumen on the Ten Commandments, asks a series of ten quite different questions, the answers to which can only reveal Wolsey's misdeeds and shortcomings—for the focus is on him, not on Church belief or us.

> What newes, what news? (232)
> What here ye of Lancashyre? (246)
> What here ye of Chesshyre? (249)
> What here ye of the Scottes? (261)
> What here ye of the Lorde Dakers [Dacres]? (271)
> What here ye of the Lorde Rose [Ross]? (285)
> What say ye of the Scottysh kynge? (345)
> What here ye of Burgonyons,
> And the Spainyardes onyons? (369–70)
> What here ye of Mutrell [Montreuil]? (376)
> Yet what here ye tell
> Of oure graunde counsell [King's Council]? (378–79)

But "speke ye no more of that, / For drede of the Red Hat" (381–82). For the Cardinal has taken over the realm, so that when the catechumen is asked the ultimate question under the New Dispensation, "'Why come ye nat to court?'" (400), he must understand it is not the King's court, where God has presumably placed his regent, but Hampton Court where true power and majesty reside (401ff.). About this the puzzled student has some doubt, but the instructor is certain—it is *not* the King's court where omnipotence is now found, it is *Hampton* Court. This brief debate within the examination is one of the most wickedly funny parts of the poem.

> "Why come ye nat to court?"
>   To whyche court?
> To the Kynges courte?
> Or to Hampton Court?
>   Nay, to the Kynges court!
> The Kynges courte
> Shulde have the excellence;
> But Hampton Court
> Hath the preemynence,
> And Yorkes Place,
> With my lordes grace,
> To whose magnifycence
> Is all the conflewence,
> Sutys and supplycacyons,
> Embassades of all nacyons (400–14).

This is the place of all petition and the dispensing of all power.

> Strawe for the Lawe Canon,
> Or for the Lawe Common,
> Or for the Lawe Cyvyll!
> It shall be as he wyll:
> Stop at law Tancrete [Tancred's canon law],
> An obstract or a concrete;
> Be it soure, be it swete,
> His wysdome is so dyscrete,
> That in a fume or an hete,
> "Wardeyn of the Flete,
> Set hym fast by the fete!"
> And of his royall powre
> Whan him lyst to lowre,
> Than, "Have him to the Towre,
> *Saunz aulter* remedy;

> Have hym forthe by and by
> To the Marshalsy,
> Or to the Kynges Benche."
> He dyggeth so in the trenche
> Of the court royall,
> That he ruleth them all (415–35).

Still the bewilderment persists—for now all of Skelton's Tudor readers were catechumens being instructed in the causes, conditions, and consequences of the New Creed, not just "All noble men" (1). Thus the last question and answer in Part 2 serve as summary and verification of what has gone before.

> Perceyve the cause why?
> To tell the trouth playnly,
> He is so ambicyous,
> So shamles, and so vicyous,
> And so supersticyous,
> And so moche oblivyous
> From whens that he came,
> That he falleth into *Acrisiam* [blindness]
> Whiche, truly to expresse,
> Is a forgetfulnesse
> Or wylfull blyndnesse,
> Wherwith the Sodomites
> Lost theyr inward syghtes,
> The Gommoryans also
> Were brought to deedly wo,
> As Scrypture recordis:
> *A cecitate cordis*
> (In the Latyne synge we),
> *Lybera nos, Domine!* (458–76).

By sharply juxtaposing the fall of Sodom and Gomorrah, by which God punished blind sinners in the Old Testament (Genesis 19:11), with the current Litany of the Mass ("From blindness of heart . . . Good Lord, deliver us"), Skelton ends Part 2 by triumphantly showing how Wolsey's usurpation of the King's rule and justice has led to a moral blindness by which Wolsey also means to usurp God's teachings to the faithful—and God Himself. Truly, he is the devil incarnate.

Part 3 of the poem is the infernal biography of Wolsey for which the first two parts have prepared us—and we shall see this judgment confirmed by Skelton's figuring Wolsey as a chronic enemy of God, an Amalekite (Exodus 17:8–16; Judges 7:12, 477), and a Mameluke (478), and by condemning him as the antitype to St. Peter (1138), lineal ancestor of the Pope, and St. Dunstan (1146), former archbishop of Canterbury who was the first to work closely with the King in an exemplary union of Church and state. But to put these and the other details of Part 3 into context, we also need to keep in mind the Nicene Creed as the figural pattern in this poem much as Psalm 93 served as the figural pattern for Collyn Clout. The Creed as said in the Ordinary of the Mass is this:

I believe in one God, the Father almighty, Maker of heaven and earth, and of all things, visible, and invisible.

And in one Lord Jesus Christ, the only-begotten Son of God, And begotten of his Father before all worlds: God of God, Light of Light, very God of very God, Begotten not made, being of one substance with the Father, by whom all things were made. Who for us men and for our salvation came down from heaven, And was incarnate by the Holy Ghost of the virgin Mary,

And was made man.

He was crucified also for us under Pontius Pilate, he suffered and was buried. And the third day he rose again according to the scriptures, and ascended into heaven, he sitteth on the right hand of the Father, And he shall come again with glory to judge the quick and the dead, Whose kingdom shall have no end.

And in the Holy Ghost the Lord and giver of life, Who proceedeth from the Father and the Son, Who with the Father and the Son together is worshipped and glorified, Who spake by the prophets. And in one holy Catholic and Apostolick Church. I acknowledge one baptism for the remission of sins, and I look for the resurrection of the dead,

And the life of the world to come. Amen.

Skelton will vary and expand these *clausulae* at will, using his customary wit and wrath, much as liturgical music tropes *clausulae* by importing them into new settings, but the outline given by the Creed will clearly direct Part 3 of the poem as it has remained the implicit reference for the ideas corrupted in Parts 1 and 2. Now the adult, in his post-baptismal renewal of the Creed, will be instructed, for one last time, in the true Creed of the Church by reviewing its inversion in Wolsey's Creed—and thus test his orthodoxy next to Wolsey's heresy.

Skelton begins Part 3 by repeating the present situation in Tudor England.

> But this madde Amalecke,
> Lyke to a Mamelek,
> He regardeth lordes
> No more than potshordes!
> He is in suche elacyon
> Of his exaltacyon,
> And the supportacyon
> Of our soverayne lorde,
> That, God to recorde,
> He ruleth all at wyll,
> Without reason or skyll (477–87).

To understand the state of the world and the condition of men we must, as the Creed teaches, look at the genealogy and life of the man who would be our Saviour.

> Howbeit the primordyall
> Of his wretched originall,
> And his base progeny,
> And his gresy genealogy,
> He came of the *sank royall,*
> That was cast out of a bochers stall (488–93),

not a stable. His birth was less miraculous than that of the One he would displace. But he continues as if he had claim to similar authority, despite his ignorance—for he was not one to teach elders in the temple at the age of twelve (Luke 2:41–51).

> But however he was borne,
> Men wolde have the lesse scorne,
> If he coulde consyder
> His byrth and rowme togeder,
> And call to his mynde
> How noble and how kynde
> To him he hathe founde
> Our sovereyne lorde, chyfe grounde
> Of all this prelacy,
> And set hym nobly
> In great auctoryte,

Out from a low degre,
Whiche he cannat se.
For he was, *parde*,
No doctor of devinyte,
Nor doctor of the law,
Nor of none other saw;
But a poore maister of arte,
God wot, had lytell parte
Of the quatrivials,
Nor yet of trivials,
Nor of philosophy,
Nor of philology,
Nor of good pollycy,
Nor of astronomy,
Nor acquaynted worth a fly
With honorable Haly,
Nor with royall Ptholomy,
Nor with Albumasar,
To treate of any star
Fyxt or els mobyll.
His Latyne tonge doth hobbyll,
He doth but cloute and cobbill
In Tullis faculte,
Called humanyte;
Yet proudly he dare pretende
How no man can him amende.
But have ye nat harde this,
How an one-eyed man is
Well-syghted when
He is amonge blynde men? (494–534).

This is a glorious trope that, in the course of expanding on the text in Luke concerning Jesus' teaching of the elders, manages to touch upon both the star that guided the Magi and on the syphilis from which Wolsey was said to suffer some blindness. It continues with a wonderful exuberance that belies the fact that Skelton was now past sixty and less than a decade from the end of his life. Skelton's joy seems uninfected. It is also boundless: Part 3 says no more than Part 1 or 2, yet it is four times the length. We learn that as Christ depended on the grace of God for His position, so Wolsey depended on Henry VIII's (535ff.). This produced "suche a myracle, / That shall be a spectacle / Of renowme and worldly fame" (566–68), although the infernality of this "miracle" leads to the birth of the seven deadly sins:

> Yet with lewde condicyons cotyd,
> As hereafter ben notyd:
> Presumcyon and vayne-glory,
> Envy, wrath, and lechery,
> Covetys and glotony,
> Slouthfull to do good,
> Now frantick, now starke wode (571–77),

such as the catechumen must recite as part of his lessons. The result is infernal:

> A prelate potencyall,
> To rule under Bellyall,
> As ferce and as cruell
> As the fynd of hell (590–93).

He boasts and blusters like the Mahomet sworn allegiance by pagans in the plays of Corpus Christi (593–637), and conceals the fact that his career began as chaplain to Henry VII when he was seventeen (640–42). In fact, promotion from this lowly position to that of chief counsel can be explained only by witchcraft, a pointed allusion to the many trials against witches and heretics then being conducted near Wolsey's palace, in old St. Paul's.

> It is a wonders case
> That the kynges grace
> Is toward him so mynded,
> And so farre blynded,
> That he cannat parceyve
> How he doth hym disceyve,
> I dought, lest by sorsery,
> Or suche other loselry,
> As wychecraft, or charmyng;
> For he is the kynges derlyng,
> And his swete hart rote,
> And is governed by this mad kote! (656–67).

Digressions follow, in which one analogy is made between Wolsey and the necromancer in Charlemagne's court (682–714) and another between Skelton's biography of Wolsey and Gaguin's biography of Jean Balue (715–48). It should have been instructive that he

> Commyted open trayson
> And against his lorde soverayne;
> Wherfore he suffred payn,
> Was hedyd, drawen and quartered,
> And dyed stynkingly marterd (736–40)—

but Wolsey has not learned from such examples (755–70) despite God's warning to Henry VIII (750–54; 771–82). Rather, when John Meautis descends to Hell (800), it is not to harrow it but "To purvey for our cardynall / A palace pontifycall, / To kepe his court provyncyall" (810–12). "It is a playne recorde / That there wantys grace" (847–48). Meanwhile, back on earth, there is folly (850–72), there is sport (873–98), and there is luxury at Hampton Court (900–904) that put to shame—and that hurt— the burghers of London (899–951). "I wolde he were somwhere ellys" (962). Indeed, the idea of Wolsey remaining in Hell, rather than passing through it to join the Father in Heaven, so captivates Skelton's imagination that he descants on it at some length (972–93)—why, "he wolde breke the braynes / Of Lucyfer in his chaynes, / And rule them echone / In Lucyfers trone. / I wolde he were gone" (989–92). But he is not; lacking "dyscretyon" and "sober dyrectyon" (1007–08) he instead keeps "the commune welth" (1023)

> But tatterd and tuggyd,
> Raggyd and ruggyd,
> Shavyn and shorne,
> And all thredebare worne (1025–28).

While Wolsey would agree that the commonwealth of England is suffering, he would blame preachers who have condemned him "Shewynge him Goddis lawis" (1053–68), and would rise against the very Church he heads (1069–77), threatening excommunication (1078–81). Yet Wolsey disregards the regulations governing Lent with a show of gluttony (1083–87); he dissolves monasteries ("all privileged places / He brekes and defaces" [1088–89]); he seizes control of St. Albans Abbey (1096–99); and he usurps the Great Seal (1101–06).

> Yet, whan he toke first his hat,
> He said he knew what was what;
> All justyce he pretended,

> All thynges sholde be amended,
> All wronges he wolde redresse,
> All injuris he wolde represse,
> All perjuris he wolde oppresse;
> And yet this graceless elfe,
> He is perjured himselfe (1107–15).

Wolsey's biography-as-sinner shows how he usurped the archbishop of Canterbury

> To whom he was professed
> In thre poyntes expressed:
> The fyrst, to do him reverence;
> The seconde, to owe hym obedyence;
> The thirde with hole affectyon
> To be under his subjectyon.
> But now he maketh objectyon,
> Under the protectyon
> Of the kynges Great Seale,
> That he setteth never a deale
> By his former othe,
> Whether God be pleased or wroth (1120–31).

To the contrary, Wolsey considers himself "equivalent / With God omnip-otent" (1134–35). Yet the prelate should instead be mindful of the position of St. Peter on whose annual feast day (29 June) he recites the story of Christ's special recognition (Matthew 16:13–19), the gospel lesson of the Proper to which the choir sang a joyful Sequence:

> O jocund band, sing forth melodious praise
> with symphonies conjoining rhythmic words;
> With special strains chant those true lights of heaven,
> who cast their golden gleams o'er all the world,
> Whose trophies flourish in the courts above,
> this bright day may their merit sins absolve.
> Upon each head a chaplet shines of triumph,
> one o'er the cross, the other o'er the sword.
> Victorious now, beyond the stars on high
> they stand superior in the heavenly realm.
> Hence by thy word, O blessed Peter, thou
> the mighty door of heaven dost shut and ope.

With favour now receive our faithful vows,
unloosing all the thraldom of our sin.

Yet even so great a man as St. Peter, the first pope, possessed a humility lacking in Wolsey. Skelton now inserts a corrective capsule biography into the larger life of Wolsey.

> The Apostyll Peter
> Had a pore myter
> And a poore cope
> Whan he was creat pope
> First in Antioche;
> He dyd never approche
> Of Rome to the See
> Weth suche dygnyte (1138–45)

as Wolsey maintains. Even closer to home is St. Dunstan—whose relics in Skelton's day took pilgrims in the opposite directions of Canterbury and Glastonbury—whose "golden age" as archbishop of Canterbury in concordance with King Edgar had produced, at a congress of secular and ecclesiastical rulers at Winchester, the *Regularis concordia* for England based on Continental customaries. He is yet another corrective model. But St. Dunstan was especially known for celibacy, for fasting, and for justice—just those things Skelton finds lacking in Wolsey—and in the Proper of the Mass for his feast day (19 May), in which the Gradual praises him for serving "the order of Melchisedech," the gospel was Matthew 25:14–23, still another lesson for Wolsey in Christ's parable of the talents.

> Saynt Dunstane, what was he?
> "Nothynge," he sayth, "lyke we:
> There is a dyversyte
> Bytwene him and me;
> We passe hym in degre,
> As *legatus a latere!*" (1146–51).

Instead, Wolsey corrupts the lesson from the Confessor Bishop Mass (a movable feast, line 1152) and canon law and the law of the provincial synods of Canterbury and his own York (1156–60). But rather than figure St. Peter or St. Dunstan, in whose names he as priest might pray, he figures Naaman the Syrian, archenemy of Israel (4 Kings 5), a leper who suggests Wolsey's own syphilitic—and spiritual—blindness given by the hand of God (1165–73) or "proude Antiochus" IV, a tyrant against the early Jews, who does not receive mention in the Scripture at all (1174). Rather, Wolsey "setteth God apart" (1179) and at the moment of his physical suffering, unlike Christ, he turns to a local doctor, Balthasar de Guercis, surgeon to Catherine of Aragon, to heal his afflictions (1181–1200). "God sende him sorowe for his sinnes!" (1200). Given such evil, who can wonder that the New Creed resembles the chaotic condition of Juvenal's Rome, which Skelton has seemed to imitate (1201–14)? Like Juvenal (*Satires* 1, 30), "*Quia difficile est / Satiram non scribere!*" (1215–16). After a short digression comparing his own work to Juvenal's (1216b–50), Skelton concludes with an Epitome (1–27)[25] and a Decasticon (1–10), which once more present capsule biographies of Wolsey, modelled on an inverted Creed. The latter is briefer and even more comprehensive.

> Proh, dolor, ecce, maris lupus, et necquissimus ursus,
> Carnificis vitulus, Britonumque bubulous iniquus,
> Conflatus vitulus vel Oreb, vel Salmane vel Zeb,
> Carduus, et crudelis Asaphque Datan reprobatus,
> Blandus et Acchitophel regis, scelus omne Britannum,
> Ecclesias qui namque Thomas confundit ubique,
> Non sacer iste Thomas, sed duro corde Goleas,
> Quem gestat mulus—Sathane, cacet, obsecro, culus
> Fundens asphaltum, precor! Hunc versum lege cautum!
> Asperius nihil est misero quum surget in altum.[26]

Thus the entire New Creed is brilliantly condensed: Wolsey's symbolic name ("wolf-of-the-sea"), his parentage ("bull-calf of a butcher"), his Old Testament prefigurations in Oreb, Zeb, and Salmana (from *Speke, Parrot*, 116–17), as well as the rebels Dathan (Numbers 16) and Achitophel (2 Kings 16:23), his usurping the crest of St. Thomas the Martyr (from "Collyn Clout," 169–74) but whose actions, even when riding a mule like Christ, are Goliardic in appearance, and therefore ludicrous. The New Creed, then, is not addressed to Our Father, but to that Father of Evil, Satan, whose arse Wolsey kisses in his infernality in the same way that the priest kisses the Host and Chalice. Wolsey will descend to Satan rather than ascend to God in Heaven; and his world without end could not be more cruel. Yet by making this condemnation, Skelton serves his Church in a tradition that started with St. Paul's instruction to catechumens in Galatia twenty-three years after the Ascension of Christ:

. . . let him that is instructed in the word, communicate to him that instructeth him, in all good things.

Be not deceived, God is not mocked.

For what things a man shall sow, those also shall he reap. For he that soweth in his flesh, of the flesh also shall reap corruption. But he that soweth in the spirit, of the spirit shall reap life everlasting (Galatians 6:6–8).

Both for men of corruption and for men of the Holy Spirit, the Holy Bible is the only source of instruction, and the catechism and grace promulgated by the historic, truly apostolic Holy Mother Church are the only means of instruction and comfort. But Wolsey seems blind to what every child of the Church is taught from the beginning.

Just as witty and certainly as energetic as "Why Come Ye Nat to Courte?" is Skelton's other major Westminster poem, "The Tunnyng of Elynour Rummyng": *"pean sua plectra sonando Materiam risus cantabit carmine rauco"* ("My paean, sounding its lyre, / Will sing the substance of laughter in raucous song," as Kinsman translates the closing Quatrain, 3–4). Through the centuries it has been—and deservedly so—Skelton's most famous poem. Yet we do not know when it was written. Some lines are similar to earlier Westminster poems, like the flytings "Against Garnesche" (?1514) and the flyting "Vilitissimus Scotus Dundas" (late 1516),[27] yet Skelton likes to repeat rhymes from one poem to another, with a penchant for particular vowel sounds (like *ou, ow*), neologisms, monosyllabic words that can be intoned as in plainsong, and long leashes, of dimeters and trimeters especially. John Harvey's discovery in the Court Rolls of the manor of Packenescham of an actual Alianora Romyng, "a common Tippellar of ale" (*"communis tiplar cervicie"*) of the Running Horse in Leatherhead, Surrey, who was fined twopence on 18 August 1525 for selling ale "at excessive price and by small measures," suggests it may have been Skelton's last major effort in Westminster. Yet we do not know when this Alianora Rummyng first began working as an alewife;[28] the pub is still operating, at the foot of a hill beside the River Mole. Edwards, following Brie's metrical tests, relates the poem to "Collyn Clout" and dates it around 1522 (pp. 122–23), and it is also true that three major themes in "Elynour Rummyng" are gluttony, witchcraft, and despotism—charges, as we have just seen, levelled against Wolsey in "Collyn Clout" (205–19, 249–61, 1166–1227) and "Why Come Ye Nat to Courte?" (662–67, 693–714, 800, 820, 1083–87, 1107–15, 1120–31, 1179–1200).[29] In addition,

Leatherhead is only six miles south of Hampton Court, and geographically then as now associated with it.[30]

"The Tunnyng of Elynour Rummyng" is the portrait of an early Tudor alehouse and the narrative of the alewife Elynour who makes her own brew with the aid of chicken dung, taking as payment anything her large degenerate crowd of women will give her, including pledges to pay later. The poem is also a narrative of her customers, who arrive one by one but stay for a drunken melée; the poet breaks off his poem only when a particularly fastidious customer, asking for additional credit, catches sight of all the goods of others that Elynour has collected and stashed under her bed.

The work opens with the portrait of the alewife.

> Tell you I chyll,
> If that ye wyll,
> A whyle be styll,
> Of a comely gyll
> That dwelt on a hyll;
> But she is not gryll,
> For she is somwhat sage
> And well worne in age,
> For her vysage
> It woldt aswage
> A mannes courage. . . .
>   And this comely dame,
> I understande, her name
> Is Elynour Rummynge,
> At home in her wonnynge;
>   And as men say,
> She dwelt in Sothray
> In a certayne stede
> Bysyde Lederhede.
> She is a tonnysh gyb;
> The devyll and she be syb (1–11, 91–100).

Nearly from the start, the poem begins to fill with her customers, who flock to her alehouse for more of her "noppy ale" (102) than they can quite manage.

> Come whoso wyll
> To Elynoure on the hyll,

With "Fyll the cup, fyll!"
And syt there by styll,
Erly and late.
Thyther cometh Kate,
Cysly and Sare,
With theyr legges bare,
And also theyr fete
Hardely full unswete;
With theyr heles dagged,
Theyr kyrtelles all to-jagged,
Theyr smockes all to-ragged,
With tytters and tatters,
Brynge dysshes and platters,
With all theyr myght runnynge
To Elynour Rummynge
To have of her tunnynge;
She leneth them on the same,
And thus begynneth the game (113–32).

Although "Some have no mony / That thyder commy, / For theyr ale to pay—/ That is a shreud aray!" (160–63), she allows them to barter freely. "In stede of coyne and monny, / Some brought her a conny, / And some a pot with honny, / Some a salt, and some a spone, / Some their hose, some their shone" (244–48), and some, in time, things they have filched from their husbands—or even sacred things, such as a wedding ring and Rosary beads. In the end, "Suche were there menny / That had not a penny" (611–12), "Neyther gelt nor pawne" (610), but, when they are able to stagger to their feet, Elynour has a solution for that too. "But, whan they shulde walke, / Were fayne with a chalke / To score on the balke / Or score on the tayle" (613–16). This, however, distresses Skelton. "God gyve it yll hayle, / For my fyngers ytche! / I have wrytten to mytche / Of this mad mummynge / Of Elynour Rummynge" (617–21). But just why he stops so abruptly and just what so disturbs him are questions that the poem invites us to consider.

However unlike Skelton's other late work this poem may appear to be, it is not a poem without precedent for his Tudor audience. A whole host of Goliardic poems deal with toping; Chaucer's parson preaches on it; Brant attacks it in his *Narrenschiff* (ch. 16); Elynour's grotesque counterpart had appeared in Lydgate's translation of de Deguileville's *The Pilgrimage of the Life of Man* (12750–64). Skelton's poem is also related to the late medieval sub-genre of poems on "Good Gossips" and "Ale-wives," "a form," R. H. Robbins tells us, "that extends from the pre-Kinsey outspokenness of a gaggle of ten matrons belittling their husbands' uxorial prowess to the black satire of the founding of a mythical order of drunkards," as found in the Goliardic poets.[31] Maurice Pollet has also called attention to significant similarities in narrative technique, names, conversation, and situation between "Elynour Rummyng" and "The Gossips Meeting," an anonymous poem printed by Thomas Wright from a manuscript of the fifteenth century in which the chief gossip is Elynore; others include Joan, Margery, Alis, and Cecely; and the poet, first stating his theme and subject in mock apology ("I shall you tell a full good sport, / How gossippis gader the*m* on a sort," st. 1), goes on to emphasize the gifts brought by the gossips to the tavern, the quality of the wine, and the drunken determination to remain joyous. Elynore swears "by the rode!" (st. 11), Anne remarks, "Wold God I had do*n* aft*er* yo*ur* covnsell, / For my husbond is so fell / He betith me lyk*e* the devill of hell" (st. 14) to which Alis replies, "God geve hy*m* short lyff" (st. 15).[32]

Gluttony is Skelton's initial concern too, but given Skelton's genius his poem figures much more. We have only to recall *The Ayenbite of Inwyt* ("Remorse of Conscience"), popular with the Tudors, in which gluttony is broadly interpreted to cover not merely intemperate eating and drinking, where man makes his belly his god, but also sins of the tongue—evil speech and blasphemy.[33] Elynour herself is guilty of this in her terrible trivialization of the Passion:

> Elynour swered, "Nay,
> Ye shall not bere awaye
> Myne ale for nought,
> By hym that me bought!" (164–67),

her oath later repeated by the alewife ("She swereth by the Rode of Rest," 271) and by her customers ("By Chryst," sayde she, "thou lyest; / I have as swete a breth / As thou, with shamefull deth!," 344–46). For Brant, the tavern also became the place for copulation, and this idea also occurs to Elynour, as she boasts at some length.

> "Behold," she sayd, "and se
> How bright I am of ble!
> Ich am not cast away,
> That can my husband say,
> Whan we kys and play

> In lust and in lykyng.
> He calleth me his whytyng,
> His mullyng and his mytyng,
> His nobbes and his conny,
> His swetyng and his honny,
> With "Bas, my prety bonny,
> Thou art worth good and monny."
> This make I my falyre fonny,
> Tyll that he dreme and dronny;
> For after all our sport,
> Than wyll he rout and snort;
> Thus swete togither we ly,
> As two pygges in a sty" (217–34)—

like the hogs, in fact, that suggestively roam with the women about the alehouse itself, "The swyne eate my draffe! / Stryke the hogges with a clubbe, / They have dronke up my swyllyng tubbe!" (171–73). Indeed, Langland could locate deadly sins in a tavern in *Piers Plowman* (Passus 5), and we are reminded of Chaucer's Pardoner's Tale, while in 1522 Skelton's fellow Catholic Thomas More was seeing gluttony as God's own token of death itself in his "Treatyce [on] the last thynges":

> If god would neuer punish glotony, yet bringeth it punishment ynoughe, wth it self: it disfigureth the face, discoloreth the skin, & disfashioneth the body, it maketh the skin tawny, the body fat & fobby, the face drowsy, the nose droppyng, the mouth spetting, the eyen blered, the teth rotten, the breth stinkyng, the hāds trimbling, the hed hāging, and the feete totteryng, & finally no part left in right course and frame. And beside the daylye dulnes and grief y^t the vnwieldy body feleth, by the stuffing of his paunch so ful, it bringeth in by leysour, the dropsy, the colike, the stone, the strangury, ye gout, the cramp, the paulesy, the pocks, the pestilence, and the apoplexy, disseases and sicknes of such kinde, y^t either shortly destroy vs, or els ye worse is, kepe vs insuch pain and tormēt, that the lenger we liue the more wretched we be.[34]

This may also be in Skelton's mind when he suggests that "A man wolde have pytty" (39) to see women like Elynour, "Her eyen gowndy / Are full unsowndy, / For they are blered; / And she gray-hered, / Jawed lyke a jetty" (34–38), while her alcoholic customers are "A sorte of foule drabbes / All scurvy with scabbes" (139–40).

Yet there is also more exuberance in Skelton's poem than in More's grim essay on God's tokens; the portraits, while grotesque, are also extremely *funny*. The high humor and indulgent wit are infectious—and this goes far to explain why this poem, above all others, has kept Skelton's poetry alive through the centuries and made him so popular with so many. Such portraits as Skelton impishly gives us here may be based on some of his own parishioners at Diss as well as on the regular customers boozing their nights away at The Running Horse, a raucous enterprise near enough to Wolsey and to Hampton Court. But they surely take their tone too from the strain of Goliardic parody that we find throughout Skelton's work, as well as from the grotesques that cavorted around the painted walls and carved pillars at parish churches such as the aisle parapets still extant at Skelton's parish church at Diss. Anticipating the later grotesquerie in early Shakespeare or in Thomas Nashe, Skelton's poem grows out of the sheer joy of poetry, the sheer joy of its strident denunciation—and reminds us pointedly that, because we indulge in such joy (as we do in pity), we should indulge in allowing, if not committing, sin. For it is also the joy of the borders of the Ormesby Psalter that nevertheless decorate liturgical texts of high seriousness; as Ecclesiasticus tells us—and Skelton—that to be merry and joyful may be an important part of human nature, yet such a perspective by itself is incomplete (2:1).

So when Skelton goes on to report that Elynour is also "gumbed,

> Fyngered and thumbed,
> Gently joynted,
> Gresed and anoynted
> Up to the knockles,
> The bones [of] her huckels
> Lyke as they were with buckels
> Togyder made fast (41–47),

he provides a ceremonial atmosphere surrounding Elynour's alehouse, which is also meant to remind us of the ale celebrations connected with Holy Mother Church. This fundamental connection had existed since early medieval times, when monastic houses served as accommodations for pilgrims and gave them food and drink. In Skelton's day one hostelry in nearby Southwark, just across the river, bore the sign of the "Three Brushes," recalling the holy-water brushes used in the *asperges* at the beginning of the Mass, while such brushes joined to ale-poles like Elynour's (525) constituted the most common signs for alehouses. But ale and churches went together during the early Tudor period; Church-ales were so common, in fact, that Skelton must have participated in a good number of them, perhaps "re-anointing" himself. Many of these celebrations were connected to sacraments of the Church, such as the Christening Ales at the time of baptismal rites and Bride Ales which followed the sacrament of matrimony. There were Give Ales to honor a donor's bequests and Parish Ales to celebrate a patron saint. And there were Wakes, where, Frederick Hackwood notes, village and city parishioners from the time of King Edgar on, at

> the birthday of the saint whose relics were deposited in their parish church, came together and made booths of the trees adjoining the church, and in them celebrated the feast with thanksgiving and prayer. Says an old author, they came "to churche with candellys burnyng, and would wake and come toward night to the church in their devocion." . . . Certain it is that as these Wakes or Watch-night festivals fell away from the original purpose of their institution, they became more popular in the sense that they afforded unbridled opportunities for the drinking of enormous quantities of ale—opportunities of which each parish in turn availed itself to invite its neighbours to patronise its special brew, then and there to take a willing tribute of them in the sale of Wake ale.[35]

Tudor canon law, which regulated against drunkenness and debauchery of the kind we see develop in the course of "The Tunnyng of Elynour Rummyng," existed uneasily alongside local regulations that saw Church-ales as lucrative fund-raising events for the local parish.

> The parishioners of Evertoon [Elveston] and those of Okebrook [Ockbrook] in Derbyshire agree jointly to brew four ales, and every ale of one quarter of malt, between this and the feast of St. John the Baptist next coming, and every inhabitant of the said town of Okebrook shall be at the several ales; and every husband and his wife shall pay twopence, and every cottager one penny. And the inhabitants of Elverton shall have and receive all the profits comming of the said ales, to the use and behoof of the church of Elverton; and the inhabitants of Elverton shall brew eight ales betwixt this and the feast of St. John, at which ales the inhabitants of Okebrooke shall come and pay as before rehearsed; and if any be away one ale, he is to pay at t'oder ale for both.[36]

There were also numerous Whitsun Ales and Clerk Ales where church-wardens were responsible for buying or receiving presents of malt with which to brew a quantity of drink; in some parishes there was a Church house where spits and cooking utensils were stored along with the vessels for brewing, in the sort of room that we see in Elynour's alehouse (189–210).

But however popular such traditions, which are associated with peasants like Elynour and her customers, they were not universally condoned. Priests like Skelton commonly spoke out against such occasions when behavior grew self-indulgent and excessive, as it does in Skelton's poem. In addition, "In the literature of the medieval English pulpit," Owst writes, "the tavern and the ale-house, apart from the acknowledged fact that they are the occasion of much gluttony and drunkenness in the ordinary way, stand for a very definite menace to the common weal. They have established themselves as deadly rivals to the ordinances of the Church, to the keeping of holydays and fast days, above all to attendance at divine service" (p. 435). Master Robert Rypon of Durham, for instance, complains that "in this time of Lent, when by the law and custom of the Church men fast, very few people abstain from excessive drinking: on the contrary, they go to the taverns, and some imbibe and get drunk more than they do out of Lent," adding,

> Most of all on feast days, also for the nights following, they go off to the taverns, and more often than not seek food such as salt beef or a salted herring to excite a thirst for drink. At length they get so intoxicated that they fall to ribaldries, obscenities and idle talk, and sometimes to brawls, by reason of which they fight amongst themselves, sometimes mutilating and killing each other. Such ill deeds, in truth, follow from drunkenness and gluttony.[37]

Owst cites other examples from Bishop Brunton of Rochester, John Waldeby of Oxford, and the Dominican John Bromyard (pp. 435–36). Clearly, it is this undisciplined outgrowth of Church-ales that Skelton has in mind when he introduces Elynour and her alehouse by noting that she especially

> . . . thynketh herselfe gaye
> Upon the holy daye,
> Whan she doth her aray,
> And gyrdeth in her gytes
> Stytched and pranked with pletes;
> Her kyrtell Brystowe red,
> With clothes upon her hed

That wey a sowe of led,
Wrythen in wonder wyse
After the Sarasyns gyse,
With a whym-wham
Knyt with a trym-tram
Upon her brayne-pan,
Lyke an Egypcyan
Lapped about (65–79).

That she finds Turkish and gypsy clothing appropriate for celebrating holy days suggests not merely ignorance or self-indulgence, but blasphemy and, worse, heresy. Furthermore, a passage in a well-known manual that circulated widely among the early Tudors, *The Book of Vices and Virtues*, argues that

> þe grete swetnesse þat þe contemplatif herte haþ and feleþ bi þe
> ȝifte of wisdom in þis dedli lif nys but a litle taste wher-by men han
> sauour and felen how God is swete and softe, and who-so tasteþ þe
> sauour of þe wyne er men drynken þer-of a ful drauȝht; but þei
> schulle see & come to þat gret tauerne where þat þe tunne is made al
> comune. Þ^t is in the life wiþouten ende, where þe wyne of loue, of
> pees, and of ioie and solas schal be ȝeue so largeliche to euery wiȝt
> þt comeþ þider þat all schul be fulfilled, as þe Sauter seiþ, þat al þe
> desire of þe herte schal be fulfilled whan God schal make aliȝht vpon
> his frendes a streme of pees, as þe prophete seiþ, wher-wiþ þei
> schulle be alle as drunken.[38]

Realizing that Church-ales resemble the sacrament of Holy Eucharist, we see the point Skelton has been making all along: Elynour and her customers are not merely congregating at a local alehouse for pleasure; they are not only attending a mock Church-ale; they are also holding a mock Mass.

This too was a traditional charge among Tudors—and the chief reason that Goliardic poetry was so despicable to many of them. As early as 1325, Walter Reynolds, archbishop of Canterbury, condemned riotous feasts celebrated after Mass precisely because they blasphemed the holiest of the sacraments. "Among all sacrifices the greatest is the mystical Sacrament of the Body and Blood of Christ. This oblation surpasses every other. It must, therefore, be offered to God with a pure conscience, and received with true devotion, and preserved with the utmost reverence. But alas! the sons of feasting and of gluttony, whose God is their belly, long since introduced into the holy Church this abuse, that immediately after they have received the Lord's Body on Easter Day, they have served to them unconsecrated bread and wine, and there sit down eating and drinking as in a tavern,—a source of many disorders."[39] It is for this reason that Langland has Gluttony enter a pub on the way to confession; or when Beton the Brewestere asks him where he is going, he replies "To holi cherche . . . to here Masse."[40] For early Tudor priests like Skelton, Mirk's *Instructions for Parish Priests* made it clear that gluttony, when it affected the reception or retaining of the Eucharist, is the most serious of sins:

> Hast þou I-synget in glotorye?
> Telle me, sone, baldelye.
> Hast þow ete wyth syche mayn,
> Þat þow has caste hyt vp a-gayn?
> Hast þow wyþ suche vomysment
> I-cast vp a-ȝayn þe sacrament? (1313–18).[41]

Although the Tudor communicant took only the Host, and did not drink from the Holy Chalice, Mirk makes a point of that too, arguing that priests must make this known:

> Teche þem þenne, neuer þe later,
> Þat in þe chalys ys but wyn & water
> That þey receyueth for to drunke
> After that holy hoselynge (250–53).

Gluttony, then, is one of the most serious of sins as well as one of the most deadly, because it directly interferes with participation in the Eucharist and excludes the communicant from the celebration of the Last Supper, the very Canon of the Holy Mass itself, and some of the most frightening (and popular) legends and stories of Skelton's day were of drunken men and women who, when dying, were damned because they were unable to receive the final sacrament.

The clues that Skelton's poem is meant to be a Goliardic topers' Mass or mock Mass are everywhere: "Now truly, to my thynkynge, / This is a solempne drunkynge" (547–48). Elynour, the high priestess, is a devil or witch practicing *maleficium*: "The devyll and she be syb" (100). She is dressed like a Turk or gypsy, we recall, in "Her huke of Lyncole grene," the devil's color (56), with "Her kyrtell Brystowe red" mocking the liturgical color of the vestments for Passion Week and Whitsunday (70); as her brewing (187–210) mocks Christ's first miracle at Cana (John 2:1–11) and its prefiguration of the Last Supper (John 2:4), so her preparations—

"God gyve it yll prevynge, / Clenly as yvell chevynge!" (185–86)—mock ablutions and Communion—

> For, I may tell you,
> I lerned it of a Jewe
> Whan I began to brewe,
> And I have found it trew (207–10).

Such burlesque or parody continues with her resurrection and blessing of "dronken Ales" (351), who as

> . . . she was drynkynge,
> She fell in a wynkynge
> With a barly-hood—
> She pyst where she stood.
> Than began she to wepe,
> And forthwith fell on-slepe.
> Elynour toke her up,
> And blessed her with a cup
> Of newe ale in cornes;
> Ales founde therin no thornes,
> But supped it up at ones:
> She founde therein no bones (370–81),

as the reference to "thornes" in the midst of this mock Crucifixion and salvation reminds us. And it is repeated in still a second curse:

> There came an old rybybe:
> She halted of a kybe,
> And had broken her shyn
> At the threshold comyng in,
> And fell so wyde open
> That one might se her token,
> The devyll thereon be wroken!
> What nede all this be spoken?
> She yelled lyke a calfe!
> "Ryse up, on Gods halfe."
> Sayd Elynour Rummyng,
> "I beshrew the for thy cummyng!" (492–503).

Indeed, her customers mobbing in one after another (118ff.) resemble the Church processional as well as another Church celebration, the Beating of the Bounds, when clergy and choristers and other Church officials led the parish about the Church property for a periodic inspection followed by a Church-ale. Here, however, the infernal occasion is signified by the grotesqueness of the entire ritual:

> Some wenches come unlased,
> Some huswyves come unbrased,
> With theyr naked pappes,
> That flyppes and flappes,
> It wygges and it wagges
> Lyke tawny saffron bagges—
> A sort of foule drabbes
> All scurvy with scabbes. . . .
> Some loke strawry,
> Some cawry-mawry—
> Full untydy tegges,
> Lyke rotten egges.
> Such a lewde sorte
> To Elynour resorte
> From tyde to tyde.
> Abyde, abyde (133–40, 149–56).

They come to a mock confessional, and to be communicants in an Offertory of various goods—some frivolous, some vital, some stolen, and some sacred—holding them up, indiscriminately, we are told, "To offer to the ale-pole" (525) or "To offer to the ale tap" (286). It is, in fact, the surrendering of these symbolic tokens of their worship (and their souls) on which Skelton spends so much time in the poem, but Theodor Klauser, in a recent study of Church liturgy, points out that just such an Offertory was central to the act of worship.

> In Christian antiquity, it had been the custom for the faithful to lay an "offering" on the altar or to hand it over at the altar rails at each celebration of the eucharist. In part these were gifts, such as bread, wine, oil, and wax, which were found of use in making preparations for the eucharist or for the other sacramental actions. Partly, also, these were gifts to help towards the support of the clergy or the charitable work of the congregation. We should not be surprised, therefore, if the sources for our knowledge of the offertory procession in the early centuries mention cheese, poultry, and other gifts in kind. All of these gifts (those used specifically at the celebration of

the eucharist, as well as those destined for the support of the clergy and for the works of charity of the congregation) were looked upon as being a contribution to the sacrifice; and in the offering of these gifts one could see how each member of the congregation expressed concretely his intention of taking an active part in the sacrifice, and of making an offering of his very self.[42]

Skelton speaks directly to this tradition when he describes Margery Mylke-Ducke's contribution:

> A cantell of Essex chese
> Was well a fote thycke,
> Full of magottes quycke;
> It was huge and greate,
> And mighty stronge meate
> For the devyll to eate;
> It was tart and punyete.
> Another sorte of sluttes:
> Some brought walnuttes,
> Some apples, some peres,
> Some brought theyr clyppyng sheres,
> Some brought this and that,
> Some brought I wote nere what (429–41),

while, more ominously, another brings "Her hernest gyrdle, her wed-dynge rynge" (280) and "Another brought her bedes," her Rosary (523), to give to Elynour. Given such unholy an occasion, we cannot wonder that

> Some lothe to be espyde,
> Some start in at the backe syde,
> Over the hedge and pale,
> And all for the good ale (262–65).

For even to them Elynour "semed to be a wytch" (458), associated, as witches were, with the witch's customary "unset leke" in which she sees only "vertue" (451).

The "tunnyng," or brew, which Elynour serves, in short, is witch's brew, and her "tunnyng," or celebration—in this punning title—is a witch's or devil's Sabbath. "Visually," Deborah Baker Wyrick writes of Elynour, "she is the archetype of the *maleficus*: her old, furrowed, hooked-nosed, hairy face frightens men with its 'lothely lere' (9–38). In addition, she is 'greased and annoynted' (43) and 'smered wyth talowe' (88)," perhaps indicating "the witch's practice of lathering herself with magic unguent in order to fly to the sabbath. . . . One suspects that Elynour is being set up as a heretical celebrant of an inverted religious rite."[43] Owst adds that *The Ayenbite of Inwyt* "pictures the tavern as the Devil's School, where his disciples study, also as the Devil's Chapel, where his services are held and his special miracles wrought" (p. 438); "The taverne is a dich to thieves, and the dyeules castel vor to werri God and his halȝen [saints]; and tho thet the tavernes sustyeneth byeth velaȝes [companions] of alle the zennen [sins] that byeth ydo ine hare tavernes."[44] Another manuscript sermon likens a bittern to the "glotons sittynge in the taverne, puttynge hire mouthes into the bolle, til thei ben drunke. Thenne thei crien with grete voice, boostynge, swerynge, lyynge and slaunderynge, and al hire evele dedes which thei have doun of many ȝeres afore freschli rehercynge and reioisynge. But suche men sittynge in the drie cherche bi hire confessour, fer fro the taverne, for to schryve her synnes, sitten as dombe and wolen speke no word."[45] Skelton may also have in mind such sects as The Brethren of the Free Spirit who "held that Satan participated in the divine essence," according to Deanesly. "They were sometimes known as Luciferans and practised horrible and debased rites at the initiation of novices. They persisted from the late thirteenth century till the Reformation" (pp. 218–19). Indeed, we recall the wall paintings of just such witch's or devil's Sabbaths in various parish churches in Norfolk—some of them painted on the west walls, so that parishioners would have their backs to them during the celebration of the Mass. Norfolk also had its convicted witches, as in the celebrated case of Margery Backster, wife of a carpenter of Martham, who had been condemned by the Bishop of Norwich.[46] In referring to the processional, offertory, anointing, preparation, ablutions, consecration, and communion, as well as the final blessing, then, "The Tunnyng of Elynour Rummyng" also figures, as Skelton's other major poems do, the liturgy and sacraments of Holy Mother Church.[47]

And this poem, like others of Skelton, is also multiple in its references. As we have seen, overnight accommodations and so the dispensing of ale were associated for the early Tudors with religious houses where, Pollet observes, "The brewing industry was long a monopoly" (p. 108).[48] As throughout England, most of the houses in East Anglia—including Bury St. Edmunds and Carrow—were Benedictine, as Skelton means to remind us when one of Elynour's customers "sware by Saynt Benet" (393). St. Benedict was popularized by the widely circulated Life included in Gregory's *Dialogues* (Book 2); his iconographical image was the broken cup, and he was installed in the Litany of Saints, which the Sarum rite prescribes for the Mass on Easter Even. His feast day was celebrated by the Tudors on 21 March, although they also celebrated his Translation on 11 July. His Office and Gradual are both taken from Psalm 36: "The mouth of the righteous is exercised in wisdom: and his tongue will be talking of judgment. The law of God is in his heart" (36:30–31). More importantly, the Rule of St. Benedict was the basis for all monastic regulations, regardless of the order: it was characterized by prudence and moderation within a framework that stressed authority, obedience, stability, and community, and it clearly opposed in every way the raucous gathering at Elynour Rummyng's alehouse. But the Rule of St. Benedict is not something else Elynour simply inverts: it may also suggest her actual behavior. For as many Tudors surely knew, "The main element in this ideal was the practice of obedience," as R. W. Southern sums.

> The obedience is of various kinds. There is the obedience of heart and body to the precepts of spiritual counsel extracted from the Gospels; there is obedience to the Rule; but immediately and constantly there is obedience to the abbot. He is the vicar of Christ within the community; his word is to be obeyed as the voice of God himself. He both teaches and commands: "the abbot's command and teaching sprinkle the leaven of the divine justice in the minds of his disciples." . . . The Rule leaves no doubt about the quality of the obedience that it required: it is to be obedience "without delay." . . . In the first place obedience must be seen in relation to its end. The end is an entire self-negation, which those living under the Rule are required to practise as an instrument of the return to God. This self-abnegation, which is the fruit of obedience, is the source of all other virtues. The monks are to have nothing of their own; they are to expect nothing; they are to put up with everything—poverty, illness, harshness—because these things lead back to God.[49]

Bishop Fox translated the Rule into English in 1516, but there were in fact a number of editions, in both Latin and English, in circulation during Skelton's residence in Westminster; reading them over now, one is struck by how absolute is the absolute quality of obedience required and the absolute authority of the abbot (Rules 5, 6ff.). This is in part initiated because, unlike some other practices among Tudor religious orders, those entering a Benedictine house were required to give everything to the head of their particular monastery or priory—just as Elynour takes everything her customers bring with them, and, in time, asks of them everything they have, to "hyde / Within her beddes syde" (605–6). Thus Elynour's infernality is also measured by the way she engages in a kind of despotism (not unlike Wolsey's) in which she rules—and rules absolutely—everyone who sets foot in her door. It is this, in the end, that the "prycke-me-denty" (582) discovers. When she is in urgent need of a drink to recover her senses,

> "I have no penny nor grote
> To paye," sayde she, "God wote,
> For wasshyng of my throte
> But my bedes of amber;
> Bere them to your chamber" (600–604).

But in surrendering her precious Rosary—her sole means of Christian meditation, it seems—she watches the outward sign of her soul treated as Elynour treats the rotten Essex cheese, placing both with her hoard of material treasures (605–6) while other customers or disciples, thoroughly indoctrinated, feel not the horror of this as the prycke-me-denty does, but only their own failure to follow suit:

> But some than sate ryght sad
> That nothynge had
> There of their awne,
> Neyther gelt nor pawne (607–10),

and so, out of compensation, they give up their future:

> Such were there menny
> That had not a penny;
> But, whan they shulde walke,
> Were fayne with a chalke
> To score on the balke
> Or score on the tayle (611–16).

The poem concludes—it hardly stops arbitrarily—when Elynour, mocking the Benedictine abbot and St. Benedict himself—gains total control over *everyone*.

The lesson for both Masses in celebration of St. Benedict is from Ecclesiasticus; and it means to suggest the pilgrimages for which other religious, such as the pilgrims and palmers and even mendicant friars, were known.

> He shall pass into strange countries: for he shall try good and evil among men.

He will give his heart to resort early to the Lord that made him, and he will pray in the sight of the most High.

He will open his mouth in prayer, and will make supplication for his sins.

For if it shall please the great Lord, he will fill him with the spirit of understanding:

And he will pour forth the words of his wisdom as showers, and in his prayer he will confess to the Lord (39:5–9).

Religious houses participated in such pilgrimages by providing guest chambers,[50] and we have already seen how prevalent pilgrimages were throughout Norfolk in Skelton's day, especially to Our Lady of Walsingham, to which pilgrims had been coming from England for more than 350 years, to see the replica of the Santa Casa, the Holy House at Nazareth, which had been built after the Virgin appeared to a devout widow of Walsingham and gave her the measurements around 1130.[51] There were also crowded pilgrimages from Westminster and London westward to Glastonbury to St. Dunstan's bones or eastward to Canterbury to the relics of St. Thomas the Martyr.[52] Many of these pilgrims—most of them, in fact—were humble people like Elynour's customers, and like her followers many were physically deformed and sought some kind of cure. Such pilgrimages expanded to include the veneration of many saints, and the faithful were drawn to such shrines, often giving all their money or gifts they could ill afford in the hopes of gaining an indulgence; "Indeed," Zacher says, "by the fourteenth century the word 'pilgrimage' had become synonymous with indulgence."[53]

But, as Chaucer also reminds us, many pilgrimages also attracted boisterous crowds, and the occasion became as social as religious. Such shrines would hardly resemble Elynour's bowzing-den with its chicken dung and loose hogs, its boasts and its stench; indeed, the very pilgrimage her women make to see her, carrying as treasure their paltry offerings (244–56), especially the two women who offer their Rosaries (523, 603), mock the prayers in the Sarum Missal's special Service for Pilgrims:

O God of unconquered power, and boundless pity, the entire aid and consolation of pilgrims, who givest to thy servants most invincible armour; we pray thee that thou wouldest vouchsafe to bl + ess this cross, which is humbly dedicated to thee; that the banner of the venerated cross, the figure whereof hath been depicted upon it, may be a most invincible strength to thy servant against the wickedest temptation of the ancient enemy; that it may be a defence by the way, a guard in thy house, and a protection to us everywhere.

But to insure that we do not miss this point, Skelton has one of them, "dronken Ales," tell of her trip to "Saynte James in Gales" (354) just before she passes out.

We have lost the force of this reference now, but to the Tudors, who possessed as their most distinguished relic the hand of St. James of Galicia in the abbey at Reading, this must have meant a good deal. Ales had gone all the way to Spain—further than many of them had, and for the same purpose—and she had seen a shrine as famous and central for the Tudors as those at Rome and Jerusalem. But James the Great, brother to St. John, had witnessed the Transfiguration that Elynour blasphemes and had been present at the Agony in the Garden of Gethsemane (trivialized in the drunken agony of Ales and the anxiety of the prycke-me-denty)—these events, in fact, form the basis for the lessons the Tudors celebrated each year on his feast day, 25 July. It was not just another feast day for these early Tudors, for St. James was someone special: there were the relics at Reading, relics in the high Norman tower at Bury St. Edmunds, and some 414 parish churches—at least one out of every twelve—were dedicated to him. And the liturgy for his feast day seems sharply, significantly apposite. The Secret, for instance, speaks to the inadequacy that Elynour's customers may well feel:

> We beseech thee, O Lord, that the blessed passion of thy blessed apostle James may make the oblations of thy people acceptable unto thee; so that what is not fit to be received through our own merits, may through his intercession become well pleasing unto thee,

while the Epistle, from Ephesians 2, reasserts the aloneness that Ales and the prycke-me-denty portray:

> Now therefore you are no more strangers and foreigners; but you are fellow citizens with the saints, and the domestics of God,
> Built upon the foundation of the apostles and prophets, Jesus Christ himself being the chief corner stone;
> In whom all the building, being framed together, groweth up into an holy temple in the Lord,
> In whom you also are built together into an habitation of God in the Spirit (19–22).

In addition, the Gospel, about St. James and St. John, speaks of drink, but this chalice holds the very blood of Christ, Who offers it.

> Then came to him the mother of the sons of Zebedee with her sons, adoring and asking something of him.
>
> Who said to her: What wilt thou? She saith to him: Say that these my two sons may sit, the one on thy right hand, and the other on thy left, in thy kingdom.
>
> And Jesus answering, said: You know not what you ask. Can you drink the chalice that I shall drink? They say to him: We can.
>
> He saith to them: My chalice indeed you shall drink; but to sit on my right or left hand, is not mine to give to you, but to them for whom it is prepared by my Father (Matthew 20:20–23).

Elynour's utter heresy, then, is in playing the devil, in mocking St. Benedict and St. James, and in pretending to become Christ. This final parody is reinforced in the Offices in which Skelton would celebrate St. James, during the Nocturne or Vespers, with homily 66 drawn from the same passage in Matthew: "They drank the chalice of the Lord and became God's friends," and in Lesson ix, "And He added, 'Can you drink of the cup of which I am about to drink, and be baptized with the baptism with which I am to be baptized? . . . This is not the time for rewards, nor will My glory soon appear; the time of death and dangers is at hand.'"

There is one concluding parody remaining in "The Tunnyng of Elynour Rummyng," one also associated with St. Benedict and St. James, with religious houses and orders, and with pilgrimages—that of the reliquary. Each parish church in England needed its own relic—the more significant the better—to house in or near the altar. We cannot overestimate the significance of such relics to the Tudor mind and to Tudor devotion. "The dynamic holiness of icons and relics," Marina Warner tells us, "did not just stir the soul to the contemplation of higher things, they also physically communicated the properties of their subject or owner. Images were alive, and so they could breathe life into the dying. Mary's peculiar qualities of bodily and spiritual integrity made her the supreme medium of healing and rendering whole again, and her shrines have always been thronged, since early Christian times, when, according to a tenth-century legend, the Empress Zoe had been cured by touching the girdle preserved in the Chalkoprateia church" (p. 293). About the very time Skelton was writing "The Tunnyng of Elynour Rummyng," the Church and Convent of St. Peter in Westminster was making an inventory of its own relics. The long, long list is an impressive one; the order had, among other treasures,

> a Cuppe of golde withe stonys with the blood off owre lorde. Item a
> whyte marble ston with ye prynt of owre lordys foote. Item a grete
> parte of the holy crosse. Item a long Coffre of Crystall with owre
> lady's gyrdyll w^t ij casys belongynge to the same gyrdle. . . . Item a
> lytle relyke lyke a lanterne with a relyke of the vestement of saynt
> petre. . . . Item a nother stondyng relyke of sylver and gylt and berell
> broken with the combe of saynt Dunston and a chayne of sylver. . . .
> Item a stondyng cuppe of sylver and gylte with the hed of saynt
> mauryce. . . . Item an ymage off owre ladye of yverey with a Crowne
> of gold uppon herr hedde and o^r lorde in here Armys with a
> Crowne of gold and a lytle Oche sett with dyamondys with a ffloure
> of golde and a Jelofre in o^r lordys hand. Item a stondynge relyke
> sylver and gilte garnysshed w^t stones and Berell w^t the relyke off
> Nicholas. . . . Two standyng square relykys of sylver with their Cov-
> erynges, yn which were some tyme relykes of saynt marke and of
> saynt luke. . . . Item a boxe made of pomawnder to putt in relykys
> gevyn by quene Elizabeth wyff to Kyng Henrey the vij^th.[54]

and this is but a small fraction. We sense once more the atmosphere of the witch's Sabbath when we come to realize, at the moment the prycke-me-denty and Skelton do (605–10), that Elynour's relics, her holy treasures, are the rotten cheese and wedding ring, Leominster wool and Rosaries that she has collected in payment for rotten ale; that she has taken them out of the domain of public devotion and hidden them in her private reliquary; and that this sacred place is beneath the bed where she and her husband rut like hogs. Little wonder Skelton would not, could not, go on. *Everything* holy has been desecrated.

Without saying exactly why, an anonymous critic of the nineteenth century remarks, "'Elynoure Rumming' is the saddest of Skelton's works; there is no relenting, no hope in it."[55] Yet we should have thought, at the outset, that Skelton wrote no more traditionally Goliardic poem than this one. When we compare any number of Goliardic tavern songs with "The Tunnyng of Elynour Rummyng," such as this one—

> Tercio capitulo
> memoro tabernam:
> illam nullo tempore
> sprevi neque spernam,

donec sanctos angelos
venientes cernam,
cantantes pro mortuis
"Requiem eternam"[56]—

we seem, for a moment, to have caught the essence of Skelton. But it is not so. An orthodox and pious priest when he wrote most of his poems and all of his major ones, he could find cause for devotion in Jane Scrope's apparent concern for the death of a pet sparrow and unceasing, bitter rage against a prelate and priest who recklessly set about destroying Holy Mother Church. And like the services in the liturgy of that Church, and its sacred music, he learned to sing songs (or intone poems) that are alive with figural meaning, that insist on multiple significances concurrently, that see into life deeply and through the glass of God's truth if only darkly. The tone seems more joyous, the situation less consequential in "Elynour Rummyng," but like everything he touched when he was at the top of his form, Skelton quietly turns even "The Tunnyng of Elynour Rummyng" into an occasion for preaching that his parish could understand, a sermon fit for every age.

5

SEASONS OF DISCOVERY

SLANDER
Bench end (hand-carved, fifteenth century),
Church of the Holy Trinity, Blythburgh, Suffolk

The Garlande of Laurell, Skelton's longest and most autobiographical poem, was published in 1523. It seems strangely unlike his other late poems, having no readily ascertainable religious or political reference.[1] Instead, there are poetic echoes of *The Bowge of Courte*, for *The Garlande of Laurell* is also a dream vision in rime royal. Here the poet (rather than Drede) goes on a pilgrimage through his past body of work, hearing much of it named and described by Occupation, who argues in his behalf before the laureate senate (225) for his election to the Court of Fame. Occupation notes that a long roll call of writings, authentic and perhaps imaginary (1169a-1476, 1492–1504), rightly places Skelton with distinguished poets from antiquity (325–85) and, more recently, with Gower, Chaucer, and Lydgate (386–526; 1100–1103). The poem closes with still another surprise—lines addressed by the poet to the King and the Cardinal asking for a prebend that they have promised him (1586a–93). On the surface this poem seems a puzzling, excessive, self-promotional enterprise, quite out of keeping with Skelton's other work composed in Westminster, and a poem conceding at last to Wolsey. Historians, however, have valuable principles for addressing such apparent aberrations. They tell us that the most major events ought somehow to reveal fundamental relationships; and that the best way to recover the most significant facts and meanings is to determine the most economical way to account for the greatest amount of material. When we apply such theorems to Skelton's life and work, the evidence seems overwhelmingly to suggest that through much of his life he had as his patron the staunchly Catholic Thomas Howard I, Earl of Surrey and second Duke of Norfolk. This alone would explain most about Skelton as well as make sense of such occurrences as the composition—and the publication—of *The Garlande of Laurell*.

The setting of *The Garlande* is "the frytthy [brushwood] forest of Galtres" (22) surrounding Sheriff Hutton Castle, eight miles northeast of York, where Skelton dreams of "a pavylyon wondersly disgysede" (38), the home of Dame Pallas and the Court of Fame. While he is awaiting his hearing, he is led by Occupation up a "windyng stayre" (767) into a chamber where he finds the Countess of Surrey, her daughters, and her ladies-in-waiting weaving a coronal for him (769–807); in gratitude he writes for each of them a short lyric of appreciation (835a–1085). The setting, then, is meant to be Sheriff Hutton itself, Henry VII's northern castle, which John Leland in 1534 found unequalled in "princely lodgings."[2] It was the castle to which Thomas Howard I was appointed constable and steward from 1489 to 1499, when he served as Lieutenant of the North, succeeding Henry Percy, Earl of Northumberland, and like him charged with keeping peace along the Scottish border and among the rebellious citizenry. (In 1500 he returned to London as Lord High Treasurer, one of three major state positions that he held, under Henry VII and Henry VIII, until his retirement in December 1522.) Moreover, the recipients of Skelton's lyric tributes—Elizabeth Howard, the Countess of Surrey (who died in 1497); her daughters Elizabeth and Muriel Howard; Lady Anne Dacre, her daughter by her first marriage (later Anne Boleyn's mother); Margery Wentworth (aunt of the mother of Lady Jane Seymour); Margaret Tylney; Jane Blenner-Haiset; Isabel Paynell; Margaret Hussey; Gertrude Statham; and Isabel Knight—were all women in residence or visiting Sheriff Hutton between 1489 and 1497.[3] The only period when this particular configuration actually existed, then, was prior to all but one of the records we have of Skelton (that in the Cambridge University Registers for 1493)—but the likeliest reason for a young scholar of no known background to be there would be as a tutor to the Howard children. That in turn would mean that he was employed by the Howard family.

And once we look for them, there are a large number of connections between Skelton and the Howards. Skelton's first extant poem, the eulogy for Northumberland, honors Howard's immediate predecessor, whose death caused Henry VII to excuse Howard from charges of treason (he had fought for Richard III at Bosworth) and to release him from the Tower of London where he had been held close prisoner. The setting for *The Bowge of Courte* is the seaport of Harwich (34) where Howard's father John owned a house and wharf left in the charge of John Powers (hence "Powers Keye," or Quay, 35).[4] Eleanor Scrope, Jane's mother, married Sir John Windham of Felbrigg, Norfolk, at Sheriff Hutton; and here Skelton might first have heard of or met Jane, while later, after Lady Windham's death, Jane Scrope married into the Brews family, of Suffolk, East Anglia, whose kitchen servant was Christopher Garnesche. Besides such alliances and connections, Howard's friendship and patronage would also explain Skelton's early political poetry honoring the Earl of Surrey at Flodden Field—the "Chorus de Dys contra Scottos" but also "A Ballade of the Scottysshe Kynge" (1513) and "Agaynst the Scottes" (1513), all three establishing "the good Erle of Surray . . . Of chevalry he is the floure" that we see as the antitype of Wolsey in "Why Come Ye Nat to Courte?" (152, 158). The first angry attack on Wolsey, "Against Venemous Tongues" (1516), was written after the newly installed Cardinal required Howard to escort him from Westminster Abbey to York Place following his elevation to the cardinalate, and marks the period when Wolsey emerged as strong opposition to the conservative faction on the King's Council led by the aristocratic, Catholic Howard. *Magnyfycence* (1516), a play about a prince who needs to be more scrupulous in choosing his counselors, was written at the time Howard decided to leave court, mistakenly thinking himself fatally ill. In 1521, as Lord High Steward, he was required to preside over the trial of his friend and ally the Duke of Buckingham, to pronounce treason, and to read out the sentence of execution despite flimsy evidence, weeping, it is said, and unable to speak. Howard's distress doubtless prompted the embittered *Speke, Parrot* (late 1520–21) followed closely by "Collyn Clout" (1521–22) and "Why Come Ye Nat to Courte?" (late 1522). Then, suddenly, there were no more strong anti-Wolsey poems. But it is not difficult to understand why. Once more Howard had left court, again in failing health; he died on 5 May 1524. This likely means, then, that the "anti-Wolsey" poems are, even more, pro-Howard poems. They are poems supported by the orthodox Catholic faction on the King's Council in its continuing opposition to the greedy, corrupting Wolsey, quite possibly commissioned by them, and almost certainly circulated by them in manuscript to aid their cause. If this does not fully justify Skelton's use of liturgy, it does explain his directness.

Other events of Skelton's life also make better sense if we view him as the Howard family's poet. As tutor to the young Catholic Howard children, he was in a good position to be recommended to Lady Margaret Beaufort when she sought a tutor to train Prince Henry to become the next chief prelate of England and the next archbishop of Canterbury. With such an influential patron, Caxton would be well advised to praise lavishly a relatively unknown poet in the preface to his *Eneydos* of 1490 and Wynkyn de Worde similarly pleased to publish his early work. When Prince Henry succeeded Prince Arthur and joined his father and Skelton was therefore dismissed from court service, the poet accepted a lucrative living at Diss—where the Howards would be neighbors at Kenninghall Place and, as the wealthiest family in East Anglia, were already owners of Thetford Priory and of Framlingham Castle, this latter neighboring lands owned by the church gilds at Diss. (Later, in 1524, when the slow cortège took the body of Thomas Howard I the twenty-four miles through flat, heavily wooded land from Framlingham, where he had lain in state for a month, to the huge Cluniac Priory of Our Lady of Thetford [a house half the size of Norwich Cathedral] for burial, the body lay at rest overnight at St. Mary the Virgin Church in Diss: the church porch was draped in black, and a solemn dirge was sung [as in "Phyllyp Sparowe"] and alms distributed that evening, while a solemn Requiem Mass was said for him there the following morning. It is difficult to believe that Skelton, still rector of Diss, was not a celebrant.) Howard probably helped Skelton transfer to Westminster around 1512, encouraged his political poems, and may even have introduced him to a fellow member of the King's Council, Abbot John Islip, who found quarters for the poet in the sanctuary of Westminster and in turn commissioned him to write important epitaphs for Henry VII and Lady Margaret Beaufort. When Henry VIII sought a poet to engage in flytings with Sir Christopher Garnesche, who had served him in France as Sergeant of the King's Tents and head of the Revels Office, he chose in Skelton a poet who knew Garnesche through the Brews, rather than Wolsey's poet, Alexander Barclay. Even a late poem, like "The Douty Duke of Albany" (1523), supports Howard but attacks Albany with a mockery so excessive that it becomes a deliberate parallel to Albany's own boasts of strength (cf. 318–26) and also suggests in its tactical excessiveness the sort of lampoon he might address against Wolsey (527–28), a joke confirmed by the off-handed envoy and the couplet (522–23). Finally, when Howard retired in 1522, Skelton completed and published a poem that paid tribute to his patron both by paying tribute to his family by recalling the early days they shared at Sheriff Hutton and by recalling the body of work that he had accomplished throughout his life with Howard's support.

Although the actual date of composition of *The Garlande of Laurell* is difficult to determine, the number and freshness of details suggest it was written in Skelton's earlier days as tutor to the Howard children. Still, the poem as it was first published near the end of Skelton's life seems on the surface needlessly arrogant, even outrageous as it establishes a grand literary tradition (beginning with the classical muses) for the poet's works, lavishes care and attention on a complete bibliographical survey of his poems, and then lays claim (through them) for immortality. But if we accept Skelton's life-long service to the Howard family as the best way to understand the poet's career, all of these factors are transformed into a poem offering tribute to Howard as patron and isolating quite securely Thomas Howard's contribution to the patronage of English poetry at the time of his retirement. *The Garlande of Laurell* can profitably be read, then, as Skelton's extravagant, personal, witty, and touching last will and testament for his patron, employer, and protector.[5]

But it also seems clear that what we have is a modification of this earlier work, because passages that rely not on the early humanist perspective at Sheriff Hutton, filled to overflowing with knowledge and love of a classical past, but, rather, on scriptural and liturgical texts, as well as allusions now easily interpreted as pointing to Wolsey (whatever their original intention), suggest that it has been in part revised. These other passages relate the work firmly to the political Westminster poems that characterize Skelton's later years. Take, for instance, the depiction of Sheriff Hutton itself: a magnificent country estate now potentially the corrective antitype of Hampton Court, an estate where there is love and generosity rather than ostentatious wealth and display. There, "As a fair olive tree in the plains, and as a plane tree by the water in the streets, was I exalted" (Ecclesiasticus 25:19, 670 rubric). Like nearly all of Skelton's major work *after* he took priestly orders, Fame's pavilion in this poem is *figural*. We are told that it is decorated with sacred jewels—"With turkis and gros-solitis enpavyd was the grounde, / Of birrall enbosid wer the pyllers rownde" (466–67)—for this is nothing less than a moment of transcendence, seen retrospectively, late in his career, as a moment in which Skelton's vision has taken us to the true pavilion of Fame, the visionary temple of the New Jerusalem. It is this temple which another John, his namesake St. John the Apostle, dreams of in *his* grand vision:

> And the foundations of the wall of the city were adorned with all manner of precious stones. The first foundation was jasper: the second, sapphire: the third, a chalcedony: the fourth, an emerald:
>
> The fifth, sardonyx: the sixth, sardius: the seventh, chrysolite: the eighth, beryl; the ninth, a topaz: the tenth, a chrysoprasus: the eleventh, a jacinth: the twelfth, an amethyst.
>
> And the twelve gates are twelve pearls, one to each: and every several gate was of one several pearl. And the street of the city was pure gold, as it were transparent glass.
>
> And I saw no temple therein. For the Lord God Almighty is the temple thereof, and the Lamb (Apocalypse 21:19–22).

It is a splendid act of the imagination, but it is wickedly funny too. For while Dame Pallas and Occupation welcome Skelton to this glorious temple, Wolsey remains outside, syphilitic, shot at, his cardinal's hat awry:

> With that I herd gunnis russhe out at ones—
> *Bowns! Bowns! Bowns!* that all they out cryde:
> It made sum lympe-legged and broisid there bones;
> Sum were made pevysshe, porisshly pynk-iyde,
> That evermore after by it they were aspyid;
> And one ther was there—I wondred of his hap—
> For a gun stone, I say, had all to-jaggid his cap,

> Raggid and daggid and cunnyngly cut;
> The blaste of the brynston blew away his brayne;
> Masid as a Marche hare, he ran lyke a scut (623–32).

Wolsey is deliberately if subtly attacked in *The Garlande of Laurell* (540–46, 602–15, 623–32) with passages that refer us exactingly to earlier accusations in "Collyn Clout" (85–89, 125–63) and "Why Come Ye Nat to Courte?" (78–83, 168–82, 1165–73, 1193–1200).[6] While Howard's patronage and Skelton's loyalty and orthodoxy have guaranteed the poet his own wonderful Revelation, the apostate Wolsey has been denied admission altogether. For he lacks all the prerequisites: the support of the Catholic Howards and their allies; accredited and serviceable Occupation cognizant of others; the wisdom and prudence sought by Dar.e Pallas; visionary faith—and grace.

Furthermore, scriptural references in scattered rubrics alongside the catalogue of Skelton's labors (1170ff.) conclude resoundingly at 1505: "*Milia millium et decies millies centena millia, etc.: Apocalipsis. Vite senatum laureati possident: ecclesiastica canti.*"[7] It is a similar colloquy. The poet's vision is from the Apocalypse, "And I beheld, and I heard the voice of many angels round about the throne, and the living creatures, and the ancients; and the number of them was thousands of thousands" (5:11), welcoming him into the temple of the Lamb. But the antiphonal response indicated by the *Vita senatum*, the Vesper hymn for the feast day of the Apostles St. Peter and St. Paul (29 June) in the Church breviary, refers us to a meditation on Herod! "Herod the king set hands on certain members of the Church to persecute them. He killed James the brother of John with the sword, and seeing that it pleased the Jews, he proceeded to arrest Peter also" (Acts 12:1–3). Wolsey, then, figures not only Moloch, Oreb, and Zeb, but Herod too. The occasion for the hymn at the Vespers is also strikingly apposite.

> A beauteous light streams down from the eternal God to grace with happiness the golden day that brought reward to the Princes of the Apostles and gave sinners a clear road to heaven.
>
> Earth's Teacher and heaven's Door-keeper, founders of Rome and judges of the world, they take their place, laurel-crowned, in heaven's assembly—the one triumphant through being beheaded, the other through being crucified.
>
> How happy, Rome, your fortune in being dedicated to God in the Princes' noble blood; for clad in a robe dyed purple with their blood, you far outstrip in beauty all else the world can show.

To God, in essence one, in persons three, the ruler of the universe,
be eternal glory, power and acclamation through all the ages of ages.
Amen.

With these final liturgical texts, all of them like the allusions to Wolsey late
interpolations after Skelton's ordination, *The Garlande of Laurell*, as pub-
lished in 1523, becomes clear and hugely significant: Skelton's laurel,
prompted and inspired by Howard, has led him to envision the glory to
come for true disciples of the Church; it has approved of the righteous-
ness of their actions and the wisdom of their faith. The indication, too, to
the failing Howard, is that it also guarantees his salvation.

Readers who have failed to recognize Skelton's referential means of
writing poetry have felt a closing envoy, addressed in part to Wolsey,
suggests a sudden change of heart and a betrayal of conscience. But if we
read closely, we will see that this is not so. Here is the envoy:

> *Ad serenissimam Majestatem Regiam, pariter cum Domino Cardinali,*
> *Legato a latere honorificatissimo, etc.*
> *Lautre Envoy*
> *Perge, liber, celebrem pronus regem venerare*
> *Henricum octavum, resonans sua premia laudis.*
> *Cardinem dominum pariter venerando salutes,*
> *Legatum a latere, et fiat memor ipse precare*
> *Prebende, quam promisit mihi credere quondam,*
> *Meque sum referas pignus sperare salutis*
> *Inter spemque metum* (1586a–93).[8]

What Skelton says here, with considerable care, is that this poem vener-
ates and praises *not* Wolsey but *the king* (*regem*): the reverence due to the
Cardinal is directly contingent on the fulfillment of a promise already
made but that must come from the King, not the Cardinal. Moreover,
forcing Wolsey's hand in a poem which honors Henry VIII's Lord Trea-
surer is tantamount to insisting that the prelate make good while Howard
yet lives: Skelton will honor his patron in a poem which secures continu-
ing patronage through a new appointment. Rather than conceding any-
thing at all to Wolsey, this envoy actually forces Wolsey's hand.

There is no indication that Thomas Howard II ever provided the sup-
port and protection for Skelton that his father had; but in the final years
of his life, Skelton suffers no abatement in energy, courage, or inventive-
ness. His final extant poem, "A Replycacion" (1528), is an attack on two
Cambridge students, Thomas Bilney and Thomas Arthur, who were de-

clared guilty of Lutheran heresy and required to abjure publicly and to bear faggots to Paul's Cross on the Feast of the Conception, 8 December 1527, as a sign of their recantation. Skelton opens his poem with a dedication to Wolsey that maintains the combination of literal convention and tonal mockery that we find in *The Garlande of Laurell*.

> *HONORIFICATISSIMO, Amplissimo, longeque reverendissimo*
> *In Christo patri, ac domino, domino THOME &c. Tituli*
> *Sancte Cecilie, sacrosancte Romane ecclesie presbytero,*
> *Cardinali meritissimo, et Apostolice sedis legato, a*
> *latereque legato superillustri, &c., Skeltonis laureatus,*
> *Orator regius, humillimum dicit obsequium cum omni debita*
> *reverentia, tanto tamque magnifico digna principe sacer-*
> *dotum, totiusque justitie equabilissimo moderatore,*
> *necnon presentis opusculi fautore excellentissimo &c.*
> *ad cujus auspicatissimam contemplationem, sub memo-*
> *rabili prelo gloriose immortalitatis, presens pagella*
> *felicitatur &c.* (a–1).[9]

The extravagant praise with the string of titles of unequal magnitude suddenly closes down to the fact that Skelton will respect the Cardinal with just the "proper" reverence "due" to him—the implication is the respect due to his performance, not to his titles—and shows how the poet could seem to placate his opponent while actually pursuing his independent way through irony. But Skelton is right to sense that they will agree on his present poem: Wolsey also supported the punishing of nascent Lutheranism, recently attacked by the King himself on behalf of the Church, for it was rapidly becoming the most dangerous heresy of them all.

In the 1520s, Lutheranism was especially strong along the Norfolk coast and, as Skelton points out, at Cambridge itself where a "Little Germany" of heretics led by Bilney and including Arthur was actively preaching direct communication between supplicant and God without the intervention of Holy Mother Church. Bilney had, in fact, been licensed to preach throughout the whole diocese of Ely in 1525; by 1527 he was preaching in and around London, arguing, as Skelton says, against the veneration of saints (especially the Blessed Virgin) and against pilgrimages—practices which were clearly central to Skelton's faith as they were important to his poetry. The young men were tried by an ecclesiastical tribunal that sat from 27 November to 7 December 1527 in the chapter house at Westminster and at the London residence of the Bishop of Norwich, Bishop

Nikke. Skelton's punning title carries at least five possible meanings: it is the reply of the plaintiff to the plea of the defendant; the rejoinder to the heretics on behalf of the poet; a repetition of the poet's defense of beliefs he had argued throughout a lifetime of poetry; reverberations of Church doctrine; and a bringing together, or summing up, of the place of the sacraments and the work of the poet in the service of faith, justice, and truth.

The poem is in three parts—the protestation, proposition, and confuta-tion—which borrows legal terminology and form only to transcend them. Each of the three sections works antiphonally in two ways: an English prose passage serves as a text for an expanded English verse; and both English prose and verse are longer descants on briefer Latin rubrics that run marginally alongside the poem. In Part 1 Skelton opens his own argu-ment by announcing that uninspired learning is itself dangerous, if not inherently heretical. The prose proem notes

> Howe yong scholers now-a-dayes
> embolmed with the flyblowen blast
> of the moche vayneglorious pipplyng
> wynde, when they can have delectably lycked
> a lytell of the lycorous electuary of
> lusty lernyng in the moche studious scole-
> hous of scrupulous Philology, coun-
> tyng themselfe clerkes exellently enformed
> and transcendingly sped in moche high con-
> nyng, and whan they have ones superciliously
> caught (a–j),

mocking the ostentatious erudition and elaborate rhetoric that are in fact hollow upon inspection, to which the poet replies,

> A lytell ragge of Rethorike,
> A lesse lumpe of Logyke,
> A pece or a patche of Philosophy,
> Than forthwith by and by
> They tumble so in Theology,
> Drowned in dregges of Divinite,
> That they juge themselfe able to be
> Doctours of the Chayre in the Vyntre
> At the Thre Cranes,
> To magnifye their names.

> But madly it frames,
> For all that they preche and teche
> Is farther than their wytte wyll reche.
> Thus by demeryttes of their abusyon,
> Finally they fall to carefull confusyon:
> To beare a fagot, or to be enflamed—
> Thus are they undone and utterly shamed (1–16a).

The two halves of the protestation thus display the students' ignorance of the Old and New Testaments that they attempt to deal with directly, eliminating the intercessory role of Holy Mother Church. The "flyblowen blast" (b) refers us to Psalm 77, in which the Psalmist asks for God's judgment against the ungrateful Israelites:

> Attend, O my people, to my law: incline your ears to the words of my mouth.
> I will open my mouth in parables: I will utter propositions from the beginning.
> How great things have we heard and known, and our fathers have told us. . . .
> That they may put their hope in God and may not forget the works of God: and may seek his commandments.
> That they may not become like their fathers, a perverse and exasperating generation.
> A generation that set not their heart aright: and whose spirit was not faithful to God. . . .
> And they turned back and tempted God: and grieved the holy one of Israel.
> They remembered not his hand, in the day that he redeemed them from the hand of him that afflicted them:
> How he wrought his signs in Egypt, and his wonders in the field of Tanis.
> And he turned their rivers into blood, and their showers that they might not drink.
> He sent amongst them divers sorts of flies, which devoured them: and frogs which destroyed them.
> And he gave up their fruits to the blast, and their labours to the locust (1–3, 7–8, 41–46).

But these young scholars of heresy ignore Scripture; instead, gathering at the local tavern in Cambridge, the Three Cranes in the Vintry, they discuss and drink in ways that mock the sacrament of the Eucharist, in which the priest performs daily the miracle of Transubstantiation, while one scholar sits in a chair as if it were the bishop's throne (on which Wolsey sat).

The second proposition, therefore, contrasts secular ignorance in the proem—

> Over this, for a more ample processe to be
> farther delated and contynued, and of every
> true Christenman laudably to be enployed,
> justifyed, and constantly mainteyned; as
> touchyng the tetrycall theologisacion of these
> demy-divines and Stoicall studiantes, and frisca-
> joly yonkerkyns, moche better bayned than braynd,
> basked and baththed in their wylde burblyng
> and boyling blode (a–i)—

with the corrective lessons of Church doctrine which, in this instance, draw on the Blessed Virgin to signify the Feast of the Conception on which they abjure:

> In the honour of our blessed Lady
> And her most blessed Baby,
> I purpose for to reply
> Agaynst this horryble heresy
> Of these yong heretikes, that stynke unbrent,
> Whom I nowe sommon and convent,
> That leudly have their tyme spent
> In their study abhomynable,
> Our glorious Lady to disable
> And heynously on her to bable
> With langage detestable;
> With your lyppes polluted
> Agaynst her grace disputed,
> Whiche is the most clere Christall
> Of all pure clennesse virgynall,
> That our Savyour bare,
> Whiche us redemed from care (18–34).

These lines look forward to Skelton's summary that while Bilney and Arthur support *latria* or supreme worship of God alone ("They saye howe *Latria* is an honour grete," 282), they deny *dulia*, the veneration of angels and saints (288), and especially *hyperdulia*, or the veneration of the Blessed

Virgin (287). In citing the miracle of the Conception of Christ here, Skelton is interceding to instruct and save the young heretics much as the Virgin has interceded for all mankind, as the Sequence for the Mass of the feast day of Conception (8 December) makes clear:

> O how happy, O how fair;
> sweet to us, to God how dear,
>   hath this conception been!
> Misery now is at an end,
> mercy doth on earth descend,
>   for sorrow joy is seen.
> A mother her new offspring bears,
> from a new star new sun appears,
>   new grace doth all inspire;
> The mother bears the generator,
> the creature brings forth the creator,
>   the daughter bears the sire.

By denying the act of God that saved mankind, Bilney and Arthur do not deny only the Blessed Virgin but Christ (and God's power) as well. Heresy is inseparable from damnation.

But while the dedication and shape of this poem suggest that Skelton means to gloss the trial of the heretics, he is actually doing something quite different. He means to elaborate on just what he has managed here—the intercession of the poet of faith, which is a holy analogy to the intercession of the Virgin. Just as the birth of Christ makes Her divine, so the art of poetry breathes divinity into Skelton. Part 3, "A confutacion responsyve" (a), opens with Skelton's own rhetorical question: "Why fall ye at debate / With Skelton Laureate, / Reputyng hym unable / To gainsay replycable / Opinyons detestable / Of heresy execrable?" (300–305). For, he argues, the position of a poet—and especially *a priest as poet*—is something special and something also ordained by God. For

> . . . there is a spyrituall,
> And a mysteriall,
> And a mysticall
> Effecte energiall
> (As Grekes do it call),
> Of suche an industry
> And suche a pregnacy
> Of hevenly inspyracion

In laureate creacyon,
Of poetes commendacion,
That of divyne myseracion
God maketh his habytacion
In poetes whiche excelles,
And sojourns with them and dwelles.

By whose inflammacion
Of spyrituall instygacion
And divyne inspyracion,
We are kyndled in suche facyon
With hete of the Holy Gost,
Which is God of myghtes most,
That he our penne dothe lede (365–85).

At once Skelton elevates poetry and the poet—deliberately giving himself (because of the inspiration of the Holy Ghost) more authority even than the abbot or bishop who tried the heretics—and more authority too than Cardinal Wolsey, *legate a latere*. The poem that began with what appeared to be a note of conciliation, then, is actually a poem that begins with subterfuge. And there is more: in arguing in the course of the poem that the young heretics were first supported by gifts of money given toward their education by several, including the chief prelate himself—

Many a good man
And many a good woman,
By way of their devocion
To helpe you to promocion,
Whose charite wele regarded
Can nat be unrewarded (134–39)—

Skelton, indirectly, argues that the chief prelate is also guilty of promoting heresy. This gives a new and quite different meaning to the dedication in which the poet writes that Wolsey was "assuredly the most excellent promoter of this present treatise" and clarifies his remark that the poet means here to give "all due reverence proper to so great and so magnificent a prince of ecclesiasts" as one who—without the benefit of the inspiration given the poet—has instead aided and abetted the very heretics under examination. In this last, glorious poem, written within a year or two of his death, Skelton manages—even without the protection of the Howards —to condemn Wolsey once again while elevating his work as a poet to his performance as a teacher of the sacred. "A Replycacion," then, is a reply to

Wolsey and to Skelton's whole life as priest and as poet; and it may be no accident that this final published poem, about an art that is "spyrituall . . . mysteriall [and] . . . mysticall," echoes his contention in the very first of his extant poems, the eulogy to Northumberland, that poetry is "Enbrethed with the blast of influence dyvyne" (157). Such a poetic governed his entire life. Because Skelton was a priest he could be a particularly inspired poet; being a poet, he was a most effective priest.

"If we think that we are not in the presence here of poetic greatness," John Holloway told the British Academy in 1958 regarding Skelton, "it is because there is a kind of poetic greatness which we have not learnt to know."[10] We have misread Skelton for some time, that is, because we have not known where to look. That was not always the case, of course; surely the very fact that he pursued a lifelong career of figural poetry, leaning on Scripture and liturgy to represent the final and most mysterious truths of the holy, suggests that originally he had an audience that understood him. Nor did they disappear with his death in 1529. In the short space between 1545 and 1563—during the Protestant reign of Edward VI—there were twenty-one editions of his work. But even then his reputation was being transformed; in the years to come, an increasing number of jests and jestbooks about Skelton would emphasize his wit and ingenuity at the expense of his piety: for to a country becoming more determinedly Protestant, a Catholic priest could only trivialize and mislead—could even be a buffoon. Even Ben Jonson, who seems to admire him as a character in two of his works, makes Skelton into a clown. And the kind of poetry Skelton forged—cut from the hard and living rock of the Church Herself—had to wait until John Donne's "A Nocturall upon S. Lucies Day" before it saw the equal again of anything like the poetic that Skelton forged for England. "We ask too often why cultures perish and too seldom why they survive; as though their conservation were the normal and obvious fact and their death the abnormality for which special causes must be found," C. S. Lewis writes. "It is not so."[11]

We have lost sight of Skelton because we have lost sight of his age. It was an age, J. D. Mackie tells us, when "there seemed to be nothing incongruous in the production by clerics of a *mappa mundi* which showed the earth as a disk with Jerusalem at the centre."[12] Skelton's age believed in the miracle of Transubstantiation along with the miracles in *The Golden Legend*—and their world was richer for it, richer and far more alive with fresh possibilities for poetry. Skelton doubtless knew, for instance, that according to *The Golden Legend* "John" means the Lord's grace, or he who is in grace, or he to whom grace has been given. He knew that, he tells us in "A Replycacion," because the grace of the Holy Ghost led him to poetry and the grace of Christ led him to celebrate the Eucharist. In a sense, drawing on Scripture and liturgy, Skelton saw poetry as an act of reconfirmation, of attesting to fresh realizations of a sacred, prefiguring past. But for him poetry was also, like grace, an act of replenishment. It is not clear how exclusively Skelton followed the *vita apostolica*, the truly Christian way followed by the most devoted monks and hermits, regular canons and clergy, but for the *orator regius* of Henry VIII, oratory must have meant primarily—as it did in the sanctuary at Diss and the Howard chapel at Sheriff Hutton—a place of prayer. It may be no coincidence, then, that when Skelton gave up residence in Diss for a residence in Westminster, he chose to live next door to where another great poet of pilgrimage, Geoffrey Chaucer, had lived before him.

"*Speke Parrot* is a typically mediaeval work of art in that the system of ideas on which it is based is external to it," Brownlow writes. "It is manifestly incomplete without the co-operation of an audience of informed readers. It is designed for a community of Christian readers, and like most mediaeval art, it cannot be wholly alive apart from such a community."[13] But what splendor that community shared with him: the Old Testament and the New; the Holy Mass and the Divine Offices; the processional, lesson, gospel, and Sequence; plainsong and motet; wall paintings and sculptures, tapestries and drama; shrines and pilgrimages—each moment of the day and each season of the year was touched by Church beliefs and Church celebrations that made life seamless and sacred and whole. The poetry that flourishes in such an environment, Brownlow continues, "refutes our aestheticisms. It originates in a belief, and it is therefore utterly serious in its demand of the reader. It is not an allegory of the artist's life, nor a poem about poetry; it reminds us that art imitates life, and the works of art belong to the history of mankind, not to the history of art" (p. 139). An anonymous reader of Skelton's own age makes the same point. Scribbled on the flyleaf of a sixteenth-century edition of "Why Come Ye Nat to Courte?" Kinsman found, "Skelton, tis pitty that thy bookes should rust / Used, they doe live, thoughe thow art turned to dust."[14]

We cannot tell now what Scripture Skelton thought of as his favorite—his allusions are too encompassing. But the Psalter is surely central to his poetry, as it is to the liturgy. It is the whole of the Offices, nearly the whole of liturgical music. And Skelton, reading through the Psalter each week at Matins and Lauds and Vespers and Compline, came often upon that last Psalm which also serves as the basis for the Mass:

Praise ye the Lord in his holy places: praise ye him in the firma-
ment of his power.

Praise ye him for his mighty acts: praise ye him according to the
multitude of his greatness.

Praise him with sound of trumpet: praise him with psaltery and
harp.

Praise him with timbrel and choir: praise him with strings and
organs.

Praise him on high sounding cymbals: praise him on cymbals of
joy: let every spirit praise the Lord. Alleluia.

In joyous praise of Jane Scrope, in stout tribute to Surrey, in his wrath at
Wolsey, his exposure of an anonymous curate, and his vengeance on old
John Clarke, Skelton knew the range that even praise could take. "A
demon in point of genius," as Wordsworth once wrote of him,[15] Skelton
knew too that every liturgical season offered a fresh invitation to discover
what it means to be Christian. Such seasons for Skelton always inspired, at
their best, occasions for poetry too: liturgical seasons like the writing and
reading of poems, all became for him seasons of discovery. They can
become seasons of discovery for us, too, as looking with Skelton into his
poems as figures of the deepest and highest of mysteries, what we can
finally discover there is ourselves.

NOTES

PREFACE

1. A. C. Spearing, *Medieval to Renaissance in English Poetry* (Cambridge, 1985), p. 225.

CHAPTER I

1. John M. Berdan, *Early Tudor Poetry* (New York, 1920), pp. 95ff.; A. R. Heiserman, *Skelton and Satire* (Chicago, 1961), chap. 2.

2. Lines 1,3; all quotations and citations are from the forthcoming edition of Skelton's *Works*, ed. Robert S. Kinsman, for the Clarendon Press. References also correspond to present editions by Philip Henderson (1959) and John Scattergood (1983).

3. Heiserman, p. 37. There he also cites "works by Hoccleve, Chaucer, Langland, Dunbar, and Caston's Chartier" (p. 58).

4. C. S. Lewis, *The Allegory of Love* (Oxford, 1936), p. 252; Leigh Winser, "*The Bowge of Courte*: Drama Doubling as Dream," *ELR* 6 (1976): 18; Paul D. Psilos, "'Dulle' Drede and the limits of prudential knowledge in Skelton's *The Bowge of Court*," *JMRS* 6 (1976): 305; Frances McNeely Leonard, *Laughter in the Courts of Love* (Norman, Okla., 1981), p. 88.

5. Howard S. Patch, *The Goddess Fortuna in Mediaeval Literature* (Cambridge, Mass., 1927), pp. 140–43, 101–5, 50–57, 61–63. Cf. John Lydgate's "To Mary, the Queen of Heaven": "Queen of heuene, of helle eeke emperesse, / Lady of this world, O verray loodsterre! / To maryners geyn al mortal distresse / In ther passage that they nat ne erre" (1–4). *The Minor Poems of John Lydgate*, ed. Henry Noble MacCracken, EETS 107 (London, 1911), part 1, p. 284.

6. Macrobius, *Commentary on the Dream of Scipio*, tr. William H. Stahl (New York, 1952), pp. 88–89; Heiserman, p. 32.

7. John Holloway, *Skelton*, Chatterton Lecture on an English Poet, *Proceedings of the British Academy* (1958), pp. 92–93.

8. Stanley Eugene Fish, *John Skelton's Poetry* (New Haven, 1965), p. 79.

9. All citations are to the Vulgate text, which Skelton used.

10. G. R. Owst traces the allegorical journey with its wayward temptations through many medieval sermons in *Literature and Pulpit in Medieval England* (Cambridge, 1933), pp. 85–109. Cf. William Langland, *Piers Plowman*, Passus 5–6.

11. "The metaphor lived naturally in the Christian imagination and it is an effort as unnecessary as it is futile to relate the [*Pilgrimage* of deGuileville upon John Bunyan] and his age." Bernard Spivack, *Shakespeare and the Allegory of Evil* (New York, 1958), p. 84.

12. Spivack gives a succinct but highly useful summary of works in this tradition, which can be considered fruitfully alongside Skelton's poem, pp. 83ff.

13. Peter Green, *John Skelton* (London, 1960), p. 16.

14. I am following here a careful and illuminating discussion, with many detailed references to the text of the poem, by Stanley J. Kozikowski; see "Allegorical Meanings in Skelton's *The Bowge of Courte*," *PQ* 61 (1982): 305–15. Earlier, Heiserman (pp. 59–60) had more generally connected Dysdayne to pride, envy, and wrath; Ryote to sloth and lechery; Hervy Hafter to sloth, lechery, pride, and avarice; and Favell to pride, envy, sloth, avarice, and gluttony.

15. This seems to have been the occasion for publication, but F. W. Brownlow, decoding the astrological opening of the poem, argues convincingly that the date at which the poem is set is 19 August 1482, in celebration (in part) of Skelton's early Yorkist connections with the Howard family. This dating would signify the court being described as that of Edward IV. Were that surely the case, there was nothing to prevent an earlier date of publication. But it seems equally reasonable (and more likely) that Skelton uses his fictional introduction to cast explicit attention away from the Tudor court of Henry VII where he now found himself in service. However, for those aware of his job of tutoring young Henry, duke of York, the alternative would always be possible—and his ordination an appropriate time for such a moral (as well as learned) analysis. See Brownlow, "The Date of *The Bowge of Courte*," *ELN* 161 (September 1984): 12–20.

16. The original documents are transcribed in Dyce's edition of Skelton's *Poetical Works*, 2 vols. (London, 1843, 1844), 1:xx–xxi, and rpt. H. L. R. Edwards, *Skelton* (London, 1949), p. 288.

17. Barbara Nolan, *The Gothic Visionary Perspective* (Princeton, 1977), pp. 207ff.

18. M. L'Abbe Bacquez, *The Divine Office Considered from a Devotional Point of View*, ed. Rev. Ethelred L. Taunton (London, n.d.), p. 521.

19. A. J. Smith, "Incumbent Poets," *MLQ* 29 (1968): 348.

20. C. S. Lewis, *English Literature in the Sixteenth Century Excluding Drama* (Oxford, 1954), p. 141.

21. I am drawing here on F. W. Brownlow's important essay, "*Speke, Parrot*: Skelton's Allegorical Denunciation of Cardinal Wolsey," *SP* 65 (1968): 124–39.

22. *The Sarum Missal in English*, tr. Frederick E. Warren (Milwaukee, 1913).

23. Douglas Gray, *Themes and Images in the Medieval Religious Lyric* (London, 1972), p. 8.

24. Augustine as cited by Brownlow, "Allegorical Denunciation," pp. 130–31. For an alternative reading of Psalm 82 to that which follows, see Nathaniel Owen Wallace, "The Responsibilities of Madness: 'Speke, Parrot,' and Homeopathic Satire," *SP* 82 (1985): 75–78.

25. Brownlow, "Allegorical Denunciation," pp. 133–34.

26. British Library Additional MS 5665, in John Stevens, *Music and Poetry in the Early Tudor Court* (Lincoln, Neb., 1961), Appendix. Parrot as Christ interceding for mankind is also discussed by Spearing, pp. 272–73; cf. Wallace, pp. 74–75.

27. *Medieval English Lyrics*, ed. R. T. Davies (London, 1963, 1966), pp. 256–57.

28. William Nelson determined the cryptic dating and explained the events alluded to in the last four envoys in *John Skelton, Laureate* (New York, 1939), pp. 161–74.

29. Bernard F. Huppé, *Doctrine and Poetry* (Albany, N.Y., 1959), p. 24.

CHAPTER 2

1. Lacey Baldwin Smith, *Henry VIII: The Mask of Royalty* (Boston, 1971), p. 93.

2. William Nelson, *John Skelton, Laureate* (New York, 1939), pp. 113–14.

3. John Foxe gives a harsh but unreliable account of Bishop Nikke because of his staunch Catholicism (followed by Strype and others, Francis Blomefield, *An Essay Towards a Topographical History of the County of Norfolk* [London, 1745 ed.]) 2:386–89. This is also partly based on his arrest and imprisonment in 1534 when he was heavily fined for ignoring an exemption from his jurisdiction (he summoned the mayor of Thetford to appear before him in a spiritual case, although the borough had long been exempt), but this is thought now to have been a way for Henry VIII to get at part of his vast wealth. He died, blind and infirm, but still fighting for Holy Mother Church long after the Reform began to take hold in England; he is buried in a small but rather prominent tomb in the nave of Norwich Cathedral.

4. Ian A. Gordon, *John Skelton Poet Laureate* (Melbourne, 1943), p. 31.

5. Maurice Pollet, *John Skelton, Poet of Tudor England*, tr. John Warrington (London, 1971), p. 160.

6. Attributed to H. L. R. Edwards in Nelson, p. 219n.

7. Quoted in Pollet, p. 2.

8. A. G. Dickens, *The English Reformation*, rev. ed. (London, 1967), pp. 25–26.

9. Rev. Leonard E. Whatmore, *Highway to Walsingham* (Walsingham, 1973), p. 26.

10. A. R. Myers, *England in the Late Middle Ages*, 8th ed. (Harmondsworth, 1981), pp. 236–37.

11. This is discussed at some length in Robert S. Kinsman, "Phyllyp Sparowe: Titulus," *SP* 47 (1950): 473–84.

12. Reproduced in William Gaunt, *Court Painting in England from Tudor to Victorian Times* (London, 1980), p. 3.

13. *Latin Liturgical Manuscripts and Printed Books* (Oxford, Bodleian Library, 1952).

14. Edward Hall, "Henry VIII," in *The Lives of the Kings*, ed. Charles Whibley, 2 vols. (London, 1904), 1:67.

15. Christopher Morris, *The Tudors* (London, 1955, 1966), p. 55.

16. Dickens, p. 28. He was not alone: the earl of Oxford arranged in 1509 for

2,000 Masses; Colet's father, a Lord Mayor of London, arranged for daily Mass for fifteen years by two priests. See Morris, p. 74.

17. Margaret Deanesly, *A History of The Medieval Church 590–1500*, rev. ed. (London, 1972), pp. 195–96.

18. Donald L. Edwards, *Christian England: Its Story to the Reformation*, rev. ed. (London, 1982), p. 303.

19. Marianne G. Briscoe, in an unpublished paper on "An Application of Sermon Design: The N-Town *Via Crucis.*"

20. *Gallicantus in sinodo apud Bernwell*, p. lv, in J. W. Blench, *Preaching in England in the Late Fifteenth and Sixteenth Centuries* (New York, 1964), p. 238.

21. John Fisher, *English Works*, ed. J. E. B. Mayor, EETS extra series 27 (London, 1935), part I, p. 181, quoted in Blench, p. 239.

22. Quoted anonymously by Robert W. Ackerman, *Backgrounds to Medieval English Literature* (New York, 1966), p. 89.

23. Benedict of Canterbury, quoted in Howard Laxton, *Pilgrimage to Canterbury* (London, 1978), p. 92.

24. J. J. Jusserand, *English Wayfaring Life in the Middle Ages*, tr. Lucy Toulmin Smith (London, rpt. 1961), p. 192.

25. See Erasmus's *Colloquies*; when agents of Henry VIII visited St. Thomas's shrine in the 1540s, they found piled up by pilgrims nearly 5,000 ounces of gold, 5,286 ounces of pure silver, 4,425 ounces of silver-gilt, and "twenty-six cartloads of other treasure." See Paul Johnson, *A History of Christianity* (Harmondsworth, 1980), p. 267.

26. Erasmus, quoted in A. F. Scott, *Every One a Witness: The Tudor Age* (New York, 1976), p. 153.

27. J. R. Lander, *Government and Community: England 1450–1509* (London, 1980), p. 115.

28. See, for example, Stanley Eugene Fish, *John Skelton's Poetry* (New Haven, 1965), pp. 14–15.

29. Nan Cooke Carpenter, *John Skelton* (New York, 1967), p. 114.

30. Carpenter, "Skelton and Music: *Roty bully joys*," *RES* 6 (1955): 284, 283.

31. Alec Robertson, *Ancient Forms to Polyphony*, vol. 1 of *The Pelican History of Music*, 3 vols., ed. Robertson and Denis Stevens (Harmondsworth, 1978), p. 139.

32. Richard H. Hoppin, *Medieval Music* (New York, 1978), p. 91.

33. John Norton-Smith, "The Origins of 'Skeltonics,'" *EC* 23 (1973): 57.

34. Skelton's use of the strophic pattern of plainsong looks forward to a slightly later poem (1530–55) based on the Sarum use, the marvelous *Harmony of Birds*, a macaronic poem which reproduces the entire Latin text of the *Te Deum* much as the *Placebo* is reproduced in "Phyllyp Sparowe." The text has recently been edited by Malcolm Andrews for the Renaissance English Text Society. See *Two Early Renaissance Bird Poems* (Cranbury, N.J., 1984), pp. 45–55.

35. Some of this is anticipated by Friedrich Brie, "Skelton-Studien," *Englische*

Studien 37 (1907): 78–83; Nelson, pp. 92–93; and Robert S. Kinsman, "Skelton's 'Upon a Deedmans Hed': New Light on the Origin of the Skeltonic," *SP* 50 (1953): 101–9, among others, posit alternate theories.

36. J. A. Burrow, *Medieval Writers and Their Work* (Oxford, 1982), pp. 47–48.

37. Anne Righter [Barton], *Shakespeare and the Idea of the Play* (London, 1962), pp. 14–15.

38. See Rosemary Woolf, *The English Mystery Plays* (Berkeley, Calif., 1972), p. 85.

39. Frederick B. Artz, *The Mind of the Middle Ages*, 3rd ed. rev. (Chicago, 1980), p. 360.

40. Eleanor Prosser, *Drama and Religion in the English Mystery Plays* (Stanford, 1961), p. 5.

41. Woolf, *The English Religious Lyric in the Middle Ages* (Oxford, 1968), p. 273.

42. O. B. Hardison, Jr., *Christian Rite and Christian Drama in the Middle Ages: Essays in the Origin and Early History of Modern Drama* (Baltimore, 1965), pp. 39–40.

43. Julian of Norwich, *Revelations of Divine Love*, tr. Clifton Wolters (Harmondsworth, 1966), p. 63.

44. Peter W. Travis, *Dramatic Design in the Chester Cycle* (Chicago, 1982), p. xv; he is referring specifically to the Chester plays.

45. See also Essays 3 and 4 in Hardison, pp. 80–177.

46. Mary H. Marshall, "Aesthetic Values of the Liturgical Drama," in *Medieval English Drama*, ed. Jerome Taylor and Alan H. Nelson (Chicago, 1972), pp. 36–37.

47. Travis, p. 109; Arnold Williams, *The Drama of Medieval England* (East Lansing, Mich., 1961), p. 117.

48. Sandro Sticca, *The Latin Passion Play: Its Origins and Development* (Albany, N.Y., 1970), p. 169.

49. A. C. Cawley, "Introduction" to his edition of *The Wakefield Pageants in the Towneley Cycle* (Manchester, 1958), p. xxiv.

50. David Bevington, *Tudor Drama and Politics* (Cambridge, Mass., 1968), pp. 28, 33.

51. Malone Society, *Collections XI* (Oxford, 1980/81).

52. "Nature's law yields / to the new creation. / Against all laws of the flesh / the virgin pure gives birth. / By a new law / nature is overcome, / by the birth of Christ. / She hears the inaudible, / keeps the virginal / flower untouched. / Against all custom / the mother breaks with usage / and keeps her modesty, / by the birth of Christ." Tr. Edna S. deAngeli in liner notes of the Musical Heritage Society recording (MHS 824437) of *The Play of St. Nicholas: A 12th-Century Liturgical Drama* (Tinton Falls, N.J., 1981).

53. Derek Pearsall, *Old English and Middle English Poetry* (London, 1977), p. 255; cf. Cawley's description of the Wakefield Master, pp. xxx–xxxi, which we might take for Skelton if Cawley had not identified him otherwise.

54. Philip A. Crowl, *The Intelligent Traveller's Guide to Historic Britain: England,*

Wales, The Crown Dependencies (New York, 1983), p. 216.

55. *Festival: A Collection of Homilies*, ed. Theodor Erbe, EETS extra series 96 (London, 1905), p. 171.

56. *Dives and Pauper*, quoted in Gray, pp. 44–45.

57. Morris Bishop, *The Middle Ages* (New York, 1970), p. 305.

58. Photograph reproduced in Morris Bishop, *The Horizon Book of the Middle Ages* (Boston, Mass., 1968), p. 131, from the Cloisters Collection of the Metropolitan Museum of Art.

59. D. W. Robertson, Jr., *A Preface to Chaucer: Studies in Medieval Perspectives* (Princeton, 1962).

60. E. W. Tristram, *English Wall Painting of the Fourteenth Century* (London, 1955), pp. 6, 4.

61. W. W. Williamson, "Saints on Norfolk Rood-Screens and Pulpits," *Norfolk Archaeology* 31 (1957): 299.

62. Quoted in Travis, p. 237.

63. Nicholas Coldstream, "Art and architecture in the late Middle Ages," in *The Later Middle Ages*, ed. Stephen Medcalf (London, 1981), p. 186.

64. Coldstream describes this more fully, pp. 187–88; it is reproduced (in black and white) as plate 5.

65. Cf. Sir John Paston's composite volume containing *La Belle Dame sans merci, The Disputation between Hope and Despair, The Parliament of Fowls*, and *The Life of St. Christopher* in H. S. Bennett, *Chaucer and the Fifteenth Century* (Oxford, 1947), p. 123.

66. "(And there appeared a great sign in heaven, a woman whose mantle is the sun, and the moon beneath her feet, and on her head a crown of twelve stars.)" Tr. Gray, p. 4n.

67. Quoted in Gray, p. 41.

68. In Gray, p. 61.

69. #77 in *Medieval English Lyrics*, ed. R. T. Davies (London, 1963), p. 166.

70. J. A. Burrow, *Ricardian Poetry* (London, 1971).

71. #73 in Davies, pp. 162–63.

72. Quoted in John Peter, *Complaint and Satire in Early English Literature* (Oxford, 1956), p. 68.

73. George F. Whicher, *The Goliard Poets: Medieval Latin Songs and Satires* (Cambridge, Mass., 1949), p. 221.

74. John Matthews Manly, "Familia Goliae," *MP* 5 (1908): 202–4.

75. "Right and wrong they go about / Cheek by jowl together. / Lavishness can't keep in step / Avarice his brother. / Virtue, even in the most / Unusual moderation, / Seeking for the middle course, / Vice on either side, it must / Look about her with the most / Cautious contemplation." Quoted and tr. Helen Waddell, *Medieval Latin Lyrics* (London, 1929), pp. 188–89.

76. "Who is truthful, who is good, / Who would help God if he could? / Have at once your pennyworth: / Death now rules in all the earth. / Prelates own him lord

and sire, / Putting sacraments to hire, / While secure in power they sit, / Making mock of Holy Writ." Quoted and tr. Whicher, pp. 150–51.

77. See J. A. MacCulloch, *Medieval Faith and Fable* (Boston, Mass., 1932), p. 282.

78. James Kinsley in *The Poems of William Dunbar*, ed. James Kinsley (Oxford, 1979), p. 280.

79. "Then quench we must / Our fleshly lust / By penance, prayer, and fasting, / That when we rise, / Our longing eyes / To heavenly joys upcasting, / We may rejoice / With heart and voice / Where life is everlasting." Quoted and tr. Whicher, pp. 154–55.

80. Quoted and tr. Whicher, pp. 106–7.

CHAPTER 3

1. Roger Lockyer, *Henry VII* (London, 1968), p. 3.

2. Colin Richmond, *John Hopton: A Fifteenth Century Suffolk Gentleman* (Cambridge, 1981), p. 175.

3. John Seymour notes an early sixteenth-century map in Sweden in which three towns only are marked for England: Rochester, Chatham, and Diss. See his *The Companion Guide to East Anglia* (London, 1970, 1982), p. 176.

4. Long associated with the Catholic Mowbrays and Howards—Mary Tudor went there from Kenninghall where she was declared queen—Elizabeth I turned it into a prison for recusants.

5. *Original Papers of the Norfolk and Norwich Archaeological Society*, 27(1939): 140; see also H. B. Walters, "Inventories of Norfolk Church Goods (1551)," *Norfolk Archaeology* 26 (1938): 245–56.

6. The Augustinian Abbot William Clown of Leicester was a favored hunting companion of Edward III; in 1368 Abbot Littleton of Westminster offered at his altar a waxen image of a falcon as a reward for recovering his best hawk. Indeed, the Book of St. Albans in 1400 assigned the sparrowhawk itself to priests and muskets to parish clerks as proper birds for their station!

7. Jacobus de Voragine, *The Golden Legend*, tr. and adapted by Granger Ryan and Helmut Ripperger (New York, 1969), pp. 509–10.

8. Henry Bradley, "Two Puzzles in Skelton," *The Academy* 1 (1896): 83.

9. Nan Cooke Carpenter, *John Skelton* (New York, 1967), p. 69.

10. "sophist"; "writer of syllogisms, pure and oversimple"; "devilist dogmatist"; "To hawk when you wish / In that church, / My master, have you coveted, / With your hawk on your fist."; "Have you said so? / Have you done so? / But where have you read this? / Or whence [comes] this, / Dr. Dawcock?" (tr. Robert S. Kinsman).

11. "Reverend liberty granted to devout poets / Of saying whatever pleases, whatever will gratify, / Or whatever is efficacious to defend just causes, / Or nip coarse clowns. /Accordingly you will grant indulgence" (tr. Kinsman).

12. M. D. Anderson, *Drama and Imagery in English Medieval Churches* (Cambridge, 1963), p. 1.

13. Transcribed in *Hymns to the Virgin & Christ, The Parliament of Devils and other Religious Poems*, ed. Frederick J. Furnivall, EETS 24 (London, 1867), part 1, p. 93. I am grateful to Thorlac Turville-Petre for suggesting this analogue.

14. Francis Blomefield, *An Essay Towards a Topographical History of the County of Norfolk*, 3 vols. (London, 1805), 3:182–83.

15. "O destruction too too tearful, O fate how lamentable!
Venerable city, you fall in hateful fires;
Whether the bolts of Jove or the ultimate fates were calling,
You perish in the fierce fires of Vulcan.
Alas, until but now, the glory, the most beautiful ornament of our land!
The city of Norwich is sinking in ashes.
O city, what shall I say to you? Briefly shall I utter a few words in your
    recompense:
Good fortune seldom endures, take advantage of your lot;
Nothing mortal lasts, fate overturns all things;
O lamentable city, farewell! Your lot is indeed to be lamented" (tr. Kinsman).

16. Kinsman cites P. Lehman, *Die Parodie in "Mittelalter"* (Munich, 1922).

17. "Adam was inhabitant; / While he lived, he carried on deceitful acts, / For he used to obtain by force / Whatever villein held, / Or free-born; therefore / He was called the ravening wolf" (tr. Kinsman).

18. "This Pilate, seed of Belial, / Violated the Church / He who trampled it underfoot / Is now violated: Perfidious, irate, / Never was he blessed: / Undersall, prostrate / Has been stripped of his goods, / Wicked, puffed-up, / Now is he flayed with curses!" (tr. Kinsman).

19. The priory built in 1146 at Carhowe ("car" meaning "a marshy spot," "how" meaning "hill"; the church was originally dedicated to the Blessed Virgin and to St. John the Evangelist. In time the priory, answerable directly to the Pope, owned land in fifty villages, some as far as London, as well as the rectories of nearly a dozen Norwich churches. It also had its own fair for four days annually at Norwich and provided priests for the oratory in the marketplace. In 1385 the Saddlers and Spurriers of Norwich moved their guild chapel to Carrow Priory. During later Tudor visitations it established itself as the only priory "of very good name." See S. H. Edgar, "The Story of Carrow Abbey." (Skelton may have the formal name of the priory in mind, too, when composing the imagery behind "Phyllyp Sparowe.")

20. H. S. Bennett, *The Pastons and Their England* (Cambridge, 1922), p. 197.

21. Quoted in J. R. Lander, *Government and Community: England 1450–1509* (London, 1980), p. 112.

22. F. W. Brownlow, "*The Boke of Phyllyp Sparowe* and the Liturgy," *ELR* 9 (1979): 8.

23. Texts for the Divine Offices are those published for the Benedictine Order.

24. There is a discussion of the relationship between the Christ child and the bird—it is one of the shepherd's gifts in the Wakefield *Secunda Pastorum*—by Lawrence J. Ross in "Symbol and Structure in the *Secunda Pastorum*" in *Medieval English Drama*, ed. Jerome Taylor and Alan H. Nelson, pp. 185–92.

25. These particular examples come from Kinsman's notes to the edition in preparation.

26. E. O. James, *Christian Myth and Ritual* (Cleveland, Ohio, 1963), pp. 203–6.

27. A. S. Duncan-Jones, "The Burial of the Dead," in *Liturgy and Worship*, ed. W. K. Lowther Clarke and Charles Harris (London, 1954), p. 621.

28. Rosemary Woolf, *The English Religious Lyric in the Middle Ages* (Oxford, 1963), p. 273.

29. *Religious Lyrics of the XVth Century*, ed. Carleton Brown (Oxford, 1938), p. 18. Some were in short dimeters resembling the Skeltonic: "Sodenly afraide, / Half waking, / Half slepyng / And gretly dismayde, / A wooman sate wepyng," quoted in Gray, p. 137.

30. Quoted in Gray, p. 110.

31. Quoted in Gray, pp. 110–11.

32. Quoted in Woolf, *Religious Lyric*, p. 257.

33. It is captured in a stunning west window in the south nave aisle at York Minster, for instance, while at the church of St. Giles, Skelton, an identical rood cross is reinforced by side altars to the Virgin (to the left of the main altar) and to St. John (to the right), flanking Christ who is crucified on the cross on the altar itself.

34. See Gray, pp. 56–58.

35. Richard Rolle in *Fourteenth Century Verse & Prose*, ed. Kenneth Sisam (Oxford, 1921, 1964), p. 38.

36. *Religious Lyric*, p. 283.

37. John Lydgate, "Saynt Valentyne, of custume yeere by yeere," in *Religious Lyric*, p. 277.

CHAPTER 4

1. Westminster Abbey Muniments, 33325, fol. 17; quoted in William Nelson, *John Skelton, Laureate* (New York, 1939), p. 118.

2. John Weever, *Ancient Funerall Monuments* (1631), p. 476.

3. H. F. Westlake, "Skelton in Westminster," *TLS* (27 October 1921): 699.

4. "Hail festive day, memorable through all time, / On which King Henry ends the Gallic war. / Our Henry the Eighth, glowing in arms, / Has levelled to the ground the walls of Thérouanne. / The scepter-bearer of the English, doughtiest Hector in war, / Bruises the proud necks of the French. / Leader but recently renowned in arms, now a leader without arms, / De Longville, say now what your

proud retinue has fallen to. / De Clarmount, a short time ago famous, say now proud Gaul, / For what reason will you be proud. Do you not groan in prison? / Learn, O other French captives, come to know / That Britain is magnanimous, and place yourselves under her. / [St. George] the Glory of Cappadocia and soldier of the Blessed Mary, / Will govern the French kingdom here under her aid. / May the English people always tell of this auspicious blessing, given by the Godhead, / And sing, exulting" (tr. Robert S. Kinsman).

5. "Hail, festive day, resounding through all eternity, / On which James the Scot, overwhelmed by sword, fell, / The barbarous breed of Scots, perfidious, full of evil / . . . . Now what is become of James, sprung from the seed of the damned? Perfidious as Nimrod, he has tumbled, fallen to the depths. / Say now, mad ex-ruler of the evil Scots, / Now you are ruled; behold, you lie dead! / Thus did the savage lion, the famous White Lion [Howard] beset you, / Through whom you, the Red Lion [Scottish royal arms], suffer the ultimate fate. / England, lead the choral dance; play your timbrels, sing to the lyre; / Give praise to God, give solemn pledges to God" (tr. Kinsman).

6. Ruth Ellis Messenger, "Salve Festa Dies," *Transactions of the American Philological Association*, 78 (1947): 208–22.

7. *Magnificence*, ed. Paula Neuss (Manchester, 1980), p. 74n.

8. "Give, O God, to him Bedell, not honey but gall, this Ishmael, / A perfidious Achitophel, ghastly, and a blackguard; / Now this Jabel [his] stinking in the ground; he is, behold, the rascally Nabel! / He was hated by, and hateful to, all; / Stumbling in the street, he died in filth: / Hating the priests, thus out of his mind he fell" (tr. Kinsman).

9. A. F. Pollard, *Wolsey* (London, 1929), p. 76n.

10. Nancy Lenz Harvey, *Thomas Cardinal Wolsey* (New York, 1980), p. 12.

11. *The Life and Death of Cardinal Wolsey* in *Two Early Tudor Lives*, ed. Richard S. Sylvester and Davis P. Harding (New Haven, 1962), p. 13.

12. Pollard, pp. 76–78.

13. See Neville Williams, *The Cardinal & the Secretary* (London, 1975), pp. 79–80.

14. Pollard, p. 102.

15. Pollard, p. 71.

16. Barclay seems to have been a rival of Skelton's for the patronage of Thomas Howard; he dedicated *Jugurtha* to him and wrote a tribute to Howard's brother Edmund, the Lord High Admiral, in *Eclogues IV* where he simultaneously attacks Skelton. If we are to believe John Bale in *Scriptorum Brytanniae Centuria*. 9, Barclay's "Contra Skeltonium" suggests Barclay was especially offended by Skelton's expropriation of moral themes combined with what he thought a low style.

17. Harvey, p. 71.

18. This list is taken from Harvey, p. 93. Cf. Pollard, pp. 180–81.

19. Roger Lockyer, *Tudor and Stuart Britain 1471–1714* (London, 1964), p. 37.

20. "And take a sum for services, / Contrary to the rule of morals, / Whether of the Black Monks [Benedictines], / Or of the [Augustinian] canons, / Or of the Bernardines [Cistercians], / Or of the Crutched Friars [Trinitarians]" (tr. Kinsman).

21. Williams, p. 50.

22. Details are from Williams, p. 56.

23. Harvey, p. 84.

24. The bibliographical situation with the opening 28 lines is especially vexed. "All noble men" is printed as a separate work in *Certayne Bokes*, STC 22598 (c. 1545), sigs. C3v–C4, at about the same time that it appears as the prolegomenon to "Why Come Ye Nat to Courte?" STC 22615 (c. 1545), sig. A2. Moreover, Rawlinson C. 813 at the Bodleian Library (c. 1537), fol. 36, presents these lines as the incipit to a fragmentary text of the poem. Kinsman takes up such tangled textual variants in his forthcoming edition.

25. As tr. Kinsman: "Next, that finely dissembled/ Pandulph, the great legate, / Not long ago a much feared prelate, / Now stretched out like Naaman the Syrian / So soon living in solitude; / Burdened with the Neapolitan affliction, / Prostrated by poultice, by plaster, / Bored through by the lancet of a quack doctor; / By nothing is he relieved, / By nothing is his condition healed; / His servants are abandoned to servitude, / By which infamy is incurred. / But a greater madman is exposed. If only that debaucher would shrink / From the whore-house, / The master badly critical / More aptly called harsh / Fanatic, phrenetic, / Just as the masterly prosodist [Skelton] / Asserts. / This type of composition/ Is not in need of examination/ in the *Centiloquium* / Or in the *Centimentrum* / Of the honored / Grammarian / Maurus.

26. As tr. Kinsman: "Alas, the grief of it, behold, a wolf-of-the-sea, and a vile bear, / The bull-calf of a butcher, and the wickedest oxherd of the Britons, / A puffed-up bull-calf like Oreb or Zalmunna or Zeeb, / A prickly thistle, and an unmerciful Asaph and reprobate Dathan, / And a flattering Achitophel of the king, the whole vice of the British / For he is the Thomas who confounds churches everywhere, / Not the famous Thomas [à Becket], a holy man, but Golias, hard of heart, / Who rides a mule! Satan, may he shit, I pray, his fundament / Pouring forth asphalt! / I pray, read this cautious verse. / Nothing is more cruel than a wretch when he shall rise to high position."

27. "Your skyn scabbyd and scurvy, / Tawny, tannyd and shurvy; / Now upon thys hete / Rankely whan ye swete, / Men say ye wyll wax lowsy, / Drunkyn, drowpy, drowsy" ("Against Garnesche," iii.131–36); "Dundas, dronken and drowsy, / Skabed, scurvy, and lowsy" ("Dundas," 56–57).

28. Court Rolls of the Manor of Pacheneshám (6/7–6/15 [1500–1525]), which included the View of Frankpledge for Leatherhead; John H. Harvey, "Eleanour Rumming," *TLS* (26 October 1946): 521. *The Victoria County History of Surrey* shows descendants there for the next 140 years (2,379). Even much earlier, Robert Gray reports, drink was plentiful with "over a thousand brew shops" in London

"where the smallest measure was apparently a quart." *A History of London* (New York, 1979), p. 127.

29. In Skelton's day, Wolsey was credited with having a magic ring and a serviceable devil as popular explanations for his power over the King. William Tyndale in "The practyse of oure tyme" in *The Practyse of Prelates* (1530), "And as I harde it spoken of diverse, he [Wolsey] made by crafte of necromancy graven to beare vppon him, wherewith he bewitched the kynges mynd and made the kyng to dote vppon him more than ever he did on any ladye or gentylwoman so that now the kynges grace folowed him as he before folowed the kyng." Cf. "An Impeachment of Wolsey" in *Ballads from MSS*, ed. F. J. Furnivall, 1: 359, v. 43; *Norfolk Archaeology*, 1 (1847): 60–61; *Letters and Papers of Henry VIII*, 9, no. 2733.

30. Peter Clark, in *The English Alehouse: a social history 1200–1830* (London, 1983), reports that in Skelton's time alewives were common but alehouses serving only women were unknown (pp. 131–32); it may be possible that we are to think of Elynour's establishment as if it were all men rather than all women—and this too would make it analogous (by inversion, as antitype) to Hampton Court. Cf. the habit of Elynour's gathering all the goods she can and storing them under her bed to Wolsey's acquisitive habits or the accusation of both of them, by the poet, of witchcraft.

31. R. H. Robbins, "John Crophill's Ale-Pots," *RES* 20 (1963): 184.

32. Maurice Pollet, *John Skelton: Poet of Tudor England*, tr. John Warrington (London, 1971), pp. 254–57. The poem is rpt. in *Early English Carols*, ed. R. L. Greene (Oxford, 1935), pp. 280–82.

33. Robert W. Ackerman, *Backgrounds to Medieval English Literature* (New York, 1966), p. 94.

34. *The Workes of Sir Thomas More Knyght, sometyme Lorde Chauncellour of England, wrytten by him in the Englysh tongue* (1557), fol. g7v.

35. Frederick Hackwood, *Inns, Ales, and Drinking Customs of Old England* (London, 1909), p. 55. It may be of interest to note that Wolsey became drunk at such a village festival at Lymington when he was a parish priest around 1500 and was arrested. See Hackwood, pp. 56–57.

36. Quoted in Hackwood, p. 55.

37. Transcribed by G. R. Owst, *Literature and Pulpit in Medieval England* (Cambridge, 1933), p. 435. Robert D. Newman compares the poem to the tavern scene in Breughel's "The Peasant Dance" in which the church is abandoned for the tavern and an equally disregarded image of the Virgin Mary is about to topple to the ground from a tree from which it has been hung. "The Visual Nature of Skelton's 'The Tunnyng of Elynour Rummyng,'" *College Literature* 12 (Spring 1985): 138–39.

38. *The Book of Vices and Virtues*, ed. W. Nelson Francis, EETS old series 217 (London, 1942), p. 274, quoted by Francis on p. 85.

39. Clarence H. Miller and Robert Bux Bosse, "Chaucer's Pardoner and the Mass," *Chaucer Review* 6 (Winter 1972): 176–77.

40. Ed. J. A. W. Bennett (Oxford, 1972), V.308.

41. As we might expect, Chaucer's pardoner, in dealing with gluttony, devotes some of his most extravagant rhetoric to vomiting: "The Pardoner's Tale" in Geoffrey Chaucer, *The Canterbury Tales* in *Works*, ed. F. N. Robinson (Boston, 1957), lines 524–28 (p. 150).

42. Theodor Klauser, *A Short History of the Western Liturgy*, tr. John Halliburton, 2nd ed. (Oxford, 1979), p. 109.

43. "Withinne that develes temple: an examination of Skelton's *The Tunnyng of Elynour Rummyng*," *JMRS* 10 (1980): 249–50. Cf. Wayne Shumaker: "The English witch . . . was typically a woman, poor, uneducated, something of a social outcast, 'queer' and perhaps partly demented, and usually old. The presumption that she was a sorceress was enormously strengthened if she was also physically repulsive, afflicted by some such evident abnormality as a drooping or crooked eye, and given to unintelligible but ominous muttering." *The Occult Sciences in the Renaissance: A Study in Intellectual Patterns* (Berkeley, Calif., 1972), p. 68. Shumaker quotes Reginald Scot, *The Discoverie of Witchcraft* (1584), "One sort of such as are said to bee witches, are women which be commonly old, lame, bleare-eied, pale, fowle, and full of wrinkles" (pp. 68–69), like Elynour (12–19).

44. Owst, p. 438.

45. Owst, p. 439.

46. In 1428; see G. G. Coulton, *Medieval Panorama: The English Scene from Conquest to Reformation* (New York, 1955), pp. 707–8 for details.

47. E. O. James, in *Christian Myth and Ritual* (Cleveland, Ohio, 1963, pp. 45–53), makes a detailed analogy between the Mass and the *Liber Regalis* directing the procedures for the coronation of a king (processional, entrance, recognition, oath, consecration, anointing, investiture, coronation, enthronement, mass, communion, and final procession), which may be another reason for finding some hints of Wolsey even in this poem.

48. Hackwood adds that "In Saxon and mediaeval times the office of Cellarer was one of the most important in English religious houses" (p. 41); indeed, in Skelton's time, the strengths of beer (X, XX, XXX) were thought of as crosses which served to indicate the monks' oath, 'Sworn on the cross,' meaning 'of sound quality, fit to drink.'"

49. R. W. Southern, *Western Society and the Church in the Middle Ages* (Harmondsworth, 1970), pp. 219–20.

50. Hackwood describes this in some detail, pp. 60–61.

51. She was honored in a fifteenth-century ballad printed by Richard Pynson: "Many seke ben here cured by our Lady's myghte / Dede agayne revyved of this no dought / Lame made whole and blynded restored to syghte / Lo here the chyef solace agaynst all tribulacyon / To all that be seke bodely or goostly / Callin to Our Lady devoutly." Quoted in Marina Warner, *Alone of All Her Sex: The Myth and the Cult of the Virgin Mary* (New York, 1983), p. 295. The best account of Walsingham—thought to be pointed to by the Milky Way—is Rev. Leonard E. Whatmore, *Highway to Walsingham* (Walsingham, 1973).

52. Southern gives a compelling picture of early pilgrimages to the shrine of St. Frideswide, Oxford, near the site of what would later be Wolsey's Cardinal College (now Christ Church), p. 306.

53. Christian K. Zacher, *Curiosity and Pilgrimage* (Baltimore, 1976), p. 46.

54. Herbert Francis Westlake, *Westminster Abbey: The Church, Convent, Cathedral, and College of St. Peter, Westminster*, 2 vols. (London, 1923), Appendix 4, 2, 499–501.

55. "A Satirical Laureate of the Sixteenth Century," *Dublin University Magazine* 68 (1866) quoted in Anthony S. G. Edwards, *Skelton: The Critical Heritage* (London, 1981), p. 139.

56. "Third, the tavern—here I dread / Lies detraction's kernel: / Long on tavern joys I've fed, / Never shall I spurn all / Till these eyes shall see instead / Choirs from realms supernal / Chanting for the newly dead / Requiem eternal" (tr. George F. Whicher, *The Goliard Poets: Medieval Latin Songs and Satires* [Cambridge, Mass., 1949], pp. 110–11).

CHAPTER 5

1. But see 183–96, 596–601.

2. Quoted in Peter F. Ryder, *Medieval Buildings of Yorkshire* (Ashbourne, 1982), p. 103.

3. For this and some other facts that follow, I am indebted to personal correspondence with M. J. Tucker and to the following works by him: *The Life of Thomas Howard, Earl of Surrey and Second Duke of Norfolk, 1443–1524* (The Hague, 1964), Table 3; "Skelton and Sheriff Hutton," *ELN* 4 (1967): 254–59; "The Ladies in Skelton's *Garland of Laurel*," *RQ* 22 (1969): 333–45; "Setting for Skelton's *Bowge of Courte*: A Speculation," *ELN* 7 (1970): 166–75; and "Skelton's More-Howard Connections," *Moreana* 10 (1973): 15–23.

4. HRO D/B4/38/10; *Borough of Harwich Muniments* (Harwich, 1931), Bundle 39/3, 21 April, 2 Richard III, and 39/26, 20 May, 15 Edward IV.

5. J. J. Scarisbrick seems to accept just such a theory: "John Skelton, a client of the Norfolks, had unleashed his outbursts against the cardinal, savaging him for allegedly ousting the aristocracy from their rightful place in the realm." *Henry VIII* (Berkeley, Calif. 1968), p. 229. The details of the poem, drawing on events of the 1480s, suggests an early composition with a few later interpolations concerning Wolsey.

6. For a helpful (and revisionary) reading of *The Garlande of Laurell*, see the important essay by John Scott Colley, "John Skelton's Ironic *Apologia*," *Tennessee Studies in Literature* 18 (1973): 19–32, from which I have drawn some references here, and the forthcoming edition of the poem by F. W. Brownlow which supplies further factual background and dates the poem's composition.

7. "Thousand thousands [ministered unto him] (the Ancient of Days) and ten thousand times ten thousand [stood before him]" (tr. Robert S. Kinsman).

8. "To the Most Serene Royal Majesty, equally with the Lord Cardinal, Most Honored Legate-from-the-side. / L'autre Envoy. / Hasten, book, venerate with lowered eyes the famous king / Henry the Eighth, making resound his rewards of praise. / The Lord Cardinal alike greet with reverence / Legate-from-the-side, and may he be mindful to request / The prebendary which he promised sometime to entrust to me, / And may you bear back this pledge of safety. / 'Between hope and fear'" (tr. Kinsman).

9. "To the Most Honorable, Most Distinguished, and by far Most Reverend Father in Christ, and in the Lord, Lord Thomas, &c., of the title of Saint Cecilia, priest of the Most Holy Roman Church, Cardinal most deserving, and Legate of the Apostolic Seat, Most Illustrious Legatus-a-Latere &c., Skelton Laureate, 'Orator of the King,' declares most humble compliance with all due reverence proper to so great and so magnificent a prince of ecclesiasts, most just moderator of all justice, and assuredly the most excellent promoter of this present treatise, &c.; for whose most auspicious consideration, under the press of glorious immortality, the present little page is counted happy" (tr. Kinsman).

10. John Holloway, *Skelton*, Chatterton Lecture on an English Poet, *Proceedings of the British Academy* (1958), p. 100.

11. C. S. Lewis, *English Literature in the Sixteenth Century Excluding Drama* (Oxford, 1954), p. 113.

12. J. D. Mackie, *The Earlier Tudors, 1485–1558* (Oxford, 1957), p. 2.

13. F. W. Brownlow, "*Speke, Parrot*: Skelton's Allegorical Denunciation of Wolsey," *SP* 65 (1968): 137.

14. Noted by Robert S. Kinsman in a review of Stanley Eugene Fish, *John Skelton's Poetry* (New Haven, 1965), in *Renaissance News* 18 (1965): 327.

15. William Wordsworth in a letter to Allan Cunningham, 23 November 1823; quoted in H. L. R. Edwards, *Skelton: The Life and Times of an Early Tudor Poet* (London, 1949), p. 90.

HYPOCRISY
Bench end (hand-carved, fifteenth century),
Church of the Holy Trinity, Blythburgh, Suffolk

INDEX